Praise for HARVEST PILGRIMS

"Vincenzo Pietropaolo's genius in these photographs is to suggest whole histories and whole worlds in the simplest of images. He takes a phenomenon most of us are hardly aware of and makes us see in it the story of a continent."

—Nino Ricci, author

"In the supermarket, everything looks poster-perfect. But Vince's camera opens our eyes to the bruises, skill, and humanity too often left out of the picture. As we strive for food that is more honest, real, local, healthy, and responsible, this fresh look at our food system shows us an important place where the fruits of labour need to be properly shared."

—Wayne Roberts, manager, Toronto Food Policy Council and board member, Food Secure Canada

"Vincenzo Pietropaolo's photographs have the intensity found in Jean Mohr's and John Berger's seminal book, *A Seventh Man*. Pietropaolo's engagement with the dignity and forbearance the workers show in their seasonal exile allows us to return, through these very fine photographs, to early notions of the honesty of documentary work."

—Meeka Walsh, editor, *Border Crossings*

"Pietropaolo's portraits of migrant farm workers and their lives show them the very respect he says they deserve for the service they give us: they grow our food and without them we couldn't do it."

—Rick Salutin, writer and columnist

"Vince's photos suggest that the old phrase "If you ate well today, thank a farmer" should read, "thank a guest worker" – or a seasonal worker, impermanent resident, or permanently temporary immigrant. Whatever the descriptive term, these men and women are the backbone of today's farming industry in Canada."

—John Sewell, political activist, recipient of the Order of Canada

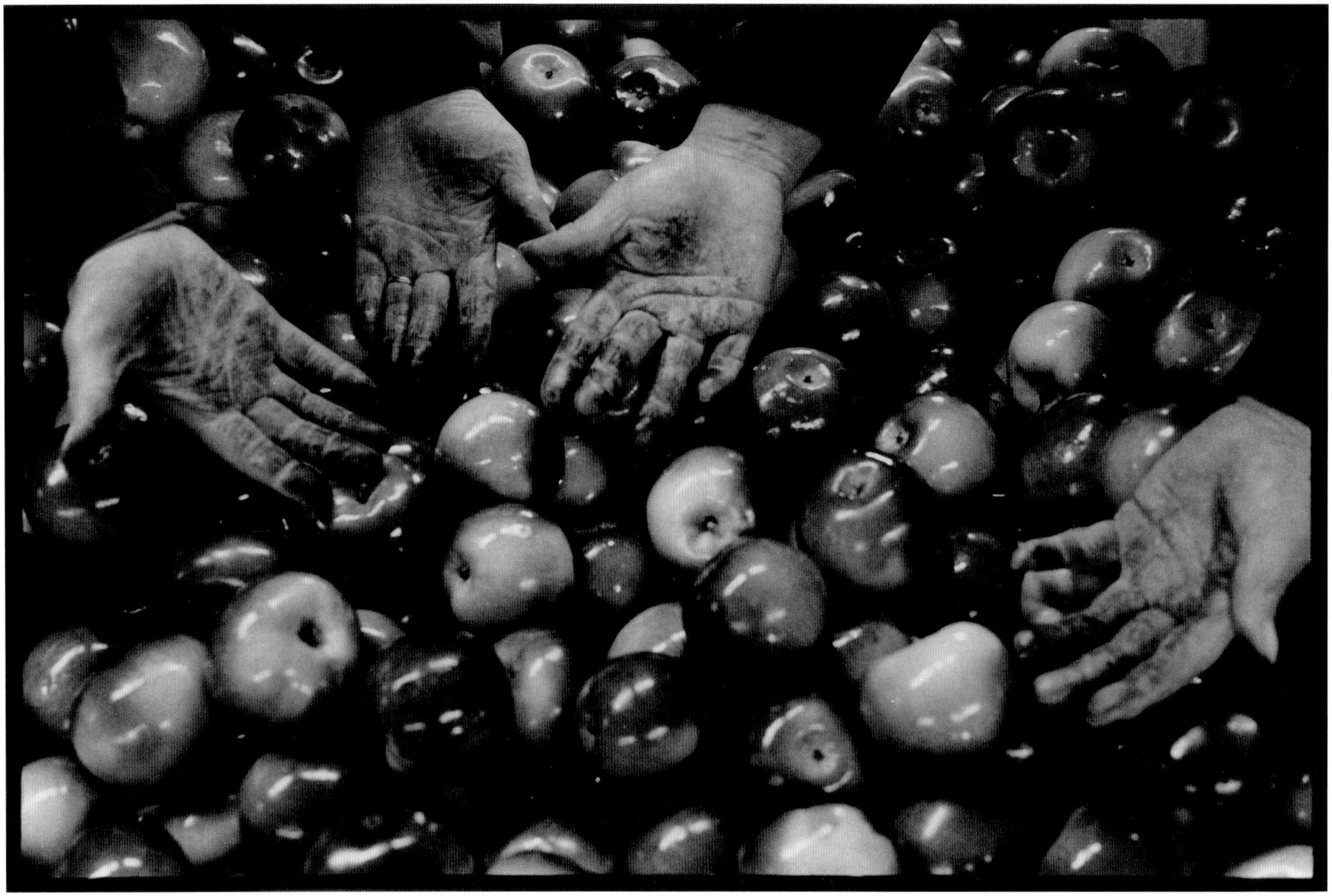

HARVEST PILGRIMS

Mexican and Caribbean Migrant Farm Workers in Canada

Photographs and Text by

VINCENZO PIETROPAOLO

BETWEEN THE LINES
TORONTO

For

Jorge Guerra
and
Denyse Gérin-Lajoie,

friends and mentors

A friend came to see me in a dream. From far away.
And I asked in the dream: "Did you come by photograph or by train?"
All photographs are a form of transport and an expression of absence.

—John Berger

CONTENTS

FOREWORD

NAOMI ROSENBLUM

THIS COLLECTION OF IMAGES of migrant farm labour in Canada by Vincenzo Pietropaolo is part of a long tradition of socially useful photographic documentation. In the past the credibility of camera images – their capacity to suggest real space and capture human expression – led to their acceptance as truthful witnesses of reality. As such, they have played a continuing role in efforts to alter disturbing aspects of society, particularly in the United States.

For a number of years following the announcement of the medium in the mid-nineteenth century, making photographs in the field was a cumbersome undertaking, requiring a large apparatus and portable processing equipment. Then in the late nineteenth century the technology began to catch up with the need for such images. Dry plates and faster-acting lenses made it easier to depict labour in the field, while the invention of easier half-tone reproduction methods provided the means for the pictures to appear as illustrations in brochures, magazines, and newspapers.

Around the same time, towards the end of the century and in the United States especially, the mechanization of planting led to much larger harvests requiring more workers than were available locally; and the workers were often migrants imported from other countries. All of these developments coincided with efforts by progressive forces to rein in the effects of unregulated capitalist enterprise by making visible socially questionable situations in both agriculture and industry.

The first large bodies of socially conceived camera images were of immigrant rather than migrant labour – that is, of recently arrived people who worked in farms and small factories for long hours and little pay. Jacob Riis, a transplanted Dane, photographed sweatshop and child street workers in New York City in the late 1880s in order to call attention to conditions that he believed were inimical to the proper functioning of civil society. Riis was a journalist who briefly turned to photography as a useful tool; but in the early twentieth century, Lewis W. Hine, recognizing the growing need for this kind of imagery, advertised himself as a "social" photographer, able to depict a range of subjects useful to reformers. Between 1908 and 1916 he travelled widely throughout the United States documenting child workers in industry and agriculture. Along with images of youngsters picking cotton, cranberries, and beets, Hine recorded names, ages, dates, and other information, amassing a visual record of child labour in the fields. These "social" images, meant to evoke an emotional response and persuade viewers of the truthfulness of dire conditions, later came to be called "documentary," a term subject to much discussion as to whether it denotes truthful depiction or rather a photographic style.

Hine had consciously created the genre of social photography, but his work in the field was underwritten by a privately supported charity – the National Child Labor Committee – which paid his salary, reproduced the images and information in its own publications, sponsored illustrated lectures using lantern slides he provided, and made the material available to newspapers and magazines. Until the mid-1930s no other large-scale projects of similar intent and scale were undertaken by either private or public entities, although a number of individual photographers continued to be concerned with agricultural labour. Among them was Doris Ulmann, a privileged New York portraitist who journeyed to the fertile plains of South Carolina in the late 1920s and early 1930s to portray field hands working on a large plantation owned by author Julia Peterkin. Published in *Roll, Jordan, Roll* – with Peterkin's text – the images reveal a pictorialist approach to field work in their softness and avoidance of any suggestion of discomfort or difficulty.

A quite different view of Southern farm labour became visible as the Great Depression of the 1930s deepened. It is apparent in the work of Margaret Bourke-White, who began her project a few years after Ulmann, working with writer Erskine Caldwell in the sharecropping communities of the South. Appearing in 1937 in *You Have Seen Their Faces*, the images were unabashedly dramatic in their exposition of the harshness of life for both African-American and white sharecroppers during this upheaval in the agricultural sector. Meant to appeal to the emotions, the images have since been criticized as too obviously composed and overly sentimental in their stress on victimization rather than grit in the face of adversity.

Like Ulmann, Bourke-White depicted folk who did farm work in the same localities in which they lived. Other photographers were drawn to the phenomenon of migrant labour. In California migrant labourers known as "bindlemen" had long existed, but they had rarely been documented photographically. Then, in the 1930s, the large influx of farmers forced by dust storms and adverse economic conditions to leave their Midwestern homesteads for what they believed might be "greener" fields in California attracted attention. *Life* photographer Horace Bristol, who had hoped to interest the magazine in the story of migrant labour in California, captured over one thousand largely descriptive images in the camps set up to house workers. Still another view of farm labour characterized the imagery of the husband and wife team of Otto Hagel and Hansel Mieth – refugees from Germany who settled in California and worked intermittently as photojournalists. They were drawn to portraying the struggles – at times violent – being waged in their adopted state in the early 1930s by cotton pickers who wanted better pay and living conditions.

By the mid-1930s attitudes about social issues had undergone a sea change, with photography now being called upon by governmental agencies to act as a witness of conditions in need of rectification. A fortuitous meeting in California in 1935 between social scientist Paul S. Taylor and photographer Dorothea Lange evolved into a state-sponsored project involving the documentation of migrant labour. Soon after, when the photographic unit of the federally sponsored Resettlement Administration under the leadership of Roy Stryker was established in Washington to pursue a similar objective in the nation as a whole, Lange transferred her efforts from the state agency to the national group. Known as the Historical Section of the Farm Security Administration

(FSA), this group eventually included John Collier, Jack Delano, Walker Evans, Carl Mydans, Arthur Rothstein, Ben Shahn, and Marion Post Wolcott; each brought a personal way of seeing to their portrayal of American rural life. They produced more than two hundred thousand images, large numbers of them picturing agrarian pursuits. In their time, FSA images were reproduced in magazines, exhibited at county fairs and in art galleries, and published in book format. One of the most notable books was *American Exodus*, which appeared in 1940 with images by Lange and writing by Taylor. Like the book you now hold, it integrated text and imagery to create both a sociological and a historical study.

With the onset of World War II in the early 1940s, many of the individuals who peopled Lange's photographs (and those by other FSA photographers) had found jobs in war-related industries. After the war's end, both farm work and farm workers also changed. Now migrants of a different order – mainly large numbers of Mexican and Caribbean islanders – came north to work on a seasonal basis. For a number of years the existence of the hundreds of thousands who travel to the United States and Canada to work on the tomato and sugar plantations of Florida and Louisiana, the fruit orchards and vegetable farms of New York, Ontario, and Oregon, and the growing fields of California was largely invisible even though their labour fed both nations.

The government-funded agencies that had emerged to deal with the economic and social crises in the United States – among them the FSA and Works Progress Administration – were no longer deemed necessary after the war. Projects that provided either a look at social conditions or employment for photographers and sociologists were phased out. (The FSA images went to the Library of Congress, and those of other agencies ended up in various federal and state archives.) In consequence, the picturing of farm labour was once again left to be undertaken by individuals – writers and photographers – who now had to market their work to magazines and publishers. Little such documentation appeared in the 1950s and 1960s as socially minded photographers concerned themselves with issues relating to racism and civil rights.

With the increased mechanization of agriculture and the new availability of larger amounts of food of greater variety, the issue of who was providing this abundance and under what circumstances began to attract individual photographers. Debbie Fleming Caffery, a native of Louisiana, concentrated on the sugar-cane harvest, suggesting through her images the choking dust of the ambience. In California, Roger Minick and Reesa Tansey sought out the more recent Mexican migrants who were engaged in the intense struggles during the 1960s and 1970s around the harvesting of grapes and other produce. As awareness grew of the undocumented entry of migrant labourers across the long border between Mexico and the United States, Ken Light attempted a sympathetic photographic portrayal of these individuals drawn to jobs in California's agricultural sector. In his book *The Migrant Project: Contemporary California Farm Workers*, Rick Nahmias provides a collection of photographs and texts revealing the appalling conditions of migrant farm work.

Canada may have fewer seasonal migrant farm workers than does its Southern neighbour, but Vincenzo Pietropaolo's *Harvest Pilgrims* seeks through photographic imagery and texts to acquaint readers with an understanding of seasonal migrant farm life in his country. An immigrant himself – he arrived in Canada from Calabria as a child – Pietropaolo recognized from an early age that work was an intense preoccupation in his own community. As a consequence, his involvement with photography led him to concentrate on those for whom work was an absolute necessity. Like others drawn to this subject, he works in black and white, believing that colour might add a degree of "prettiness" to images that show workers picking fruit and other vegetation. Bilingual himself, Pietropaolo is able to empathize with the workers as they attend religious services, study to learn English, make friends (on occasion with the employer), take care of their domestic chores, and miss their families back home in Jamaica or Mexico.

This view of migrant life in Canadian fields continues the older tradition of social documentation in that Pietropaolo's images are not manipulated digitally. Perhaps in this age of digital replication the idea that such images can evoke a sympathetic response is too hopeful. So accustomed have we become to the seamless montages and adjusted imagery that we see in print illustrations or on the screen – whether of mechanisms or people – that the "real" may seem unexciting in comparison. Nevertheless, neither overly dramatic nor coolly distanced, the ordinary human activities that Pietropaolo makes visible in *Harvest Pilgrims* suggest that the real world of labour still can be powerfully and sympathetically evoked, revealing the world, once again, as it appears in the camera lens.

Naomi Rosenblum is a photographic historian and author of *A World History of Photography* and *A History of Women Photographers*.

ACKNOWLEDGEMENTS

THE MAKING OF THIS BOOK began long ago, and many people in several countries have played a part in its creation, some directly and others indirectly. I would like to take this opportunity to acknowledge and thank them all.

First of all I am deeply grateful to Wayne Hanley, national president of UFCW Canada (the United Food and Commercial Workers Canada union), who believed in the book from the moment when I first showed him the photographs. And I am equally grateful to Victor Carrozzino, who in his capacity as an excecutive assistant to the national president, shepherded the project successfully through the process. UFCW Canada's generous financial commitment towards its publication was crucial, and without this expression of solidarity it would not have been possible to publish the book at this time. I am also very grateful for additional financial support by the Sisters of Providence of St. Vincent de Paul (Kingston) and the Sisters of St. Joseph (London). The photographs were produced with the help of the Canada Council and Ontario Arts Council.

The book began to come to life when Paul Eprile, then editorial co-ordinator at Between the Lines, became interested in pursuing the project. The book was shepherded through the publishing process by his successors, Anjula Gogia and Amanda Crocker, and by Jennifer Tiberio, design and production co-ordinator, and Paula Brill, promotion and marketing co-ordinator.

I would particularly like to thank Naomi Rosenblum for her enlightened foreword and Maia-Mari Sutnik for an insightful article; Tony Macfarlane for transcribing the Caribbean interviews and for his assistance in Jamaica; Alejandro Monsivaís for help in transcribing and translation of the Mexican interviews; Robert Clarke for his thoughtful and thorough editing; Jamie Swift for his wise counsel at all times; David Vereschagin for his creative design; and Giuliana Colalillo, my wife and partner, who has tirelessly contributed her insights and all forms of support throughout.

I would like to thank the following farmers and growers who kindly permitted me to take pictures on their properties and/or agreed to be interviewed: Glenda and Tony Boerkamp, Evelyn Brown, Tony Drescher, Esther Dobrenski, Ken and Steven Enns, Mary and Dave Gibson, Jean and Murray Glover, Dave and Ray Harlings, George Kapitor, Henry and Muriel Kozec, Neal Lehn, Bill and Marty Lenaers, Fernando Loffredo, Helen Magalas, Fred Mayo, the Moyer Family, Danny Mucci, Rick Pajor, Joseph and Gabriel Radvanyi, Eugene Scotch, Henk Sikking Sr., Tony Smyrecinsky, Russell Stangl, William Stetler, Bob and Wanda Winters, Annie and Paul Zaluski, and W. Zawada.

I am also grateful to a number of people who have provided support and/or logistical help, artistic advice, research assistance, exhibition space, and other insights that aided the development of the project and creation of the book: Neyra Alvarado, James Aquila, Kathryn Bates, Carole Condé and Karl Beveridge, Hugh and Wanda Brennian, Leesa Bringas, Stephen Bulger, Liliana Cerón, Rev. Steven Chambers, Jill Delaney, Eduardo del Buey, Glenn Dierker, Janusz Dukszta, Melanie Fernandez, Joan Fillimore, Denyse Gérin-Lajoie, Cassandra Getty, Manuel and Virginia González, Jorge Guerra, Delfina Valle Gutiérrez, Martha Hanna, John Howsen, Sister Pauline Lally, Catherine Macleod, Ezequiel Martinez, Richard McCallam, Patricia Mendoza, Ingrid Meyerhoff, Guillermo Monteforte, Rev. Frank Murphy, Henry Neufeld, Rosario Ortiz, Brent Poulton, Ceford Providence, Ann-Seigel Robertson, Lew Rosenbaum, Chris Scoggins, Lynne Sharman, Maureen Shaw, Murray Shaw, Hettie Schipperheijn, Barbara Sibbald, Carole and Howard Tanenbaum, Meeka Walsh, and Diane Wolfe.

Finally I would like to deeply thank all the migrant farm workers who graced my camera and shared their thoughts and feelings with me. Where possible, I have recorded their names in the book so that they would not be rendered without identity in history. As we strive towards greater social justice, I would like to think that their struggle is *our* struggle.

A Note on the Text

The quotations accompanying the photographs are from interviews that I carried out in 1984, 1986, 1987, 1993, 1994, 1996, in Ontario, Montserrat, Jamaica, and Mexico. The Mexican interviews were transcribed in Mexico, and the extracts used in the book were translated from the Spanish by the author and Alejandro Monsivaís. The Jamaican and Eastern Caribbean interviews were transcribed by Tony MacFarlane, and the extracts were translated from the patois by the author. Complete transcriptions of the interviews will be deposited in an appropriate institution.

Throughout the book I have taken every care to identify people correctly, and regret any errors or omissions. I welcome any corrections and additions of new names, which will be included in the project files for archival purposes, and in subsequent editions of the book.

V.P., Toronto

VINCENZO PIETROPAOLO

The Challenge of Documentary Photography

MAIA-MARI SUTNIK

VINCENZO PIETROPAOLO works in the challenging field of documentary photography. As a category of photographic representation, this genre is often complex and demanding. In practice the photographer needs to know the history of the subject, be aware of the associated issues, have a point of view, and, most importantly, have the vision to communicate all of the various elements in a meaningful way. While documentary photography is often associated with a specific "look" or style of expression, the genre has no adequate definition – indeed, one could say that it is more a matter of constantly shifting definitions depending on the historical moment and the approach taken by the individual photographers.

Clearly, much of the early photography of the nineteenth century was carried out as the production of "documents." An early example was the work of Scottish photographer Thomas Annan, who in 1866 captured stark and powerful images of Glasgow's narrow streets and derelict passageways, revealing the haunted look of people who were living in overcrowded housing, suffering from poverty and illness, and about to have their only homes demolished. The photographs were commissioned as documents for the city's Improvement Trust. Today, Annan's carbon prints are highly desired works of art that contribute great insight into nineteenth-century urban realities and also make us aware of similar phenomena in our contemporary culture.

In the late 1920s British filmmaker John Grierson became synonymous with the term "documentary" – which he himself described as "the creative treatment of actuality" and others have seen as depicting "the real world," representations formed by the observation and selection of subjects for dramatization.[1] In still photography the concept is more complex. The genre of images seen as documentary leans towards the material evidence of social and cultural conditions, ideology, and the arts, consequently united into a discourse centred on the "fine art" of documentary photography. Unlike photography per se – with its ideas and vision concentrating on the intensity of the individual image or a series of formal concepts – documentary photography, as an extended genre, suggests the actual conditions as confronted by a socially conscious photographer who enters into an ideological explication of the subject.

Since the mid-1980s, Vincenzo Pietropaolo's documentation of Mexican and Caribbean migrant farm workers in Canada has captured their worlds, situating with clear-sighted images the disparate conditions engulfing his subjects. One of the characteristics that Pietropaolo brings to his project, with its symbolic title of *Harvest Pilgrims*, is a distinctive quality of lucid awareness of his subject-matter. Even with such insight, a documentary photographer nevertheless needs to approach his subject with empathy and through an interpersonal relationship, characteristics that are deeply seated throughout Pietropaolo's work. The dynamics of his engagement are revealed in the faces of the men and in their responses to his presence among them; and no doubt his own immigrant background plays a large part in the sensitivity he brings to this approach. On the other hand, a challenge for a documentary photographer is to maintain, in one sense, an "invisible" vantage point and not to detract from the integrity of the subject. Having a subjective point of view is an important emphasis, but so too is balance – to avoid overtranscribing. It is satisfying, then, to look at Pietropaolo's images, to sense their authenticity, and learn from his insights that sharply convey the full care that he takes in portraying the individual workers.

Pietropaolo's unadorned approach depends on capturing the essence of gestures – the small and the subtle, as much as the dramatic. One senses, for example, the isolation of the three workers riding in the back of the Ford pickup truck as they travel along a soul-less road surrounded by poles of electrical wires and strip-mall fast-food outlets (see p. 72–73). This image contrasts with that of the "buddy pose" of Tony Smyrecinsky, the Simcoe-area vegetable farmer, and Mike Clive and several other migrants from Jamaica, in a photo that is hopeful in its depiction of threads of mutual appreciation and the countering of isolation (see p. 86). A valued characteristic of photography from its early beginnings – one often taken for granted – is that the medium is well positioned to capture images persuasively and convey compelling communication. The means, then, of connecting quick impulses becomes as significant as exploring the larger social issues of the workers' "waiting game" in Jamaica to become migrant workers in Canada.

Issues of export labour have profound global implications and cause weighty disruptions due to the economic lines between those who have and those who do not have. Canadian migrant workers are part of that struggle, and the subordinate structure of their relationship is poignantly evident in these black and white images. Socially motivated, Pietropaolo effectively reveals the consequences of a nomadic life, the harsh character of existing on the margins, and the critical impact of poverty on people who are lacking in certain resources and power. Desperate to feed their families, which are left behind to live in humble circumstances, migrant workers toil with pride to uphold their Canadian opportunity. Over the years the acceptance and conditions of migrant workers have improved, mainly because Canadian farmers cannot sustain their production under any other arrangements. Large collectives of migrant workers have evolved into temporary communities; in Leamington, Ontario, Pietropaolo captures celebrations that momentarily serve to reclaim their indigenous customs and practices (see pp. 108–9).

Throughout much of the 1980s, in one of the critiques of documentary practices, a number of artists and critics positioned the need for an "alternative" to documentary photojournalism, arguing that, essentially, such narratives celebrated an aesthetic of suffering and pain, and that empathy was a misdirected and futile emotion because it never did alleviate the suffering.[2] However, if we consider Tony Peart's letter written to his wife in 1986 (see p. 90), it becomes on close reading a marker, not only revealing his anxiety and motivation to communicate with "home," but also being in real terms a fragment of memory. Presented as a "shrine," the image is an abstraction of Peart's actual "writing moment," but as representation it holds up a reality that implicates emotions that could hardly be captured in any other visual way with the same intensity. One may wonder whether there would be more efficacy in an image of Peart writing the letter, or is the content of his letter actually more telling of his reality? Pietropaolo chose the issue of content to be more revealing of the conditions yielding the thoughts and emotions of the worker, and the representation of the Peart writing moment becomes both reflective and addresses a larger public issue. As such there would hardly be any displacement of empathy with the subject.

Images have a way of "talking to us" – often directly and at other times in an uncharted way. Pietropaolo uncovers a remarkable way of depicting this sense of dislocation in his image of the workers' hands sorting masses of apples (see frontispiece). The subject is deceptive in a lustrous way – the sheen of the apples appears to be seductive, and both cultural lore and mythology create an association with the potency of "the apple." On the other hand, the image unmasks the action of wax-apple-polishing as revealing a kind of labour far removed from the invested cultural image that we normally hold of the perfect shiny apple. Although we do not see the specific context of this scene, the image clearly defines a powerful sense of a place in which economic necessity is being played out for the purposes of mass markets, casting a less desirable perspective on the historically romanticized fruit.

Pietropaolo's independent perspective on these Harvest Pilgrims is not a singular point of view but depicts the complexity of the everyday, with the unimposing moral sense that he focuses on his subjects, with the honesty and intelligence that he brings in allowing viewers to share his experience. As a documentary photographer he instinctively makes pictures as much for the eye to discover as for the mind to unfold, and this work of prolonged study and research joins his many other important projects of social discourse. The question of "truth" and subjectivity comes to the fore in all documentary work, and is an interesting question; but in the end it is redundant because of the impossibility of locating "truthful" objectivity. It is perhaps more important to discover and to focus on images and the critical ideas that make them stand apart.

Documentary photography is a difficult and subtle art, and in contemporary practice we are learning and relearning constantly what to make of it. The medium has slowly overcome the notion that only beauty and persona are equivalent to creating expressive art. There is an increasing acceptance of more direct markers and candid forms of expressions in the art of the actual and in the large visual terrains that embrace ideology and social critique. Today many photographers uphold the challenge of creating new validations in the belief that the medium acts with both a stronger historic consciousness of its own history and social memory. Pietropaolo has taken the medium to task and has fashioned an exemplary visual record of the Harvest Pilgrims, transforming this recent – and current – history into an immensely profound subject.

Maia-Mari Sutnik is the curator of photography at the Art Gallery of Ontario.

Notes

1 Beaumont Newhall discusses this topic in his *Observations: Essays on Documentary Photography*, ed. David Featherstone (Carmel, Cal.: Friends of Photography, 1984), pp. 1–5.

2 See M. Reinhardt, H. Edwards, and E. Duganne, eds., *Beautiful Suffering: Photography and the Traffic in Pain* (Chicago: University of Chicago Press, 2006).

INTRODUCTION

In 1974 I had an unexpected opportunity to photograph César Chávez, the leader of the United Farm Workers of America. It was at a rally held in a park by the riverside, in Buffalo, New York, one of many such gatherings in support of the boycott against California grapes that was spreading across the United States and Canada. I had travelled from Toronto with two busloads of sympathizers, and after arriving at the border in Fort Erie, Ontario, we got out of the bus and crossed the International Peace Bridge on foot, carrying an assortment of placards for the rally. We paused right at the midpoint of the bridge to unfurl a United Nations international flag. (It was decidedly a simpler time, then, and such things were indeed possible.)

Chávez was the key speaker in the Buffalo park that evening, and his simple but emotional plea for solidarity with the farm workers movement was spellbinding. His struggle for social justice had by then captured the attention of people across the continent. Although the migrant farm worker of his youth had become transformed into a formidable leader, the tone of his words resonated with deep humility, and his crackling voice with sincerity. He had been dubbed the prophet of non-violence, and I too was swept up in the euphoria of that evening.

Determined to photograph him from as close as possible, I worked my way right to the front of the crowd. I was excited, for as a photographer I had been intent on exploring my own immigrant, working-class community, and now in the viewfinder of my camera was a Mexican-American farm worker who had become a legendary labour leader and civil rights activist of international stature. The experience would instil in me a deep and life-long passion for migrant farm workers.

Some ten years later, in 1984, I went to Simcoe, Ontario, as a participating artist in a small exhibition of photographs at the Lynnwood Arts Centre on the theme of "Ontario at Work." In the town I noticed small groups of men who did not appear to be of local extraction, and that was when I first learned about migrant farm workers in

Canada. The more I investigated, the more astonished I became at how invisible these migrant workers were in our society. Most people outside the area had simply not heard of their existence. Migrant farm workers are one of those subcultures of people who live on the fringes of society, part of the worldwide phenomenon of migration. This is something I am familiar with personally, because immigration has been a defining element in my own life. I had grown up in the rural south of Italy, where subsistence farming was a way of life. I was familiar with aspects of farm work and found it relatively easy to relate to farm workers in Ontario. Moreover, my father, as a new immigrant, often spoke of his experiences working on tobacco farms in Southern Ontario – he had gone there during times of high unemployment in Toronto, where we lived. He, too, was a migrant farm worker.

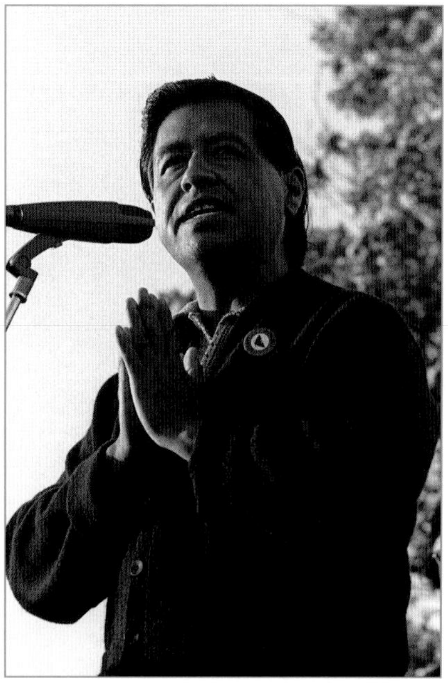

César Chávez, 1974.

As it turned out, one of the board members at the Simcoe gallery, Jean Glover, was a tobacco farmer, and she invited me to visit her farm in nearby Waterford. By then I had decided to start photographing the tobacco farm workers, and she helped me with leads and introductions to other farmers, and offered me a place to stay. But more than that: she understood. I remember roaming the countryside of Haldimand-Norfolk County all day long, locating farms on topographical maps, and then having a place to return to at night, or even for breaks in the middle of the day. Once I attempted to explain to Jean Glover how I was planning to apply to the Ontario Arts Council for a grant to fund my project. She cut me off and said matter-of-factly, "I know all about arts grants, son ... My son is a writer." Lady fortune was smiling on me just as I was getting started, only I didn't know that the project was going to take more than two decades for me to bring to a closure with this book.

I called the first phase of the project "Primers and Kiln Hangers: Tobacco Farm Workers in Ontario," which I promptly exhibited in the Steelworkers Hall in Hamilton as part of a program organized by the Photo Union Gallery, the first gallery of photography in Hamilton and one of the earliest in Canada. I continued to photograph the farm workers throughout Ontario, but now concentrated on migrant workers in the fruit and vegetable sector. I was working full-time at a different job, and when possible I took days off to work on this project. Therefore I was initially limited to areas to which I could reasonably travel back and forth in one day; but I eventually ended up covering all the various Ontario regions that drew migrant farmers. I exhibited the resulting work regularly in community galleries, and published it in a variety of media.

Early on I realized the importance of documenting the workers in the reality of their own homes in their own countries. I first visited the tiny island of Montserrat, a British colony in the Eastern Caribbean, in 1987. In Waterford I had met some workers from Montserrat, notably John Howsen, proud to be a British subject. Upon my arrival on his island he had said, "I will be your passport in Montserrat." And he was, opening doors for me everywhere I went.

A year later I travelled to Jamaica, accompanied by my wife, Giuliana Colalillo, and a Jamaican-Canadian friend, Tony Macfarlane. With Tony's help I located several of the Jamaican workers whom I had photographed in the apple orchards of Clarksburg, near Georgian Bay. All of them lived in remote villages, and they were all astonished to see me there. Stanley Rollston, one of the workers I was looking for, gave me a great bear hug in the middle of the street in Clonmell, and from that moment on I felt a special link to the village.

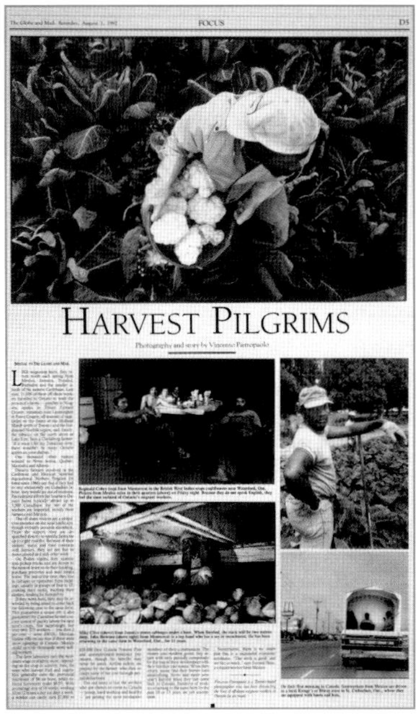

HARVEST PILGRIMS

The Globe and Mail, Aug. 1, 1992.

In 1993 I went to Mexico, but the process was a little different. A few months earlier I had made arrangements for the visit with two Mexican workers in Canada, and I travelled south to their country a few days before they were scheduled to leave. I waited for them at the Mexico City airport. When they first saw me there, they exclaimed both pleasure and incredulity that I had kept my word, for they had been a little sceptical at my unusual interest in them. For my part I had almost not recognized them because I had last seen them hard at work in an Ontario peach orchard, where they were sweaty, dirty, and tired-looking from having worked all day. Now they had new haircuts and were clean-shaven, with freshly ironed shirts and new clothes – when a migrant worker returns home, he wants to arrive looking like a success story. They carried bulging suitcases and cardboard boxes. After warm embraces all around, I was introduced as the *amigo de Canadá* to the dozen people waiting for them. That was to be my moniker for the remainder of the trip, as I first went to Querétaro, and later to the village of Monte Prieto, in the state of Guanajuato. I was a guest of Manuel González and his family, but I was more than a guest; I was a guest of honour. I photographed and interviewed people in the village and the surrounding area extensively, leaving time to visit friends in Mexico City who were also assisting me with this project.

Photography is an empowering medium. Not only does it provide information, but it can tell stories that transcend cultural boundaries and ideologies. Documentary photography is singularly powerful because it is immediate, realistic, and inherently believable. On my second trip to Monte Prieto, word spread quickly that I had returned, and so deep was the welcome I almost felt like a prodigal brother. I returned during a period when the men were in Canada, specifically to photograph the women. I wanted to hear their opinions without the influence of their husbands, brothers, or fathers. The two trips to Mexico were among the most memorable in my life. I brought pictures to give to the people I had photographed, the very least that I could do. Everyone was grateful and appreciative, especially because cameras were next to non-existent in the community. But soon there was a murmur in the village, that Señor Vincenzo's photographs "*salen bien. Lástima! salen solo en blanco y negro!*" – that is, my photos "come out good! Unfortunately, they only come out in black and white!"

Different configurations of this work have been exhibited in many locations: in Mexico City, as part of the Fotoseptiembre Festival; in a travelling show curated by the Canadian Museum of Contemporary Photography, and circulated in Mexico, Jamaica, Trinidad and Tobago, the United States, and across Canada; in Toronto at the Mayworks Festival, Harbourfront Centre, Stephen Bulger Gallery, and Gardiner Museum; in Windsor at the Art Gallery and Artcite Gallery, and at the nearby Leamington Arts Centre, where many workers were able to see it; in Gatineau's Montcalm Gallery, to mark the official visit of the president of Mexico to Canada; in Halifax, Montreal, Edmonton, and in numerous small communities.

In the intervening years I kept photographing migrant workers from time to time; in an effort to update my work, but more because I was reluctant to declare the project completed until the opportunity for this book presented itself. The last pictures I took for the book were in 2006, a span of twenty-two years from the first ones. The extracts of the workers' voices are from interviews that I did mostly in the 1980s and 1990s. In some ways little has changed since then. In some ways, much has. For certain, today the migrant farm workers are on the cusp of major change.

LIVING BETWEEN TWO WORLDS

The Workers Who Grow Our Food

Migrant farm workers have become a fixture across the country's agricultural hinterland. In Ontario in particular they are out on the land early in the spring, pruning fruit trees or tending newly planted fields. They can be seen harvesting by hand or with machinery from the intensive vegetable farms of Holland Marsh north of Toronto to the apple orchards of Georgian Bay, from the tender fruit farms of the Niagara Peninsula to the vast tomato farms and greenhouses of Essex County at the tip of Southwestern Ontario. They work in the Fraser Valley of British Columbia and the Annapolis Valley of Nova Scotia. They cultivate most of the tulips that adorn the city of Ottawa every spring.

Until recently the news media mostly ignored migrant farm workers, and therefore their existence went largely unknown by the wider public. Like migratory birds, most of the workers arrive in time for spring planting and leave in the autumn after the harvest is done. And like migratory birds again, it happens that their flights also arrive and depart mostly at night or in the early dawn. From a Canadian perspective, the ritual passage from one country to another might seem routine, effortless, and without incident, with everyone returning from whence he came. Goodbyes are said, hugs are given, a handshake or two, and the harvest comes to an official closure at the airport. *Hasta el año que viene*, until next year.

Migration

Never in history has migration been a greater phenomenon than in recent decades. Today some twenty million people are on the move yearly across the globe.[1] As a result of war and poverty, people are either being forcibly displaced as refugees or voluntarily seeking a way out of their region or country, moving... to somewhere – anywhere they hope to find opportunities for a better life.

If a time-lapse picture of migration patterns on the globe could be made from outer space, it would show surges of humanity in continual movement through airports, train stations, and seaports, and on endless roads. The multitudes travel from continent to continent. They somersault from deep within Africa into the heart of Western Europe, or from Latin America into North America. They push across the boundaries of both large and small states, as in Guatemalans going to Mexico or Haitians crossing over to the Dominican Republic in the shared island of Hispaniola. They move within the boundaries of sovereign states, as in the massive migrations in China, or go across seas and oceans, as in the ships that depart from Northern Africa, overloaded with refugees, packed like cattle – ships that capsize or drift, powerless, with tragic regularity in the Mediterranean Sea. They trek from rural areas to urbanized enclaves, as in rural Asians flocking rapidly to places like Mumbai and Beijing on one side of the globe, or Latin Americans making their way to the megalopolises of São Paulo and Mexico City on the other side.

Canada is not immune to this migratory phenomenon. Historically it has been one of the most important immigrant host nations, and from 1951 to 2007 it permitted entry to between 70,000 and 236,000 people annually, depending on the level of economic growth rates and population levels desired at different times. Within its boundaries residents have always been on the move, travelling from the Maritime provinces to the Western provinces to work in resource industries, or from north to south to work in manufacturing and service industries. In the process Canada's population has been transformed from rural- to urban-based; 80 per cent of the population now lives in urbanized areas. In most of the larger cities the "immigrant experience" has decidedly become deeply rooted and entrenched in everyday life.

Temporary Immigrants

In recent years, while immigration levels have more or less been kept at traditional postwar levels, a new concept – that of temporary immigrants – has crept into play, representing several government programs of a different nature.[2] At best the term "temporary immigrants" is contradictory because immigration is by essence a permanent disjuncture from the land of one's birth and home. Many immigrants, in the process of adjustment to a new life, have likened immigration to a process of social or cultural amputation. In contrast, a temporary workforce, or a mobile pool of workers, is a different phenomenon altogether. This workforce can be dispatched with regularity to where it is most needed, or customized to meet the need at hand with respect to the type of work and scale of a given project. It has radically different social and ethical ramifications. Indeed, it may signal a policy shift or a break with the enlightened tradition of giving immigrants a real stake in the country that they are helping to build, first through permanent residence and subsequently through citizenship. It does away with a sense of mutual belonging.

A temporary workforce in a Canadian context fits seamlessly with North-South geopolitical dynamics, to whatever extent Canada's economic output is made possible and sustainable by the importation of temporary workers paid at wages lower than what would be required for a minimum standard of living by permanent residents of the country. It is a project that began with the federal government's Canadian Seasonal Agricultural Workers Program (CSAWP) in 1966 and has continued in recent decades through several other temporary work arrangements.[3]

Seasonal Agricultural Workers Program

Canada is a member of an elite group of nations – the G8 nations – and none of them can completely grow its own food without the importation of foreign workers because agricultural salaries are too low to appeal to the local citizens. It is in this context that I photographed the workers that I call Harvest Pilgrims, all of whom came to this country as part of the CSAWP in Ontario.

In the beginning, in 1966, about 250 Jamaicans were contracted to work in tobacco farms along the shore of Lake Erie, an area that had been transformed into the cultivation of tobacco: the sandy soil, while too poor for growing food, was ideal for this crop. Tobacco quickly became the most lucrative crop that could be grown, and more and more land was turned over to its cultivation. The importation of migrant farm workers on a temporary and seasonal basis was a convenient and reliable solution to the uncertainties of a low-wage labour supply. The success of the program was immediate. For those first few Jamaican workers who had been selected to come to Ontario, it was a godsend; a rare opportunity to earn much-needed cash in Canadian dollars, which was of even greater value after being converted to U.S. dollars for use in Jamaica. By all accounts, those workers must have experienced a rather special excitement at the time. Like a proverbial chosen few, they were whisked out of isolated rural communities in an island country for a taste of adventure and work – and higher wages – in a foreign land of the North.

The program was soon expanded to include the member states of the Organization of Eastern Caribbean States and other island countries of the region, all of them of British colonial background – Barbados, Trinidad and Tobago, St. Lucia, St. Vincent and the Grenadines, Dominica, St. Kitts and Nevis, Antigua and Barbuda, Anguilla, and Montserrat. The infusion of a Caribbean black workforce in the tobacco belt of Southern Ontario, an area whose population was almost exclusively of white Anglo-Saxon and European origin, must have been conspicuous if not out of the ordinary. Yet little attention was paid to the presence of these workers. They arrived and departed with every harvest and in a short time were also working on fruit and vegetable farms.

The success of the program led to a further expansion, with an agreement between Canada and Mexico in 1974, and today Mexicans make up over one-half of all migrant workers. Eventually all provinces except Newfoundland and Labrador joined the program, although the overwhelming majority of the workers (over 80 per cent) are in Ontario. In 2008 over twenty thousand migrant farm workers came to Canada to be involved in virtually every aspect of fruit and vegetable farming as well as in the work of flower cultivation, apiary production, greenhouse vegetables, nurseries, and canning. In Ontario alone the migrant farm worker labour force accounts for an astonishing 55 per cent of all horticultural workers.[4] The program, employer-driven, is administered on behalf of the government by the Foreign Agricultural Resource Management Service (FARMS), and by its French-language counterpart, Fondation des enterprises de recrutement de main-d'oeuvre agricole étrangère (FERME). These are private non-profit organizations composed of farmers and growers. The individual farmers select the sending country from which they want workers, and after that initial involvement in the program, through a practice called "naming," they are in a position to also request specific individual workers for the following year's harvest.

Between Two Worlds

The migrants live between two worlds, North and South. Although they are "guest workers," the local populations traditionally refer to them as "offshore workers." The term "guest worker" is European in origin, and is perhaps associated too closely with the generations of intra-Europe migration (south to north) from the 1950s through the 1970s, a phenomenon with many negative connotations in the context of exploitive labour practices and human rights concerns. Possibly the term "offshore" worker is more acceptable in popular usage because it appears to have been initially coined in reference to the first workers in the program having been exclusively from island countries of the Caribbean. Although it may reflect a touch of discomfort, or perhaps represents an outright denial that a temporary worker program can be exploitive by nature – and therefore a potentially unethical practice – the term is more consistent with the historical self-image that Canada has rightly cultivated as an international promoter, if not always a defender, of human rights.

Eager and vulnerable, the workers are carefully selected back home. They must be young, healthy, and strong; muscle and brawn are what is needed. They are carefully screened. They have to pass medical checks and be in optimum physical condition. They must go to Mexico City or Kingston (or another major city in their homeland) for registration, medical examination, and other paperwork. Often they have to make several trips from remote villages, mostly at their own expense. It is overwhelmingly men who are sought for the program, and they are usually between the ages of twenty-two and forty-five (except in the case of returning migrants) – the most productive stage of their lives. Only 3 per cent of the migrants are women. Family members are not permitted, and the only eligible women are the few widows and single mothers who by virtue of their acquired marital status are the principal breadwinners. Often the migrants are the strength of the communities they leave behind. In Mexico and in the Caribbean they usually have small subsistence farms, which the women and children they leave behind must now look after. As one such mother in Mexico stated, "When the men go to *el norte* or Canada, we the women have to be both husbands and wives at the same time."[5]

The migrant farm workers believe themselves fortunate and privileged to have the opportunity to work in Canada, for they are the few selected as qualified from within their communities. When they return to their villages, it is they who now feel in control, for they have money to show, gifts to give, and stories to tell. They quickly attain a new status, improving their houses and displaying consumer goods purchased in Canada. They become the envy of those who were not chosen to work in Canada. But to maintain the higher standard of living, they have to migrate again the following year. Thus migration becomes entrenched in their lives as a self-perpetuating phenomenon: migration begets migration. Annual migration becomes a way of life, and the migrant farm worker is caught in a paradox. His life is a repetitive voyage that always ends where it started, with no hope of opportunities for lasting change for his family.

The migrant farm worker is destined to be always on the move; yet he is frozen in time, for all he can do is try to keep moving on an economic treadmill that will not let him advance to the next stage of his migratory journey. He is the centrepiece of an economic cycle that benefits all the players around him to a much greater extent; and the cycle only works as long as he is maintained in that pivotal role. To be sure, the annual increments in economic benefits that result from his work do improve his lot in life, but they come at considerable social cost and paradoxically keep him in a life of basic subsistence or poverty, for he will never be allowed to step out of that circle.

As a government program, CSAWP works extremely well, with an efficiency that both Canada and the sending countries sometimes tout as a model program. The original objectives of providing a reliable workforce at peak harvest time have been achieved with minimum bureaucratic complications and virtually no political fallout, especially when compared to other temporary work programs, which have tended to experience multiple unforeseen problems. Similarly, CSAWP stands out very favourably in comparison with the temporary work programs of other countries. Nevertheless, in the context of global geopolitical and social dynamics, it is hardly a concept to emulate as a permanent solution to the demand and supply of agricultural labour. Even if it carries considerable economic benefits at the individual worker level or macro regional level for the sending countries, the program has many undesirable social implications.

On the Canadian farms the workers live in virtual isolation from nearby communities, except for weekly trips to local shops for groceries. They have a contractual obligation to work for a particular farmer or grower, and they are dependent – beholden would be more accurate – on their employer for almost everything. They may not leave the farm without permission, or travel overnight, and are not free to look for work on any other farm except by prior agreement from the authorities in both the Canadian and their own governments. Employers have the power to administer repatriation, for any number of reasons at their discretion, and no independent dispute resolution system is in place. Employers set the hours of work, which can vary from day to day depending on the need and requirements.

The structure of the program is such that it is susceptible to abuse, though the majority of employers are fair and considerate of their workers. Arguably, the principle of being "beholden" to your employer for all your needs, even after work, is reminiscent of the indentured labour practices of the nineteenth century, whereby immigrants came to North America on contract to work for a number of years in exchange for passage and accommodation. Although the practice today is different – migrant farm workers in Canada work for wages and pay one-half or more of their own passage – the principle of near total dependence on the goodwill of the employer is not.

An example of the potential for abuse with no recourse appears in the practice of "naming" specific individual workers from one season as candidates to return for the next season. This practice is of benefit to both employer and employee, for if "named," the worker is guaranteed a return trip in the next year, and employers ensure themselves a worker with experience and familiarity of the conditions on the farm. However, a worker who is not named will most likely not be allowed to return. There are plenty of other workers back home eagerly competing for the opportunity to work in Canada. In fact, the sending country must maintain a reserve list of 10 per cent of the number of workers initially requested, and any of these could immediately be dispatched upon request from Canadian authorities in case of emergency conditions or unforeseen events on the farm.[6] Therefore the incentive for the worker to "perform" is great, reflecting the enormity of the employer's threat held over his head. The practice can result in a tense working environment: workers become reluctant to complain about day-to-day issues or working conditions lest they forfeit an opportunity to return. On average, about 70 per cent of the workers return each year. Some of them return for upwards of ten, twenty, and thirty years. These individuals have thus truly lived a significant portion of their working lives in between two worlds.

This practice of holding a reserve of workers who may or may not get to come to Canada keeps the individuals involved in a state of heightened anticipation. No doubt they experience much disappointment, especially after having gone through the elaborate screening process. For some individuals, their state of desperation and desire to work in Canada are such that they sometimes go to their country's main airport days ahead hoping for an opportunity to get into Canada. At the Benito Juárez International Airport in Mexico City, I met a man who had been waiting for three days. His luck turned in his favour when a scheduled worker did not show up due to illness, and he was selected as a replacement. The illness of one *paisano* (fellow countryman) was the other's ticket to Canada. Later, during the flight, he told me that the airplane meal had been his first "real" meal in three days. I asked him where he was going, and he replied "RR3 Ontario," but it was clear that mere details like that mattered little to him. He was just happy to have made it, to be in that select group who will have work.

Earlier in the year, after I had finished photographing some workers in a small village in Jamaica, a man approached me, addressed me as "Canadian photographer," and said, "I have strong hands. Working hands. Take me to Canada."[7] He raised both of his hands, holding the palms open in front of my eyes for me to see his calloused fingers.

Wages

The employers prepay airline tickets but recoup some of the cost through payroll deductions. There is no increase in pay based on experience for those who have worked on Canadian farms in previous years.

The pay is usually set at the minimum wage or slightly higher, but it varies from province to province. In Ontario, in 2009, it was $9.75 per hour. Workers in some crops such as tobacco earn slightly more, in recognition that it is harder work. There is no possibility of overtime under the law, which means that the only way of increasing earnings is to work longer days. Although their wages are higher than what they could earn back home, there are substantial costs and deductions, such as visa fees, private health insurance for off-work hours, and travel costs. The workers pay income tax to the Canadian government. They collectively make significant contributions to the Employment Insurance Commission (EIC) and Canada Pension Plan through regular deductions from their paycheques, but they are not entitled to receive any (substantial) benefits from the programs, other than parental benefits in certain cases.[8] As "temporary" guest workers they cannot be in Canada and be in a state of unemployment at the same time. As soon as their contracts expire, or if a job is finished prematurely and a transfer has not been prearranged to another farm, they must return home. If not, they would be in Canada illegally and subject to deportation. The requirement for these payroll deductions is absurd and ironic, for ultimately it translates into a direct subsidy for Canadian worker programs. In 2001 alone, migrant farm workers contributed some $3.4 million to the Canadian Employment Insurance Commission.[9]

Jamaican and Caribbean workers experience an added element: the Compulsory Savings Scheme. The employer is required to withhold 25 per cent of the workers' wages, and remit them directly to the respective sending countries. The worker receives the money at the end of the season, sometimes several months later, after administrative fees of at least 5 per cent have been deducted. This scheme has been likened to a sort of "forced savings" mechanism, but it is clearly paternalistic and creates an unnecessary bureaucracy paid for by workers. It also results in an unnecessary waiting time for workers to obtain their complete earnings.

Living and working conditions

Living in bunkhouses, cottages, or trailers right on the farm, the workers are usually close to the fields in which they labour, often only a few metres away. It is a convenience not only to them, no doubt, but also to the employers, who benefit from the knowledge and security of having the workers at the ready at all times. The workers are therefore available for work at all times, which is particularly important for farmers during the harvest season, when extreme amounts of work must be carried out in a short period of time. Harvests cannot be planned too much ahead of time. Ripe fruit and vegetables cannot wait for the convenience of schedules, and rain or drought are always a risk. As a result, at peak harvest workers sometimes work ten, twelve, or more hours per day, sometimes up to sixteen hours. Often they get no time off except for rainy days. Workers are paid only for actual hours worked; if the weather is favourable they end up working on Sundays too. No opportunity for work is passed over, as each worker tries to make the most of his sojourn in Canada.

It is true that farmers have usually lived and slept near to their fields, and have also worked long hours with little or no remuneration, especially on the traditional family farm. But farm workers face a different situation: as employees they cannot derive any tangible benefits from the farm other than their pay. Farm work, when performed by hired employees, cannot be considered a "labour of love." It is, simply, "work" – a paid service provided by workers.

The living conditions vary as much as the working conditions. The accommodations are basic, with shared rooms and cooking and bathroom facilities. I have seen some very spartan facilities, in spaces carved out of warehouses, but also some decent cottages or trailers, with proper heating. As a result of the day-to-day living arrangements on most farms, sometimes the only privacy is when a worker happens to be picking fruit in a remote corner of an orchard. The accommodations are supposed to be provided free of charge, but I did hear of abusive employers who charged for housing by requiring extra work. One employer, though, told me of his plans to build private bedrooms for his workers. He recognized the basic need for privacy, and understood that it would result in increased efficiency from a better-rested worker.

Farm work is one of the most dangerous occupations in Canada. Training in workplace safety is not a concept that has taken hold in farming culture, with tragic consequences. Farmers and farm workers account for 13 per cent of all occupational fatalities. In real numbers, an average of 115 work-related fatalities and 1,500 accidents occur every year.[10] In Ontario agricultural workers are excluded from the Occupational Health and Safety Act. Aside from the complex machinery and equipment used under trying conditions, the potential for serious accidents is heightened by the long working days, especially during harvest, or when there is a threat of rain and workers are pressured to hurry to finish off a certain amount of harvest.

Without organized unions to oversee workplace health and safety programs, the Canadian farm remains a dangerous place in which to work – for migrants and for Canadian farm workers alike, as well as for the employers and their families. Chemical and pesticide use is of particular concern because the effects are sometimes not immediately apparent. One day I watched a farmer spray his tobacco field with a machine that had fourteen nozzles. The cloud of spray hovered right above his head as he pulled the machine with his tractor across the field. He later remarked to me, in reference to his migrant workers, "If it's good enough for me, it should be good enough for them."[11]

It is difficult to obtain accurate data on health and safety infractions because they often go unreported except for truly dramatic occurrences. Certainly, sometimes workers are expected to work in recently sprayed fields and orchards, and, if necessary, alongside the farmer himself. A vegetable farmer who employed Eastern Caribbean workers once said to me, "We prefer them, I mean, myself I prefer them because if I need them in the middle of the night, I can go and get them." He clearly preferred them over local labour, and his attitude was at least partly based on his spraying practices. He said he sometimes sprayed at eleven or twelve during the night, when it was quiet and no-one was around. "It's safer that way," he said. "You might get it into your face, you don't want it drifting and getting into people's faces." In those cases, if he needed the Caribbean workers he could go to their bunk during the evening or night and say, "I need you for a half an hour, come out." And, he said, they would come out. Whereas the local workers, by seven or eight o'clock, "They've gone home to be with their husbands or their kids or whatever. You can't call 'em up and say 'I need a hand' 'cause they just don't come."[12]

Greenhouse Vegetables

In recent years migrant workers have become particularly indispensable to the newly established and unimaginably vast greenhouse vegetable farms of southwestern Ontario. These are nothing more than acres and acres of "fields" covered in glass, a recent development that is rapidly transforming the nature of horticulture. By 2005 Southwestern Ontario had at least 1,600 acres of greenhouses, up from only 300 acres a decade earlier.[13] Some of these structures are as large as football fields, and among the largest of their type in the world. The floors of these indoor farms are made of cement, and the buildings are completely climate controlled. The distances within some of the larger greenhouses (up to 50 acres) are such that managers and supervisors routinely travel through them in electric golf carts – a routine that is not that different from the practices in sprawling automobile assembly plants.

These are farms that have no soil. The seedlings are planted in small containers of a specially formulated growing medium, and tomato and pepper vines are programmed through a computer-controlled environment to keep growing through most of the year, irrespective of the seasons (except for the dead of winter, when the greenhouse is cleared of the previous year's growth and reprogrammed for the following year's cycle). The plants can grow up to five metres in length, or more, in climate-controlled conditions in which light, temperature, and irrigation are constantly monitored and adjusted for optimum conditions by computer. The vines are trained to grow on long and tall trellises, positioned for easy harvesting through the use of specially designed cherry pickers. The plants have almost no resemblance to the natural growth of open fields. The vegetables are perfectly shaped, consistent in size, with no blemishes, almost as if they were stamped out artificially in a factory.

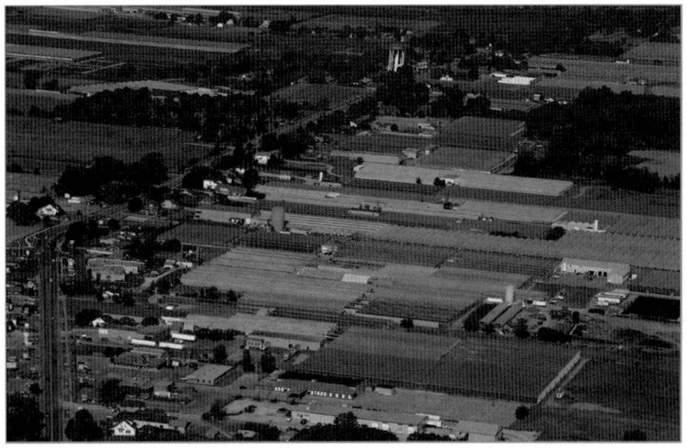

Greenhouses in southwestern Ontario, 2006.

At the very least this new kind of horticulture is industrial farming, and it is a remarkably efficient system for productively growing vegetables almost year-round in Canada's harsh climate. But the implication of having de facto industrial workers considered as agricultural workers raises fundamental issues in labour relations. Wayne Hanley, the national president of the UFCW Canada, suggests that "a greenhouse or a mushroom plant is no different than a pork-producing plant. We're dealing with a perishable product. The difference between a traditional factory and a greenhouse is the equipment that's being used to produce a product. Rather than having a drill press, it's a vine that's growing and something that's being picked."[14]

The large-scale cultivation of vegetables in greenhouses represents a radical shift in age-old farming practices, and will have an erasable impact on farm life and culture, regardless of whether the ownership is family-based or corporate-based. It is in this context that efforts to establish formal labour relations through unionization have captured the interest of the wider community beyond the agricultural sector.

Unionization

Labour legislation in Canada is a provincial matter, and the right of all classes of farm workers to collective bargaining thus varies from province to province. In Ontario and Alberta agricultural workers are not permitted to unionize. Given that Ontario is where most of the migrant workers are employed, this restriction has had significant consequences in labour relations. Attempts to introduce amendments to the Ontario Labour Relations Act, which governs all labour relations in the province, have been consistently repudiated. In 1993 the provincial New Democratic Party government introduced a bill to permit collective bargaining for farm workers, only to have it abolished by the subsequent Conservative government. In 1999, in a landmark ruling, the Supreme Court of Canada decreed that farm workers enjoy the same rights as other workers to associate freely without fear of intimidation or coercion. The Ontario government responded by enacting the Agricultural Employees Protection Act, which permits employee associations but does not compel employers to negotiate labour issues with workers if they do not want to do so. Employee associations are powerless in collective bargaining if employers do not want to negotiate and enter into formal agreements on any such matter, which was precisely what occurred at the two Ontario mushroom-growing plants of Kingsville (in 2003) and Milton (in 2009).

UFCW Canada, which has been active in farm-belt communities since the early 1990s, has taken the initiative of organizing and mobilizing migrant farm workers. Not surprisingly, it has faced daunting obstacles, especially in Ontario.

The union has embarked on a multidirectional strategy, working simultaneously on several fronts. First it opened a string of "migrant worker support centres" in eight key farming communities across Canada, including four in Ontario: Leamington, Bradford, Simcoe, and Virgil; two in British Columbia: Kelowna and Abbotsford; one in Portage la Prairie, Manitoba; and one in Saint-Rémi, Quebec. The centres offer workers a variety of much-needed services that have either fallen into the grey areas of bureaucracy or been ignored out of hand. These include assistance with worker compensation claims; preparation of income tax returns; translation assistance in medical care, banking, and insurance claims; questions with CPP contributions and EIC parental benefits; assisting sick or injured workers at hospitals and with doctors; and many other essential services. The centres have become an essential lifeline to the workers, who in the past would reluctantly rely on their employers or their sending country's representatives, or occasionally volunteers in the community who had become aware of their plight.

Second, the union also challenged existing Ontario legislation in the courts, seeking the repeal of the Agricultural Employees Protection Act of 2002 and its replacement with appropriate legislation allowing collective agreements. Both of its challenges at the Supreme Court of Canada proved successful, although the province of Ontario took no action in response. In 2006, after a challenge by the union, the Occupational Health and Safety Act of Ontario was extended to include coverage for farm workers. In 2007 the union launched an appeal against a mushroom factory farm operation that refused to negotiate a collective agreement. In a historic decision brought on by this challenge, the Ontario Court of Appeal ruled that farm workers, including migrant farm workers, have the right to collective bargaining.[15] The Ontario government was mandated to enact appropriate legislation within twelve months, but it opted to launch an appeal at the Supreme Court. In 2008 the union made labour history when workers ratified the first-ever contract for migrant farm workers in Portage la Prairie.

Given the legal precedents, it is likely that the final decision, when it comes, will be in the workers' favour, and the union is gearing up to organize workers in Ontario, which has been its third point of strategy. It has already been working to organize farms in Manitoba, where so far three locals have been established, and in Quebec. In Manitoba, not surprisingly, certification is being challenged. In Quebec the union has also challenged legal roadblocks in court.

As part of its strategy, the union embarked on a program of extensive community outreach. Instead of working in isolation, it has worked collaboratively with various community groups, faith-based organizations, local labour leaders, academics, research groups, and artists concerned about social justice and the plight of the farm workers. The efforts have led to increased awareness and community-building.

Finally, the union has gone outside the country to forge links with the Mexican Congress Commission on Population, Borders, and Migration. Given that the migrant farm workers from Mexico cannot achieve a status of permanent residency in Canada, and that they return yearly to their homes in Mexico, Mexican authorities must be involved in the ongoing discussions to guarantee them better working and living conditions. With both countries being members of the North American Free Trade Agreement (NAFTA), these discussions could be especially relevant in the context of the demand for increased numbers of workers. According to the UFCW Canada's Hanley, there was no other way of dealing with the labour impasse. In March 2009 the union launched a complaint about the matter with the International Labour Organization of the United Nations. The union had to develop an approach that, according to Hanley, was "totally different." He argues that because "there is no agreement procedure, there's no arbitration procedure, and if we are to help these workers . . . we've got to provide different types of services." The union, Hanley says, has to work to extend the health and safety laws to farm workers, to set some enforcement mechanisms in place. As it is now, "It's not like we can file a grievance, and say, 'if you don't fix a problem we'll go out and arbitrate.' It's totally different. . . . The family farm as we knew it forty years ago is considerably different. These are corporations that are running farms now."[16]

Symbiotic Relationship

The migrant farm worker system has now become completely entrenched in the agricultural cycle of Canadian farms. In fact, it could be argued that the greenhouse vegetable industry would not have developed, or at least would not have developed so rapidly, without the presence of and security provided by a reliable supply of low-wage labour as manifested in a migrant farm worker program.[17]

The overwhelming dependence of Canadian farmers on foreign migrant farm workers was dramatized during the H1N1 swine influenza outbreak in Mexico in April 2009. Early in the crisis – which occurred just as the farming season was getting underway – Canadian growers feared that as a health precaution the federal government would place an embargo on farm workers from Mexico. This move would have thrown the growers, with their half-planted fields, into complete disarray. They would have had to scramble to recruit workers from other countries, an unlikely prospect given short notice. "If they put an embargo on this program," said Jacques Notaro, a lettuce grower from Quebec, "it will be catastrophic for me and the great majority of other growers." Ray Duc, a grape grower and member of the board of the Ontario Fruit and Vegetable Growers' Association, expressed the same fear: that Mexican workers are a "good, reliable source of help, and we're dependent on them."[18] Fortunately for all, no embargo was declared. Canada and Mexico agreed that the standard medical examination of would-be migrants, coupled with increased medical monitoring, was sufficient safeguard.

Prior to the development of the greenhouse vegetable industry, the area around Leamington was already reliant on migrant workers, and it is unlikely that massive agribusiness investments would have been made without the expectation that a reliable workforce would continue to be at the ready. As in family farms of earlier times, a symbiotic relationship has evolved between the greenhouse owners and their workers; each is dependent on the other.

The "temporary" nature of the migrant farm worker program is in reality a myth, because the benefits of the program to the employers can only exist through the preservation of the program in the long term. The unique attraction of the program is the contradictory concept of "permanent temporariness," which can be surmised as the reason why landed immigrant status is not allowed for these workers. This feature is ironic; for these workers would seemingly comply with many of the requirements under immigration guidelines, such as skilled trades, operational equipment knowledge, and work experience. The migrant workers also happen to have what other prospective immigration applicants do not: Canadian experience.

Migrant farm workers have never taken jobs from Canadian residents – a point that is widely acknowledged. Evelyn Brown, an elderly apple grower in the Thornbury area, echoed the sentiments of most farmers as she worked alongside her employees packing apples in large, heavy crates. When I asked the grandmotherly farmer why she hired people from outside the country – in her case, Jamaicans – she said, "Why do I hire them? Because I want to pick my apples, and I want to pick them seven days a week. Canadians wouldn't pick apples seven days a week. No! You can't get them to work five days, even. You just can't get five days, thirty-five hours a week, or forty hours a week. . . . Without my Jamaican boys I'd be stuck."[19]

Hanley goes further, stating emphatically that these workers "are not people that are replacing the kind of jobs that Canadians aspire to, or even Canadian families aspire their children to." He suggests that there are moral issues around the questions of temporariness, and "that there's a social obligation for us advocates of workers to take on that responsibility ... it's truly a social obligation to help the most oppressed, the most needy, and this group of workers falls into that category." Any temporary worker program that allows workers to come into the country, he says, should also "allow that worker to be a landed immigrant and eventually a Canadian citizen. You're bringing someone to Canada who will make a contribution ... they're making a huge contribution already, and then we say thank you very much, goodbye."[20]

The benefits of temporary workers to Canadian society are many and far-reaching. Aside from the hugely positive impact on the sustainability of both Canadian agriculture in general and the family farm in particular, aside from their contributions to the EIC and CPP, temporary workers leave little trace of themselves behind, except some of their hard-earned money. Before returning home, they spend a substantial portion of their earnings for living expenses, and they purchase materials and goods as presents and investments for later resale at home. The retail shops in the farm belts of Canada are the prime beneficiaries. According to one estimate, the workers inject about $82 million annually into Ontario alone.[21] When they leave, they also take with them whatever social problems they might have had or developed in the future were they to remain permanently in Canada. In cases of injury, efforts are quickly made by government authorities on both sides to repatriate them, lest they become a burden on provincial workers' compensation programs and the Canadian health-care system.

The program provides other economic benefits that are easy to overlook, principally to the Canadian, Mexican, and West Indian airline companies; the airlines benefit from the annual sale of about twenty thousand seats. The flights represent guaranteed ticket sales for which the airlines can plan with certainty ahead of time – the sales are not dependent upon the strength of the tourism dollar or the competitiveness of vacation packages. There are no advertising costs incurred, unlike the heavy advertising that fills entire pages of Canadian newspapers in the winter months. The same airplanes that carry Canadians to the famous resorts of Acapulco in Mexico and Runaway Bay in Jamaica also deliver workers to and from Canadian farms. The economic impact on the airline industry is enormous. If the migrant worker program was not seasonal, these flights would not be reoccurring year after year, like clockwork.

The 100-Mile Diet

In recent years Canadians have become increasingly interested in what can be loosely termed "food culture." Supermarket shelves are perennially overstocked; merchandising practices like supersizing and wholesale purchasing encourage excessive consumption; and food is omnipresent through larger-than-life pictures on billboards, in delectable colour in the pages of glossy magazines, and in convincing television ads. More than ever before, people are keenly interested in talking about organic food, slow food, fast food, junk food, gourmet food, diverse food, heritage food, urban food, ethnic food, comfort food, country food, fair value food, and, lastly, local food. Chefs are the new celebrities. The term "foodies" has entered our lexicon, and consumers clamour for the latest cheese made from raw milk. Writers produce an abundance of food books that are guaranteed virtual success almost overnight. Who would have taken the concept of the food channel seriously only a decade ago?

This obsession with food has led to a debate on the social benefits of the "100-mile diet," which challenges consumers to favour locally produced foods, preferably those produced within a symbolic 100-mile radius of their homes. The desire for local food initially grew out of environmental concerns, especially the need to reduce greenhouse gases by avoiding trucking or flying in food from long distances. Other benefits immediately became apparent, namely the positive economic impact on local producers, the almost forgotten experience of tasting truly fresh fruit and vegetables, and the strength of community building through mutual support among local consumers, producers, and vendors. Farmers' markets, almost forgotten relics in urban areas, have re-emerged strongly in recent years to claim their traditional role as community anchors.

But one crucial component has been missing in this continuing debate: the role of the farm worker, especially the migrant farm worker. Low wages have been the rule in the history of farming in Canada. The principle of low wages goes back to the origins of the family farm, to a time when all members of the family contributed their labours and stoically accepted the seemingly endless workday, from dawn to dusk, as being normal. The evolution to larger farms, and to the industrial-type operations on the rise today, could not have occurred without the explicitly lower wages established in earlier times. As a corollary, consumers have for generations become accustomed to paying low prices for fresh food, in contrast with the relatively higher prices that are the norm for non-perishable and processed food items. For example, it is usually not questioned why a typical chocolate bar should cost the equivalent of one pound of fresh Ontario apples, especially because the chocolate bar has a long shelf life and does not have to be sold quickly.[22]

Arguably, there is a basic social contradiction in the 100-mile diet, for in essence it cannot be sustained without the importation of non-local labour, and in reality it must translate mostly into a foreign guest-worker force. Given our pricing structure for food production and distribution, farmers have found it necessary to import workers from up to 5,000 miles away. From this perspective, it is particularly disheartening to see the reluctance of popular commentators and interest groups to introduce workers' issues into the ongoing love affair with food that we see in magazine articles, food events, radio talk shows, and the like. Food policy analyst Wayne Roberts notes "the inevitable and extensive poverty, inequality and disruption that come from underpaying food workers."[23] Nevertheless, the tone in the popular media in Canada continues to be one of wide-eyed wonder at the splendour and beauty of fresh food, seldom linking the food we eat to the host of labour issues arising in its production, processing, packaging, and delivery to our restaurant tables and kitchen counters. The consistent disregard of workplace issues is reflected even in the promotional efforts of some environmental agencies, one of which has even taken out full-colour advertisements in Toronto newspapers extolling the value of locally grown diverse vegetables (and rightly so) in places like Holland Marsh. The ad quotes a farmer saying, "In Ontario we shouldn't have to import produce. We can grow it locally.... Growing [vegetables] here means they don't have to be shipped from half-way around the world."[24] Unfortunately, the advertisement did not mention that Holland Marsh farmers are forced to import farm workers from halfway around the world, or that the area has one of the highest concentrations of migrant farm workers in the country.

We do import foods from distant places such as California, Mexico, Chile, Argentina, Brazil, Central America, Europe, and even more remote locations like Uzbekistan, Asia (which sends us fresh garlic!) – foods that are often similar to produce grown in Canada. In grappling with environmental issues, the high cost of gasoline, and "carbon footprints," people arguably experience a sense of collective guilt about this long-distance practice. The concept of fair trade food value has been applied to food products from foreign countries, typically coffee, tea, and some fruit. By paying fair trade value, consumers agree to pay a premium for a product in an effort to rectify poor wages and working conditions for workers and to improve environmental measures for farmland – and both of those measures will result in substantial community benefits. This is a concept that has taken hold in a major way in Europe, especially in England, the Netherlands, and Italy, and the Scandinavian countries. According to Roberts, the city of Malmö, Sweden, has made fair trade in food a hallmark of its civic culture: "a Swedish-owned fairtrade coffee chain, Barista, is unionized, its owner says, 'because we believe in applying fair trade at home as well.'"[25] Given that our own Canadian food is produced with wages set at rates too low to be acceptable to anyone except foreign migrant workers, has the time come to apply the fair value food benchmark to at least some of the fresh food produced in Canada?

Community

The migrant farm worker population has gone from being completely unseen and ignored to establishing itself as a strong presence, even if it is only for a part of the year. In the early days of the program, the only mention of farm workers would have occurred in the odd article that might have appeared as a human interest story in a local newspaper. Indeed, in the first twenty-five years of the program, fewer than a dozen feature-length articles appeared in mainstream magazines or newspapers in Canada.[26] Contact with workers was usually limited to the family that was employing them and to the shopkeepers who supplied their basic needs. In the case of family farms, long the hallmark of Ontario agriculture, strong relationships flourished between employer and employees. Sometimes the two worked side by side, stooping in the same rows of vegetables, enjoying breaks at the end of the long rows, sharing stories about their families. Some farmers arranged bus trips to scenic places – Niagara Falls, perhaps – if conditions on the farm were right. Others took a personal interest in their workers' welfare and arranged for medical care and other services. In the traditional family farm, with its usual ambience of camaraderie, farmers often relegate day-to-day operations to their trusted offshore workers of many years. One farmer, Frank Lehn, of Wheatly, Ontario, tried to help a worker obtain landed immigrant status in gratitude for her many years of excellent service. He found that was not possible under the program. Still, other than these personal relations on the work site, contact with people outside the farm was minimal beyond the weekly outings to town for groceries.

In the late 1980s, as the number of workers increased, local churches began to offer services for migrant farm workers. In Simcoe, Rev. Steven Chambers of St. James United Church and Rev. Michael Beacom of St. Michael's Catholic Church began offering services to Caribbean workers as early as 1987. By the late 1980s Mexicans were numerous enough in Southern Ontario that they began to mark their national day of independence, Fiestas Patrias, by gathering together in La Salette, Ontario. A local priest, Rev. Ted Slamen, who once worked in Guatemala, and later Rev. Frank Murphy offered regular services in Spanish, at Our Lady of La Salette Catholic Church. The Mexican workers soon began to hold a procession by solemnly carrying a small statue of the Virgin of Guadalupe, the patron saint of Mexico, along the main street all the way to Byer's General Store. That store operated a gasoline service station that turned out to be a convenient open space for a large gathering. Following the religious part of the festivities, the Mexicans listened to impromptu performances of *ranchera* (Mexican country) music by the farm workers themselves. They consumed doughnuts provided courtesy of the gas station.

It was the beginning of the founding of a community, a somewhat virtual community because for half of the year its members lived thousands of miles away and in the other half they lived isolated in small groups in hundreds of farms across the province. This trend continued, with organized activities in many towns, in particular Simcoe and Bradford.

By the mid-1990s, with the greenhouses in full operation, the town of Leamington was "bursting at the seams with Mexican flavour," as a local resident remarked to me during a tour of the town. Stores and restaurants catered to the new population (at least for eight months of the year) and quickly became meeting places of note, including the Tacos Tony restaurant in the heart of downtown. The variety of goods available rivalled even Toronto's famed Kensington Market as a place to locate specialty goods from Mexico.

Given that the greenhouses are located on the edge of Leamington, workers are easily able to walk to the town centre from their homes. A profusion of restaurants, shops, and services cater to the migrant farm workers. The

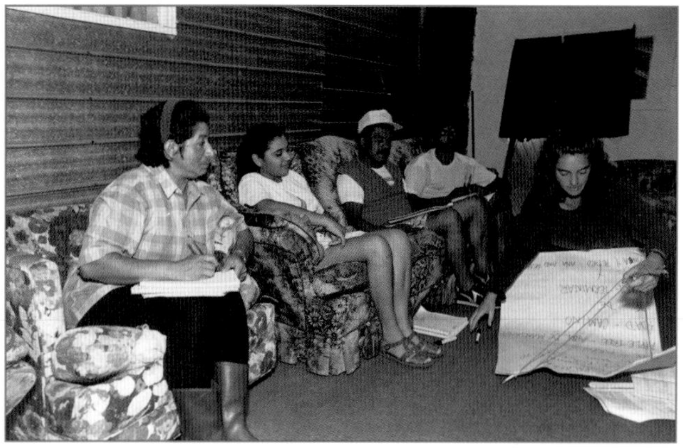

A Frontier College ESL class, 1995.

Leamington Arts Centre was supportive in holding numerous activities of interest to the population of Mexicans, including art shows, English language classes, and seminars on traffic safety and rules of the road for bicycles.[27] Some of the town merchants did the reverse: they took Spanish lessons, reflecting a desire to communicate better with their customers. UFCW Canada opened its first migrant farm worker centre in Leamington. It was followed by a branch office of the Mexican Consulate in Toronto, followed again by a Jamaican Liaison office.

The frenzy of activity culminated with the founding, by local community groups, of the festival Dos Culturas/Two Cultures, an annual mid-September celebration of the national day of independence of Mexico. The main street, Talbot Avenue, is closed to traffic, and an extensive program of entertainment, dancing, and music featuring professional mariachi bands, folk dancers, and singers takes place on a giant stage. The growers, who support the event financially, have a place of honour. Blue plastic chairs are reserved for them at the front. Specialty vendors line the streets with their wares, as do food vendors providing Mexican delicacies. The festival attracts people from all around the region, especially people of Latin American background, and between two and three thousand people dance the day and night away. At the end of the evening, one of the largest stores in the area, El Campeon Variety, holds a friendly draw for the hundreds of migrant workers present. Everyone wins something.

The festival is transforming Leamington, and is a dramatic contrast to the town's "official" Tomato Festival, which involves a beauty pageant and massive parade, but from which the migrant farm workers have been conspicuously absent among the dozens of floats that represent virtually every business and social group in the town. Regardless, the Mexican migrant farm workers have ostensibly left their imprint, and Leamington, the tomato capital of Canada, will never again be the same.

Many organizations have devoted substantial resources in assisting farm workers. Most notable among these is Frontier College, which has been teaching English as a Second Language to migrant workers since 1989, during a period when almost no other organization was aware of their existence. Frontier College's motto of "hard work and low pay" seems eerily ominous at first, because it is not a university college but a placement service for university students who, among other things, want to teach literacy to workers on farms. It recruits students and trains them as "labour-teachers," and then finds a placement for them on a willing farm for the summer months. The farmer has to agree to hire the teachers under the same conditions and wages as the migrant farm workers. Employers often have to be persuaded that the labour-teacher from university can actually handle the arduous work on the farm and will not quit after the first few weeks of stooping in a strawberry field. At the end of the workday, to the astonishment of both the workers and the employers, the labour-teachers hold English classes for the workers. Classes, organized until recently by Brent Poulton, are held regularly in about thirty to forty farms.

Some of the labour-teachers have become advocates for the workers, on the job and beyond, and hundreds of lifelong relationships have been established between Mexicans and Canadians as a result. Canadian labour-teachers have sometimes travelled to Mexico to visit their former "students." In describing the enriching experience, one of the labour-teachers, Chris Scoggins, told me, "I may have taught the farm workers a few words and phrases of basic English, but they have taught me much more about life."[28]

Since the early 1990s a virtual explosion of interest and activities has centred on migrant farm workers. According to an informal survey, no less than twelve community-based organizations have sprung up to help and advocate for migrant farm workers. No fewer than five universities and research institutes have produced theses or in-depth studies. Feature articles in the Canadian media now appear with regularity. Annual soccer tournaments of migrant farm workers take place in Simcoe, Niagara-on-the-Lake, and Bradford. The Canadian Museum of Contemporary Photography, Art Gallery of Windsor, Mayworks Festival, and others have mounted photographic exhibitions. The Gardiner Museum of Ceramic Art has held clay workshops on farms that employ Mexican workers. At least two documentary films have been made, and many radio and TV spots have been broadcast. The critical mass of migrant farm workers is such that mobile tortilla vendors now regularly visit farms throughout Southern Ontario, capitalizing on a new market by selling their specialties principally to Mexican workers.

A disproportionate amount of this attention, it seems, is directed at the Mexican workers. Most of the community-based organizations have Spanish names. Does this simply reflect that the Mexicans are the majority of workers? Is it because, unlike Caribbean workers, they don't speak English, and are therefore more vulnerable in the eyes of Canadians? Does it reflect subtle attitudes that are remnants of prejudicial times of the past in Canadian society? These are some of the questions that will need to be addressed in coming years.

In any case, the migrant farm workers, as a class, have finally captured the interest of Canadians. In so doing they have spawned a cultural and media industry, and not an immodest one at that, since all the articles, research projects, academic literature, and art projects translate into tangible and cultural benefits for their creators as well as for society in general.[29] In Jamaican patois, one might say, "Walk good," meaning "Until next time." Yet a bitter aftertaste remains in the migrant farm worker program, which can be summed up best by a Mexican saying "*todo sigue igual*" – "nothing ever changes."

Up to now, perhaps. For migrant farm workers are finally on the agenda, and the rest of us in Canada will surely have to sit up and take notice.

Notes

1 International Organization for Migration, "World Migration 2008: Managing Labour Mobility in the Evolving Global Economy" at <http://www.iom.int/jahia/Jahia/about-migration/facts-and-figures/global-estimates-and-trends>.

2 It is a new concept in postwar Canada, but not a new concept altogether, for temporary workers were brought to Canada from China as early as the 1880s to work on the Canadian Pacific Railway. See Immigration Watch Canada website <immigrationwatchcanada.org>.

3 The Live-in Caregiver Program, established in 1992, allows temporary workers into Canada as nannies. The Temporary Foreign Worker Program allows workers on a temporary basis to work in some agricultural operations, such as mushroom farms. The Project for Occupations Requiring Lower Levels of Formal Training, introduced in 2002 and modified in 2007, allows employers to hire employees in occupations that usually require at most a high-school diploma or a maximum of two years of job-specific training, for sectors such as cleaning, hospitality, manufacturing, and oil and gas and construction, for a maximum of two years. In 2008 a specialized program was organized through Okanagan College, Kelowna, B.C., designed to further train already experienced Jamaican workers in skilled trades in response to the needs of the Canadian economy. Upon graduation and certification from the college, these special status workers will be able to apply for permanent landed immigrant status.

4 Leigh Binford, "The Seasonal Agricultural Workers Program and Mexican Development," Canadian Foundation for the Americas (FOCAL) policy paper, FPP-06-07, Ottawa, September 2006, p. 2.

5 Quoted in Vincenzo Pietropaolo, "Nosotras, We the Women," *BorderCrossings*, 58 (May 1996), p. 30. In Mexico, the term "*el norte*" is commonly used to mean the United States.

6 Maxwell Brem, "Migrant Workers in Canada: A Review of the Canadian Seasonal Agricultural Workers program," policy brief, North-South Institute, Ottawa, 2006, p. 6.

7 This particular incident occurred in the village of Aboukir, Jamaica, and is similar to requests that I also received in Mexico.

8 As a result of recent initiatives taken by the United Food and Commercial Workers Union Canada, many workers have begun to apply for parental benefits under the EI, something that had been largely overlooked by relevant authorities. Some 4,000 such claims were made between 2003 and 2006. UFCW Canada, *Report on the Status of Migrant Farm Workers in Canada 2006–2007*, Rexdale, Ont., n.d.

9 Brem, "Migrant Workers in Canada," p. 8.

10 Veema Verma, *The Mexican and Caribbean Seasonal Agricultural Workers Program*, report, North-South Institute, Ottawa, November 2003; UFCW Canada, *Status of Migrant Farm Workers in Canada, 2006–2007*.

11 This conversation took place on a farm in Otterville, Ont., in 1984.

12 Interview with author, Holland Marsh, Ont., 1986.

13 Jodi Di Menna, "Vineland," *Canadian Geographic*, September–October 2007, p. 74.

14 Interview with author, March 5, 2009.

15 The Court of Appeal for Ontario, *Fraser v. Ontario (Attorney General)*, 2008 ONCA 760, Nov. 17, 2008.

16 Interview with author, Toronto, March 5, 2009.

17 This is a position supported by a number of studies. See, for instance, Tanya Basok, *Tortillas and Tomatoes: Transmigrant Mexican Harvesters in Canada* (Montreal and Kingston: McGill-Queen's University Press, 2002). She also makes this argument, on p. 85: "It is the need to have workers who are available on demand, and not economic vulnerability, that makes most Leamington greenhouse growers dependent on offshore labour." In the same book, one of the growers, in an interview on p. 119, states: "Without the offshore labour, we wouldn't be the size we are now."

18 Notaro and Duc both quoted in Ingrid Peritz, "Flu Outbreak Leaves Mexican Workers in Limbo," *The Globe and Mail* (Toronto), April 27, 2009, p. A7.

19 Interview with author, Clarksburg, Ont., 1993. Several studies have substantiated this position.

20 Interview with author, Toronto, March 5, 2009.

21 Brem, "Migrant Workers in Canada," p. 10.

22 In March 2009 in a Toronto supermarket, one pound of Ontario apples cost between $1.29 and $1.99, depending on the variety; a typical chocolate bar of four ounces cost between $1.19 and $1.99, depending on the brand.

23 Wayne Roberts, *The No-Nonsense Guide to World Food* (Oxford and Toronto: New Internationalist and Between the Lines, 2008), p. 131.

24 Quoted from an advertisement by the Green Belt (number one in a series), *The Toronto Star*, Feb. 3, 2009, p. A8.

25 Roberts, *No-Nonsense Guide to World Food*, pp. 150–51.

26 My research has uncovered eleven articles, which could be considered of feature length, published in Canada.

27 In 2003 the Leamington Arts Centre invited me to exhibit a selection of work from this book that I called "Essential Workers." An a cappella choir of Mexican women workers had been organized in the area, and they performed at the opening night of the exhibit. To my great surprise and delight, one of the members of the choir was Delfina Vale Gutierrez, whom I had photographed nine years earlier in another part of Ontario, and was also in one of the photographs displayed. In the ensuing years, she had changed farms and regions in Ontario.

28 Interview with author.

29 Including this book.

AN IMAGINARY LETTER TO A MIGRANT FARM WORKER

March 26, 2009
Toronto, Ontario

Dear Fermín,

As I look over my pictures in Toronto and listen to the tape of the words that you spoke to me years ago in Monte Dorado, my thoughts are dedicated to you.

I remember how you carefully told me your full name so that I would understand it – Fermín Antonio Guitiérrez Sánchez. Your name alone declares that you are a citizen of Mexico. But you are also a worker, the truest of essential workers: you grow our food. You are like a harvest pilgrim: you return to the same area, often to the same farm, year after year, in an annual pilgrimage. You live between two worlds, North and South. Like the *golondrinas* (swallows), you migrate north every spring, and return home every fall.

Home? Where can home be for you and your compatriots who live in Canadian farms, four, six, or eight months of the year? The world of your birth is a rural community in the state of Oaxaca, or maybe Michoacán, or Tlaxcala, or Guanajuato; the world of economic survival for you is a farm in Ontario, or maybe in British Columbia, Manitoba, or Quebec. In your first home, you have a family, a culture, an identity, all braided in your history. In your second home, you are a migrant farm worker, a visitor and guest – always a transient. For you live fully neither here nor there. Year after year.

The seeds of your journey were planted when you first travelled by bus from your *rancho* (village) to Oaxaca City, then overnight to Mexico City. How did you like *la capital?* One of the largest cities on the planet – weren't you wide-eyed with wonder at the strangeness of all things? You had been there before, for a physical examination, to prove that you were perfect enough and strong enough for working on Canadian farms. Nervous, even afraid, as you entrusted your fate to the virgin of Guadalupe, and made the sign of the cross on the very instant that the airplane defied the forces of gravity and took you magically into the skies above the clouds. It was your first flight, and you couldn't have known it then, but you would become very familiar with Benito Juárez International Airport in your annual journeys to Canada.

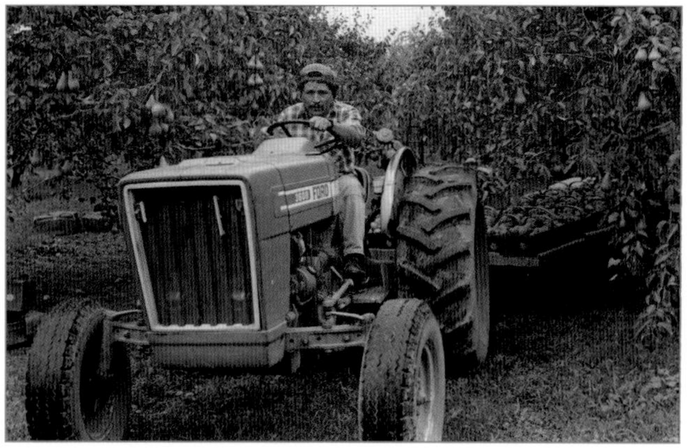

The next morning, you had arrived somehow on the Canadian farm. *Gracias a Dios*! Was this the place written on your instructions – RR3 Brantford, Ontario? You looked out the window of the room that you shared with four *paisanos* (compatriots), strangers to each other until last night at the airport. You marvelled at the size of the farm, the vast landscape, the neat and tidy farm buildings with lawns, and tall maple trees that seemed to stand like sentries all along the driveway. And flower gardens all around. Pretty like a postcard, so different from the small parcel of land at the foot of the *cerro* (mountain) that you share with your brothers in Mexico. The flat fields of Ontario reassure you. Yes, here there will be *mucho trabajo* (lots of work), the very reason for this distant journey.

It all seems like a dream, at first. But then you get a feeling of emptiness in your stomach for your beloved *esposa* (wife), your children, and your aging parents, even for the sound of the village dogs yelping at the church bells. You miss everything already.

Your first job was tobacco. You ripped the huge leaves off the plant fast, to keep up with the machine that was moving down the rows. A back-breaking job that drenched you with sweat and covered your arms with sticky black tar, and in those first few weeks your bones ached like they never had before. Canadian farmers saw value in your labours, and everyone said "*el mexicano rinde*" (the Mexican is worth it). Of late you have been picking cucumbers, cauliflower, and celery. But I remember that you once said the best work was in pears, because you could stretch your body in all directions to pick them off the branches, carefully, one by one, so they wouldn't bruise.

You have eyes to see, you feel many injustices, yet you are grateful for your good fortune. You earn the minimum wage. Last year they raised it to $8.90 an hour. Not a lot. But you are thrifty, and back home Adelina knows how to stretch those dollars a long way. Ah, she will be so happy to see you again! You are so proud of how little Francisco wrote you that letter, with every word made out neat and perfect. And Alejandra – she's already grown into a beautiful *señorita*, and next year you'll have to bring her a special gift from Canada for her *quinceaños* (fifteenth birthday). This is why you keep coming back, even if they don't pay you a cent more for all the years of experience that you have with every season. And when it rains, it's worse. You have to work another day to make up for it. No work, no pay, remember? *Hora trabajada, hora pagada*.

Worst of all you are forced to do whatever the boss wants. He's good to you, usually, he's a family man too. But you're good to him too, aren't you? You work so hard, even though you know you will always be a guest. And guests walk on tiptoes. You must show respect, even when they don't show you any. You shake your head at all the food you see piled in the store. How could there be so much food for so few people? The apples you see in magazines look more real and beautiful than the ones you pick, and the orchards on television are even more neat and tidy ... but where are the *paisanos* picking them? You can think only this: the fruit was grown in Canadian earth, yes, but it was the sweat of Mexicans that nurtured it. *Tierra canadiense, sudor mexicano* (Canadian soil, Mexican sweat). You won't forget to take some home as gifts, will you? The boss won't mind. He already said he'll be calling you back next year, as soon as the snow melts. Then you'll start the new season of work by pruning the pear trees again, your favourites. You're a master at it, you know how to shape a tree, how to make it yield the biggest fruit. Yes, over the tree you are lord. And in the summer months you'll be keeping an eye on those trees, just to make sure that you did a good job with the pruning shears. And you'll be bursting with pride. I can just see you now on that tractor as you drive by – did you get the picture that I sent you when you posed by the tractor, resting one foot on the front wheel, just like a *patrón* (boss)?

I know you'll have lots of stories to tell, don't exaggerate too much – you sometimes do that, you know? Just to impress your neighbours and friends. Don't forget to say how dangerous the work is, though. Don't get upset when your old friends in the *rancho* don't seem to understand your point of view sometimes, and make you feel like a stranger in your own home. You've seen places that they haven't. How could they understand? And don't lose your temper either when they talk about the latest gossip, and ignore you, and say, "You weren't even here, how could you know what we're talking about?" They mean well, but they're right after all. For your home was in Canada. Ah, Fermín, sometimes you're so tired you forget where you really are, just like old Manuel. Remember him? His children grew up and he wasn't there for them half the time. He was too busy working, travelling back and forth – so that he could provide for them. Then one day the boss didn't call him back. He was too old, the boss said. "*Ya no rinde, el mexicano.*" (The Mexican isn't worth it anymore.) Be careful that you don't become like Manuel, but give him my regards when you next see him.

I must go now. Be well.

Me despido y te abrazo.
Vicente, tu amigo de Canadá

HARVEST PILGRIMS

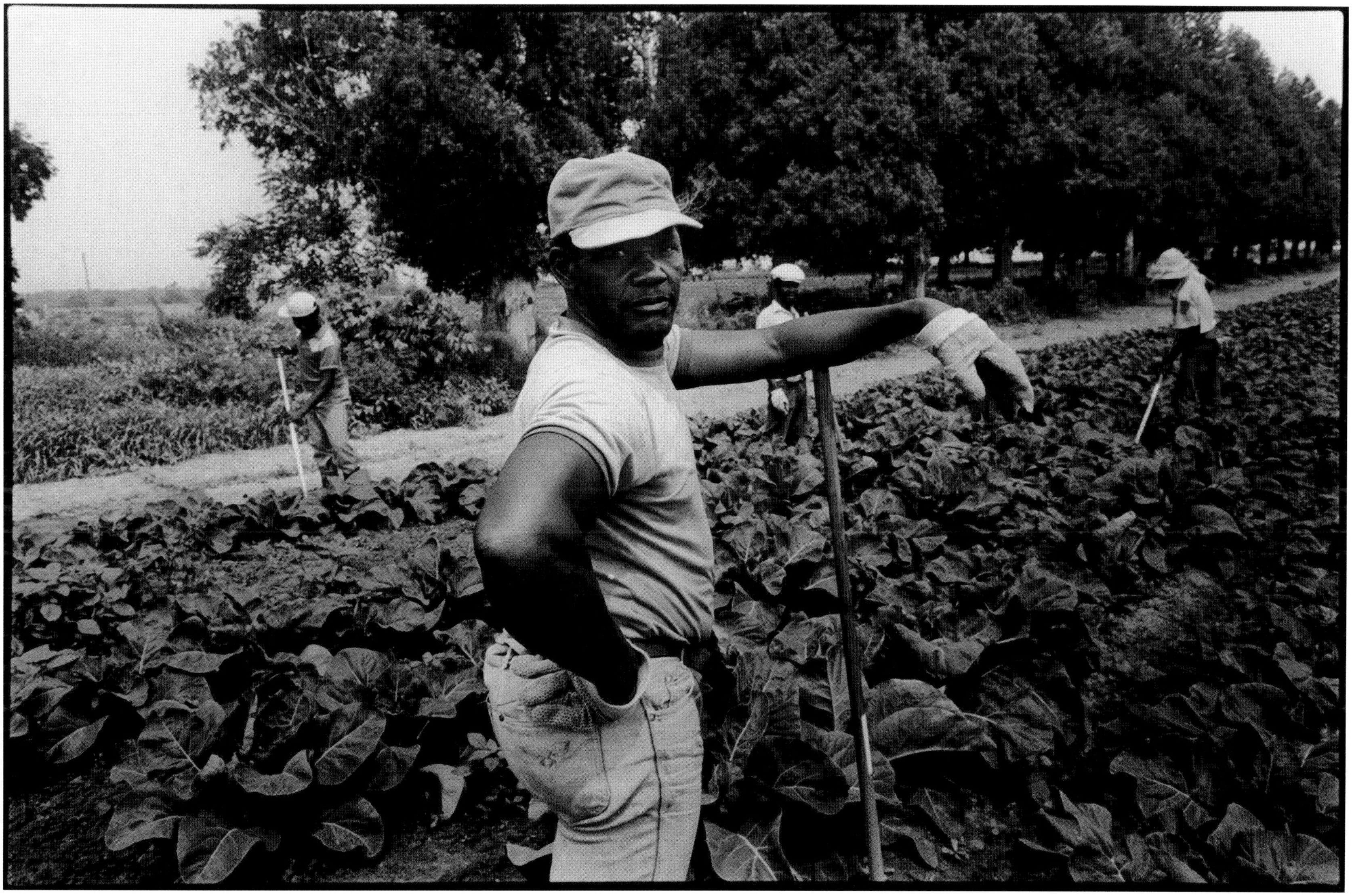

Well, the young people go away because they have this idea, you see, to find a new way of life over there. That's what they really think. Those who go away, they go because they have obligations. They're married. And they can't make ends meet here. Like Manuel, the one who just returned, with the little money that he brought back ... it didn't last long, and it's all gone. That's the reason why people have to keep going away. The poverty.

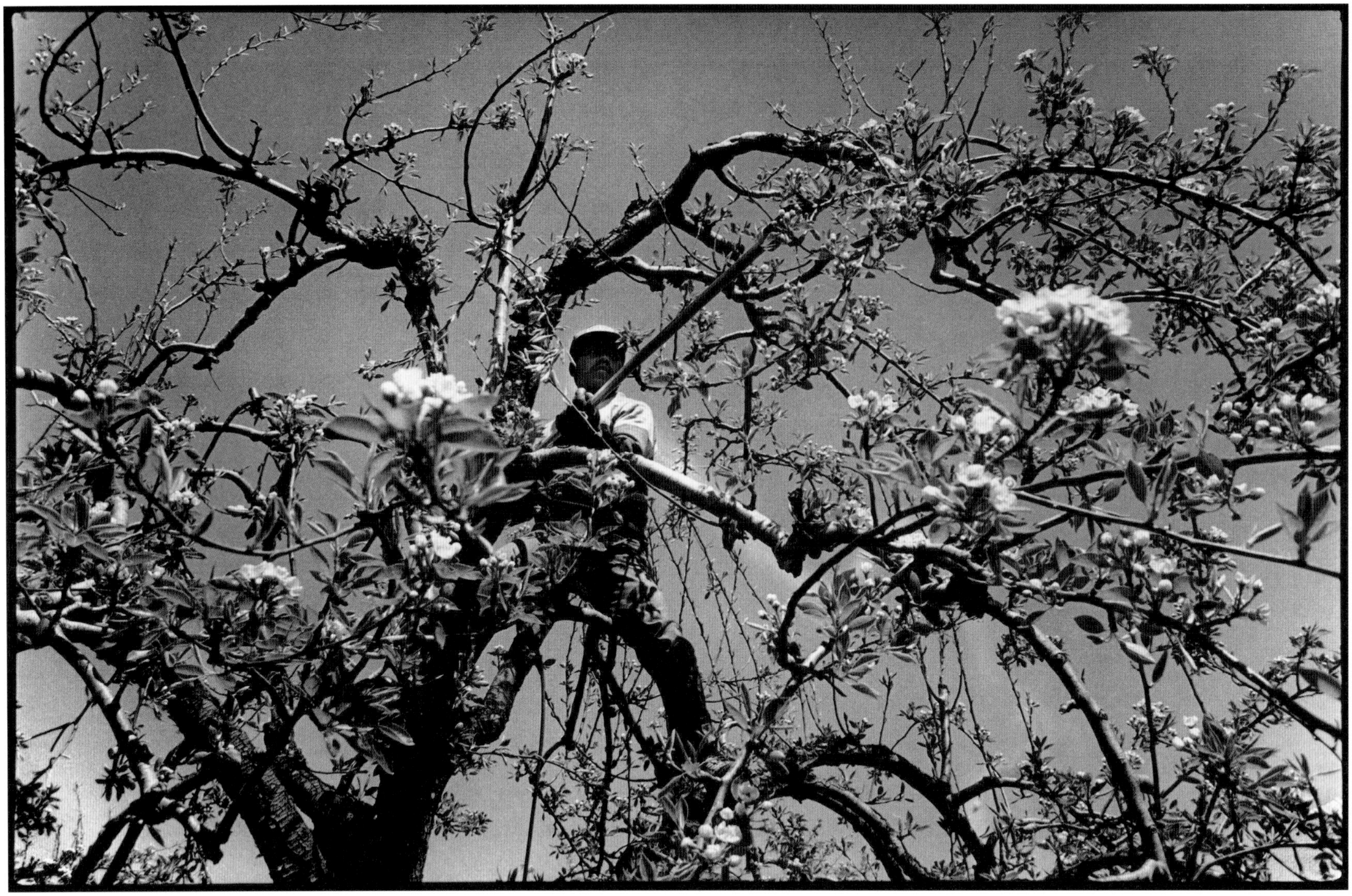

I am going to the Niagara area, and I'm going for seven months and twenty-nine days. Almost eight months.

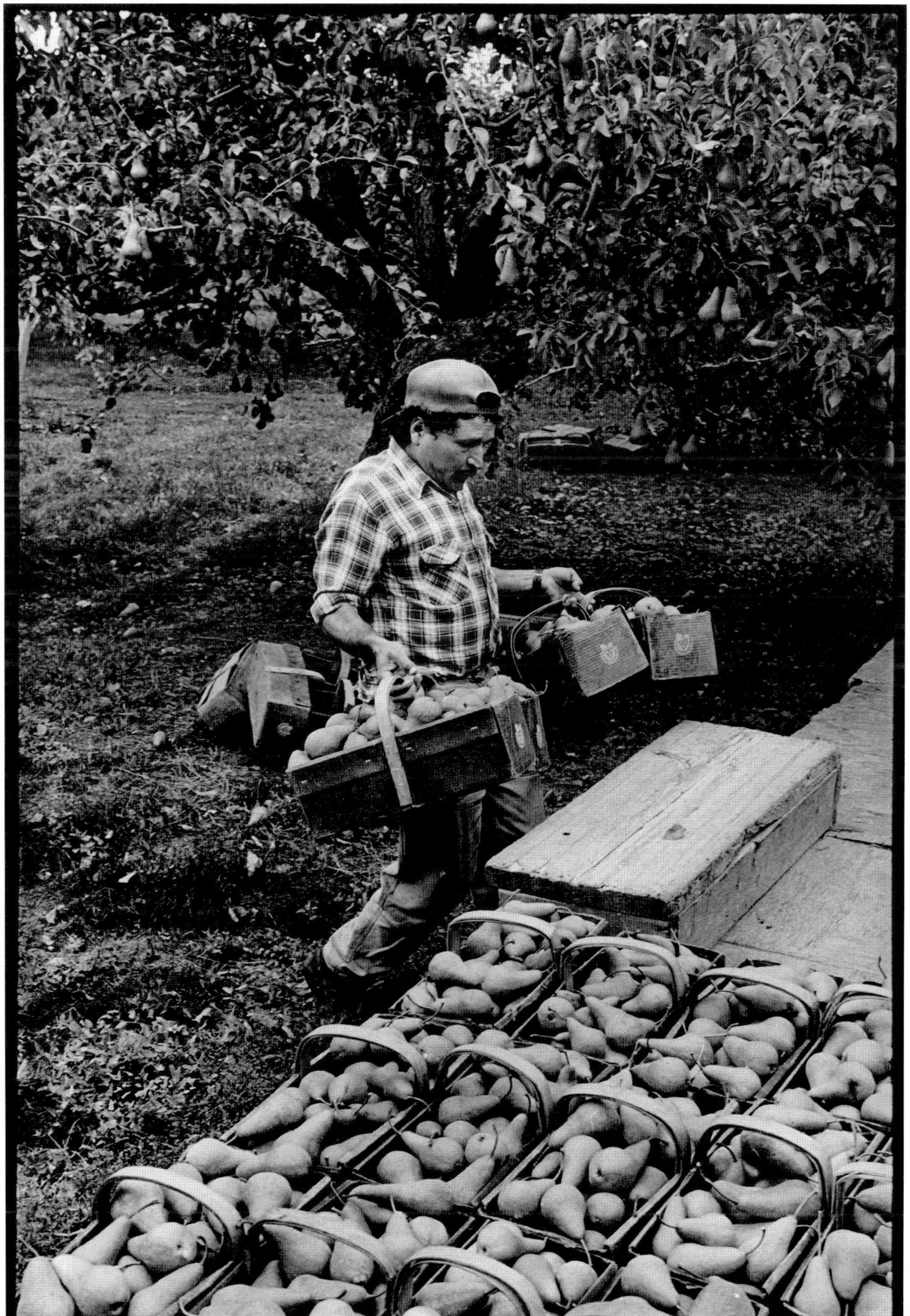

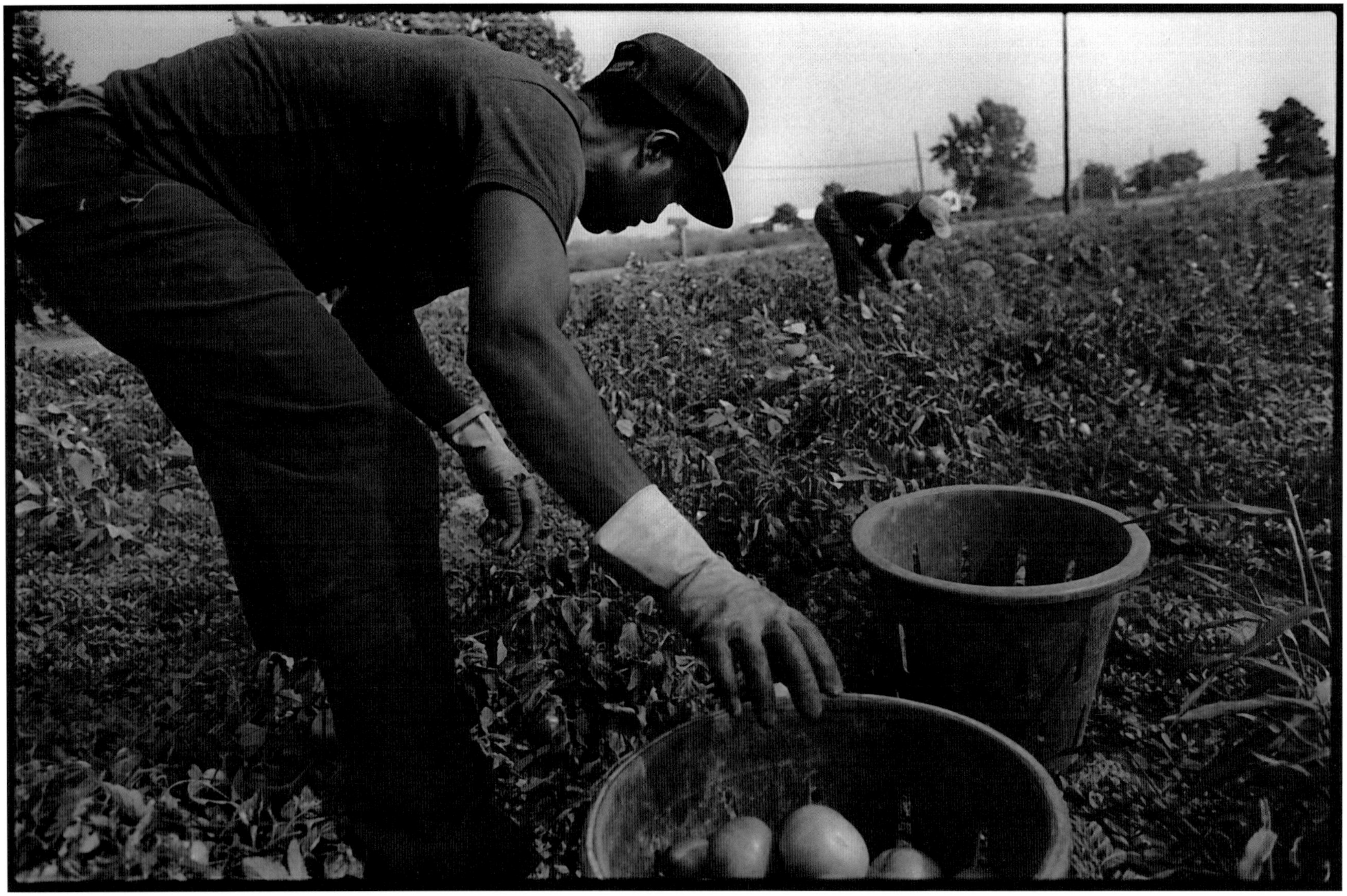

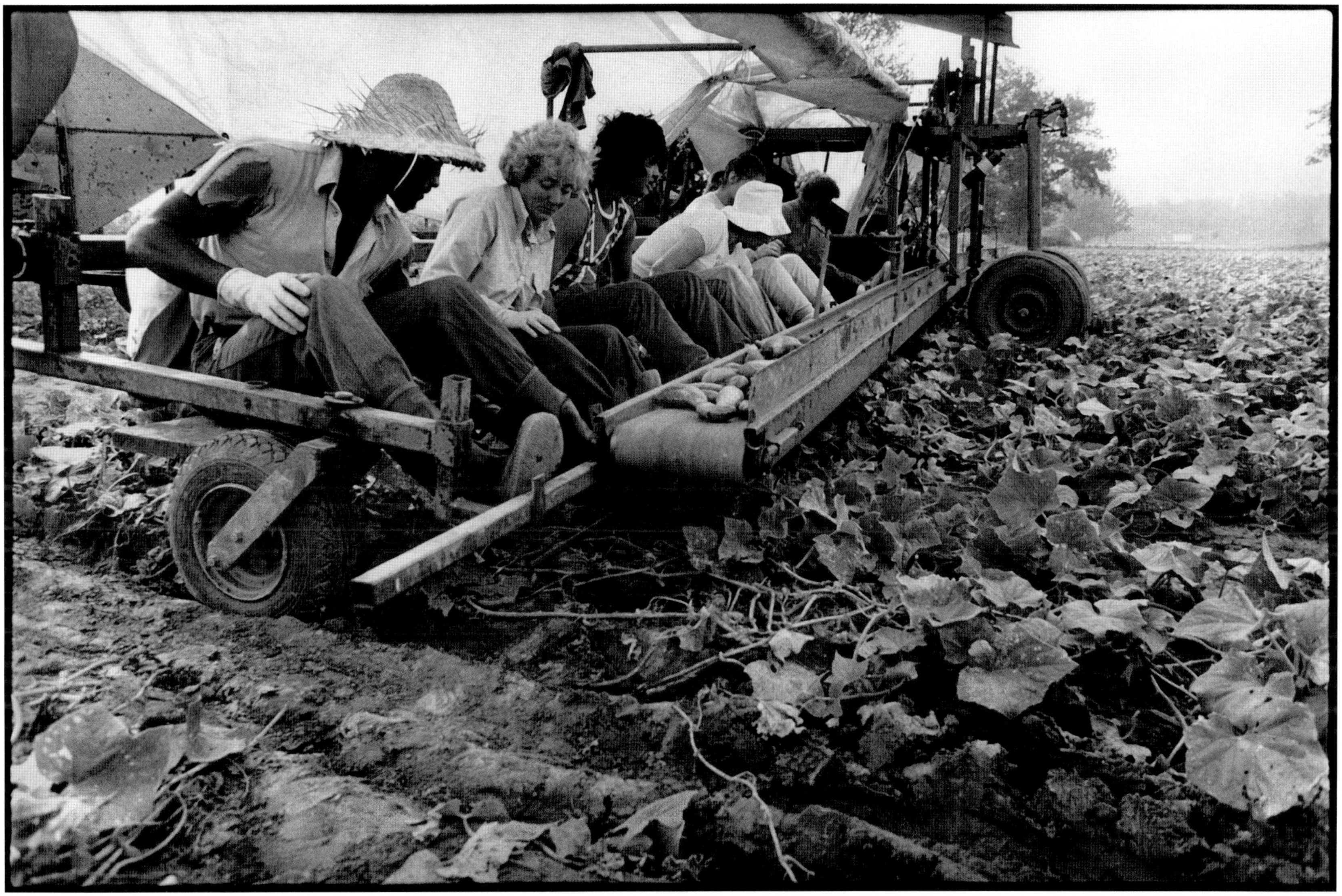

If they would say to me, you could stay in Canada indefinitely and bring your family, I would accept with the greatest of pleasure, but unfortunately you can't. From the very first moment that I arrived in the country, I liked Canada very much. If I could have my family with me, I would be more content in my work, but it's not possible.... Every time you return home, the children are older, and you miss them as they grow up.

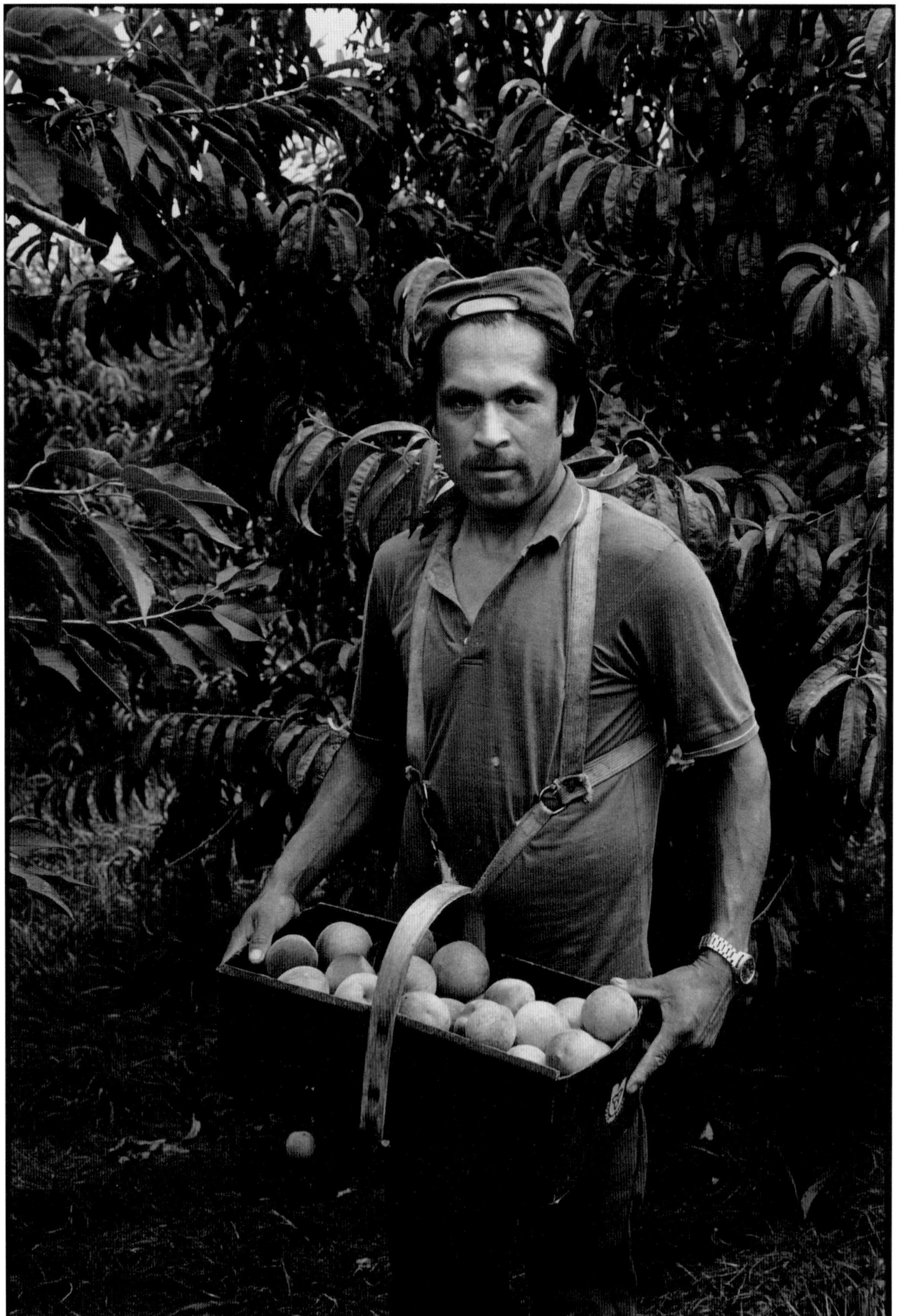

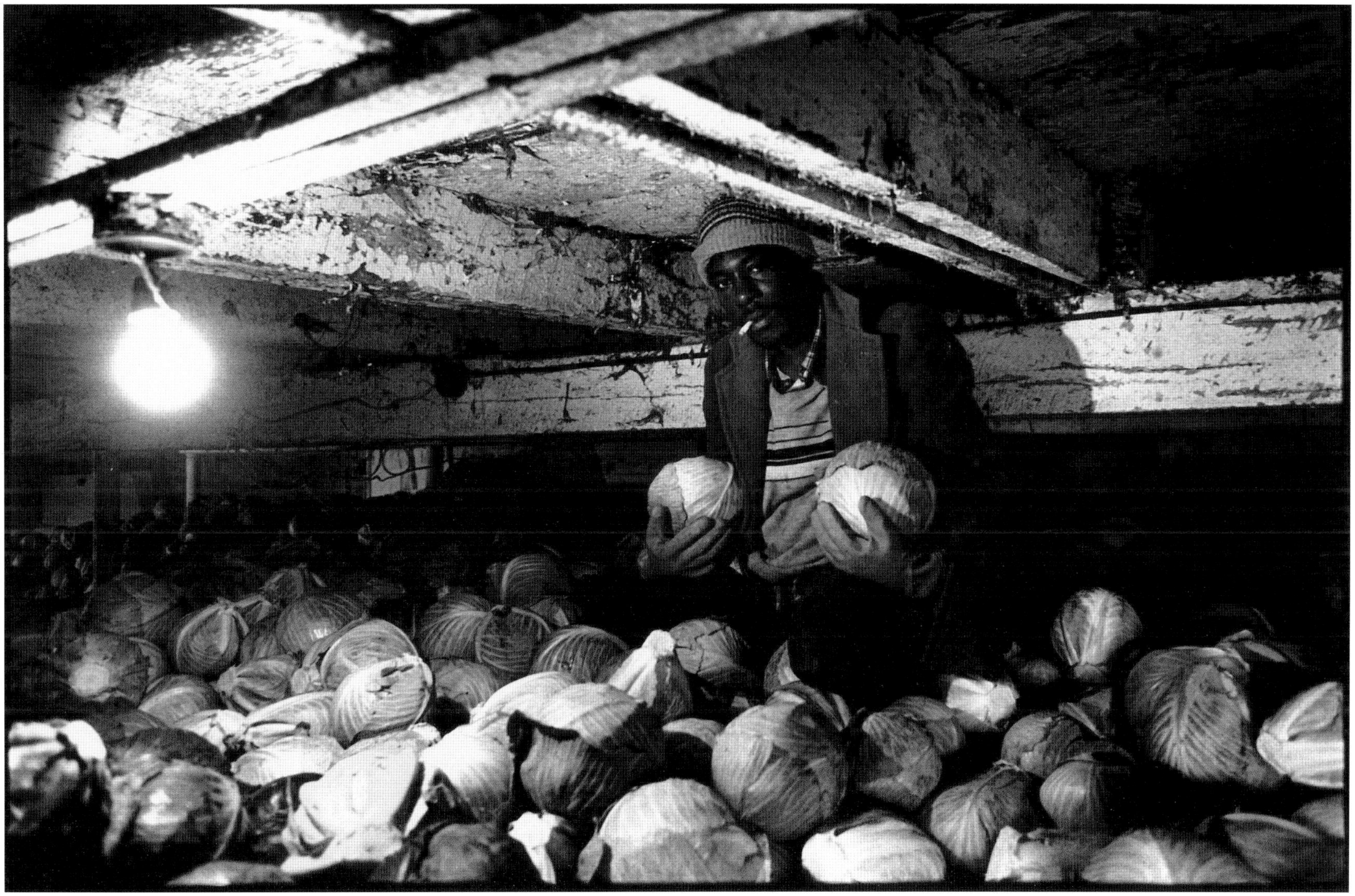

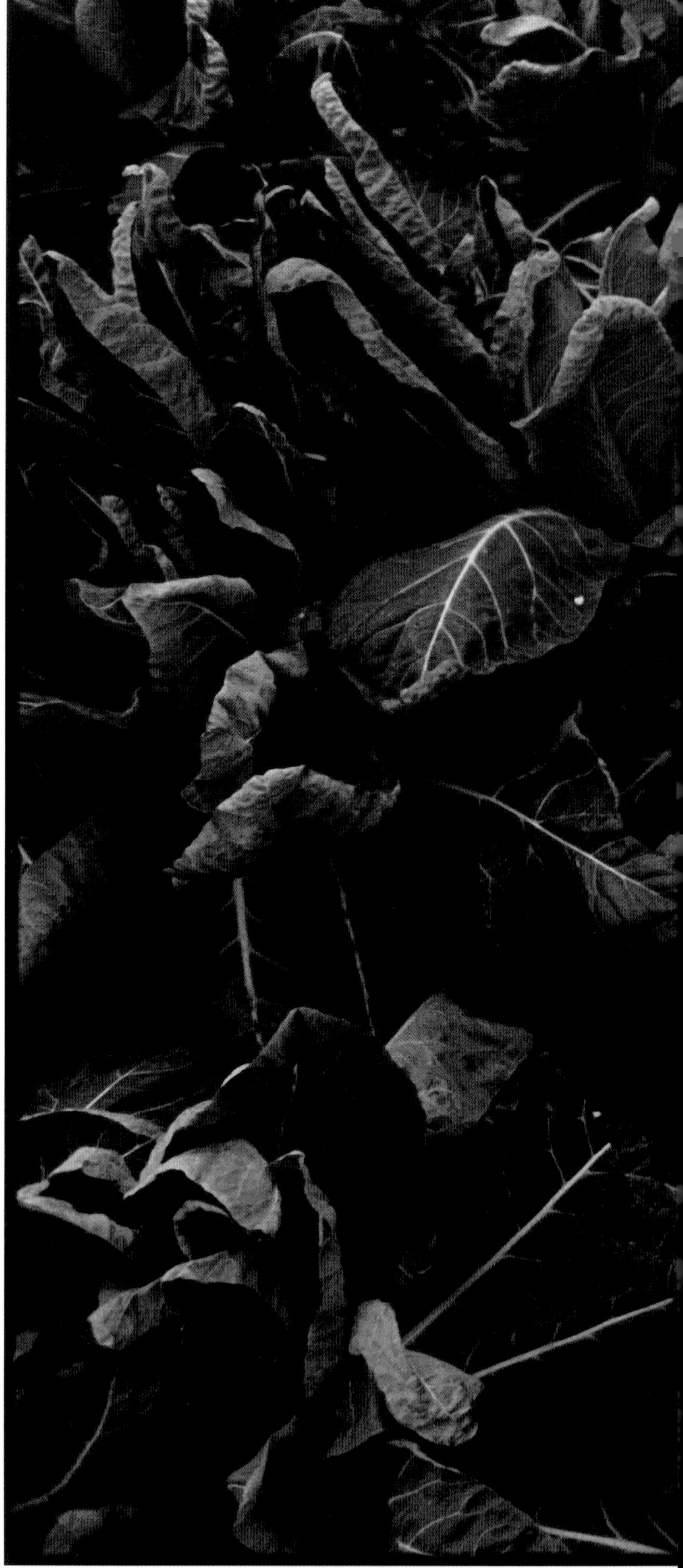

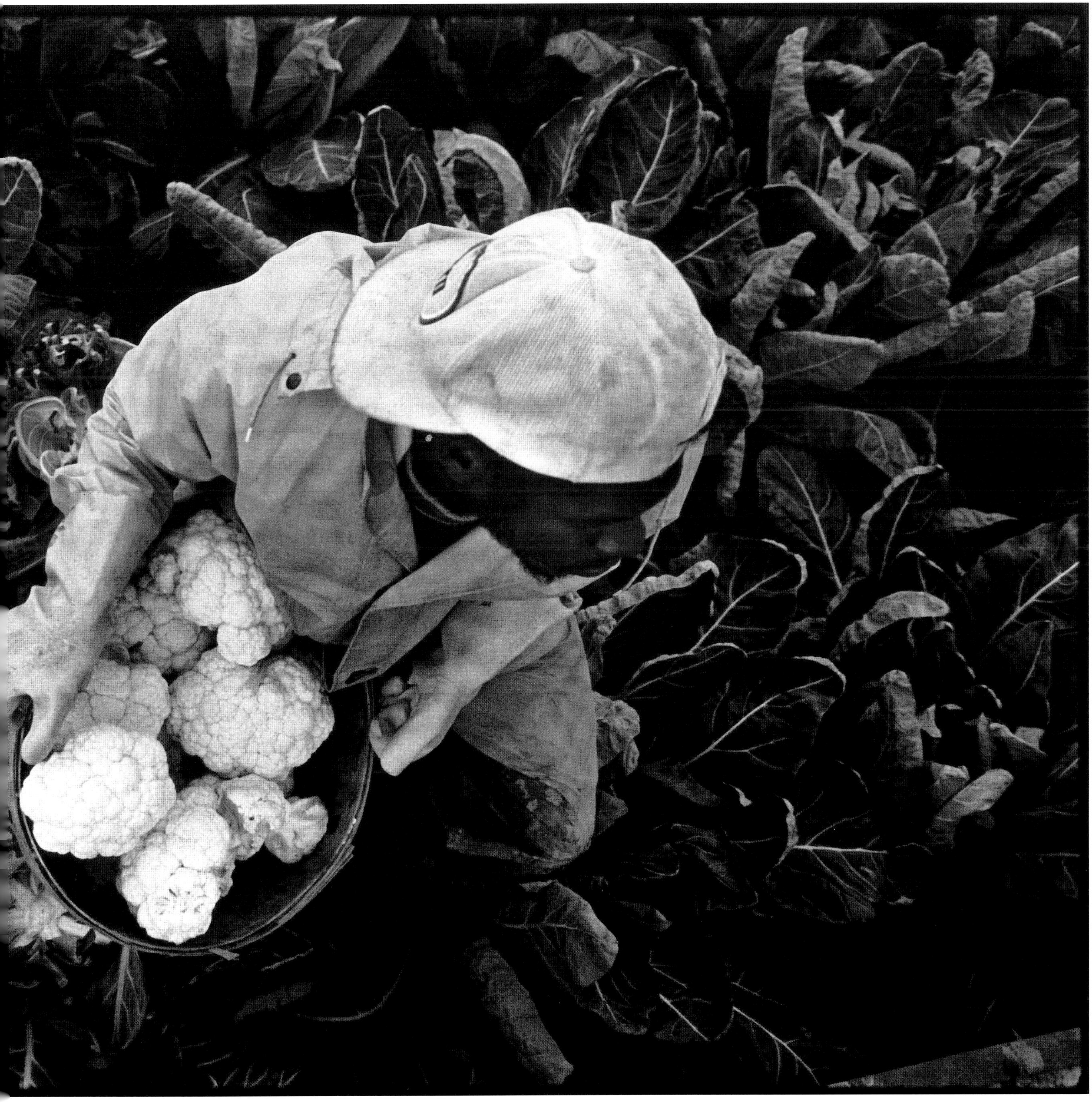

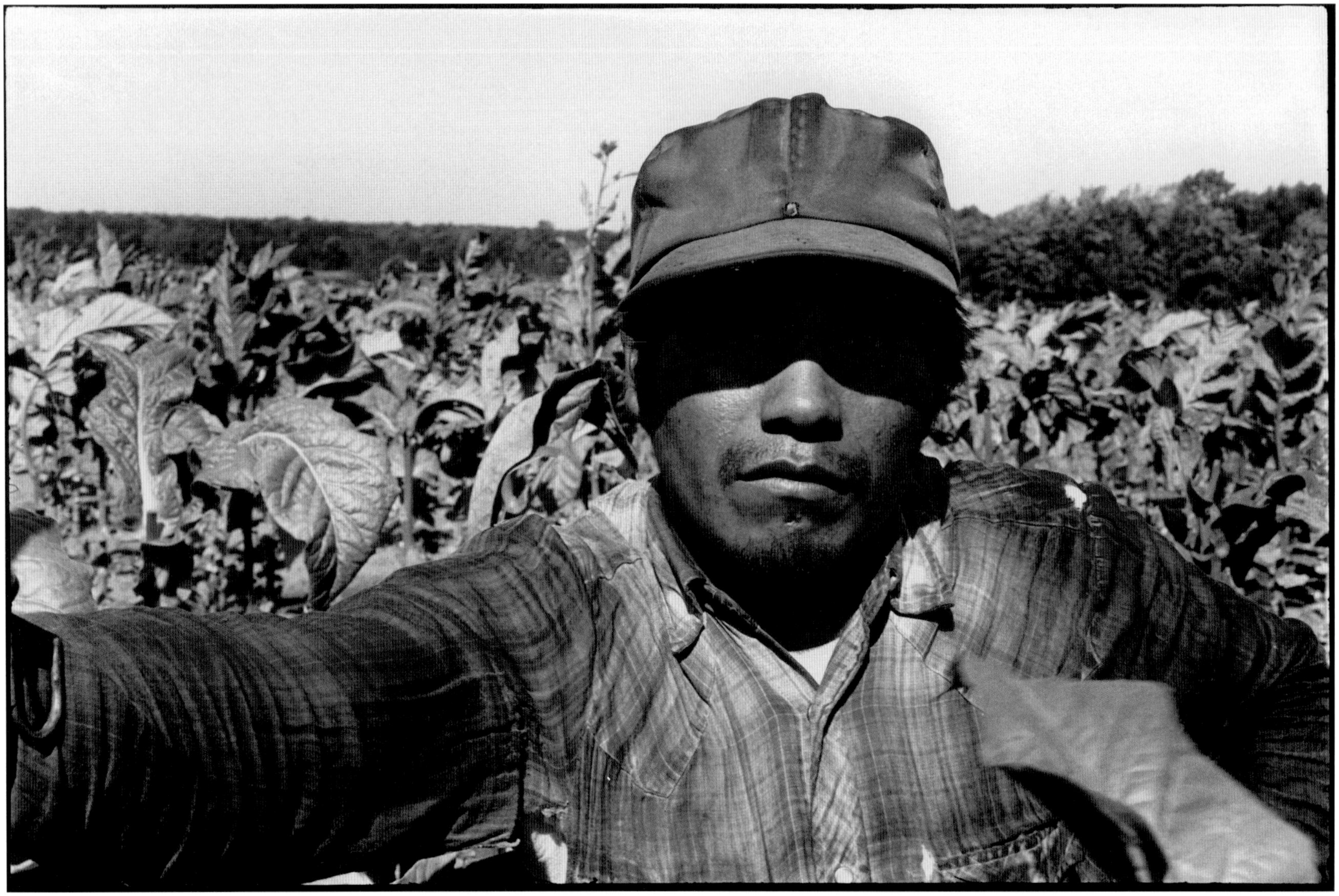

Age doesn't make so much difference so long as you can work.

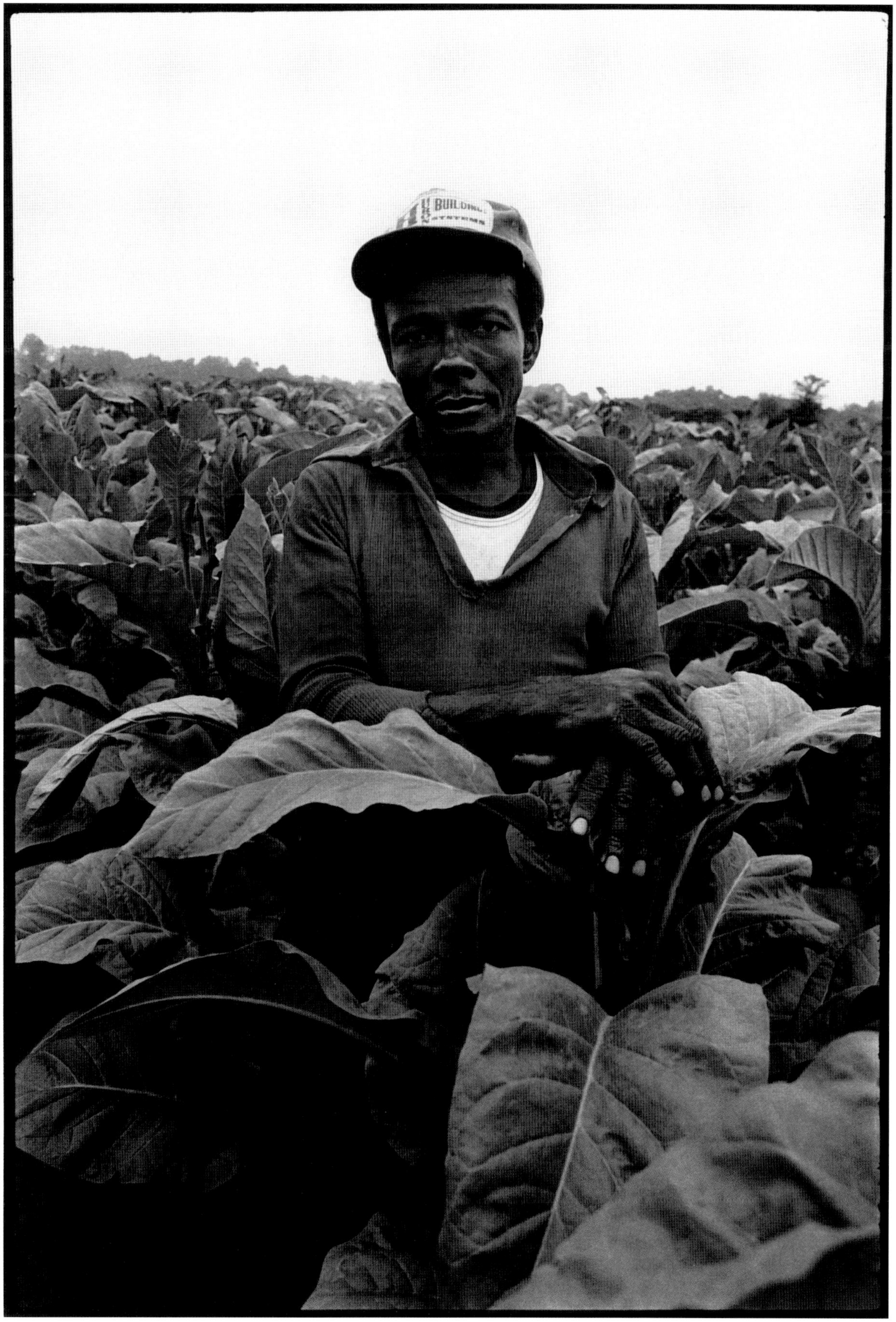

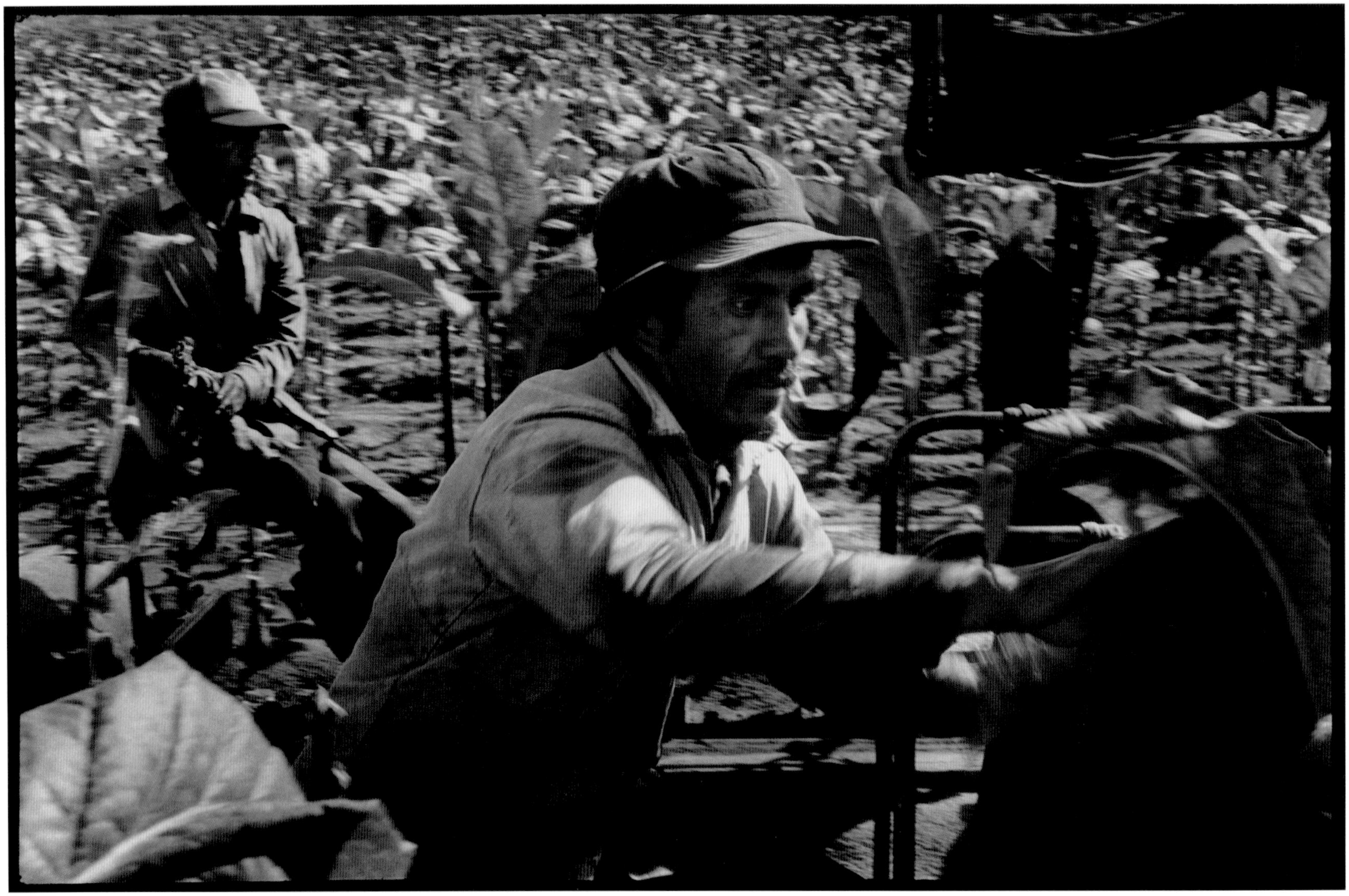

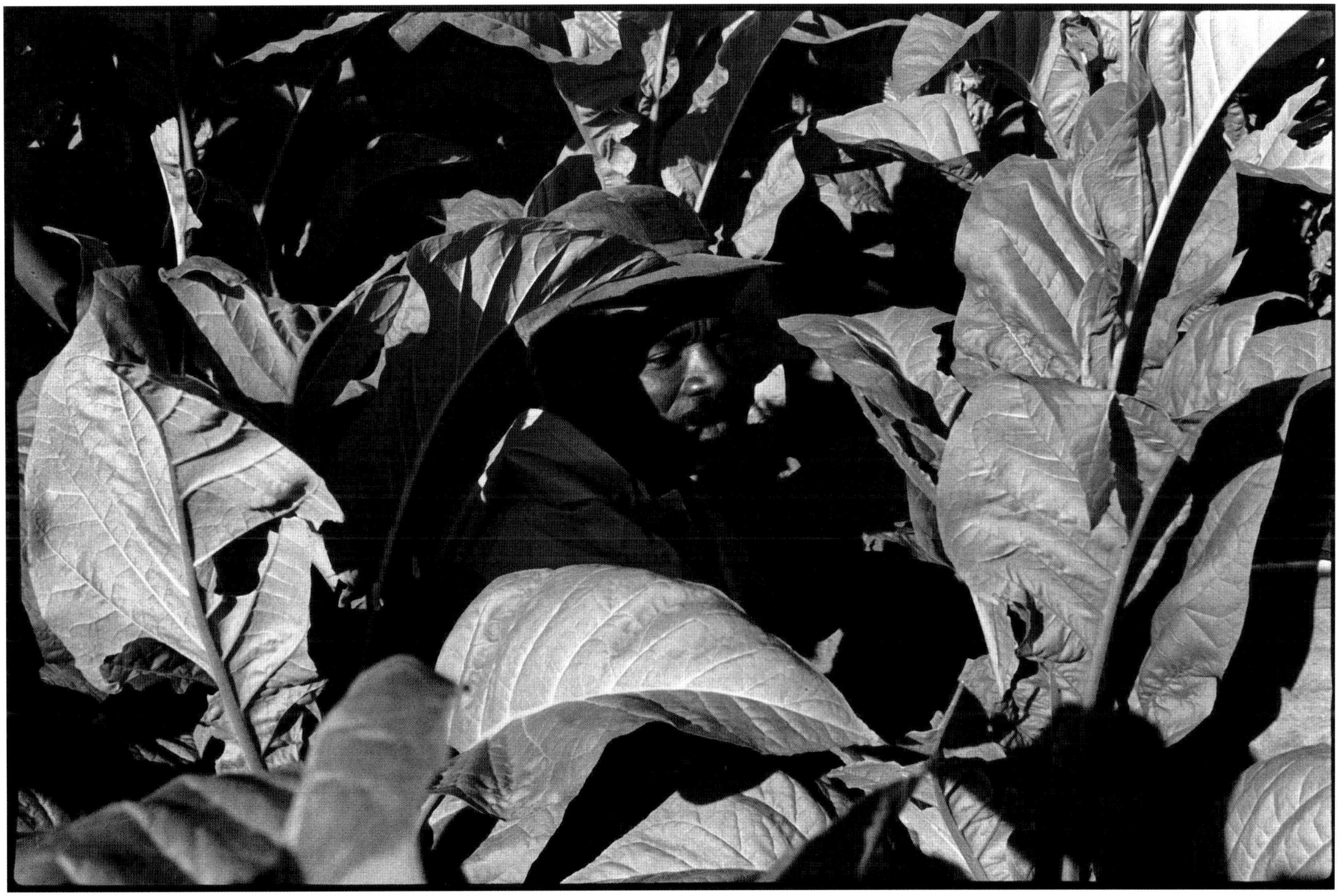

When we get off the plane we go to the immigration and they sign up our documents and the liaison office comes up and calls your name and asks you to fill out the form for the farm you are going to work on and the number of the bus and the number of hours you are going to work, and you have to cook and wash for yourself and you have to buy work clothes and your own food ... When you first go up the farmer lends you $100 to buy food and working clothes to start you off.

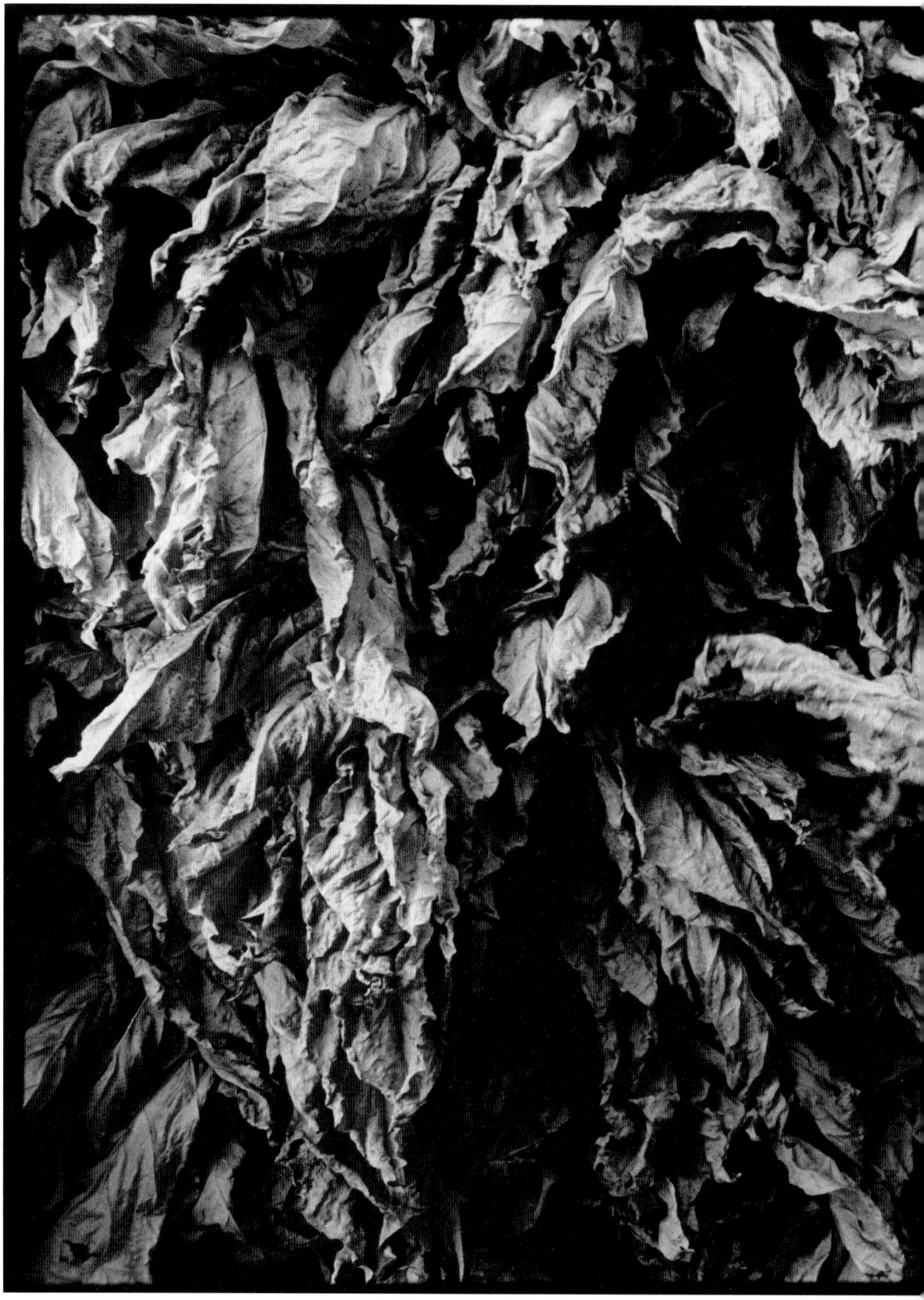

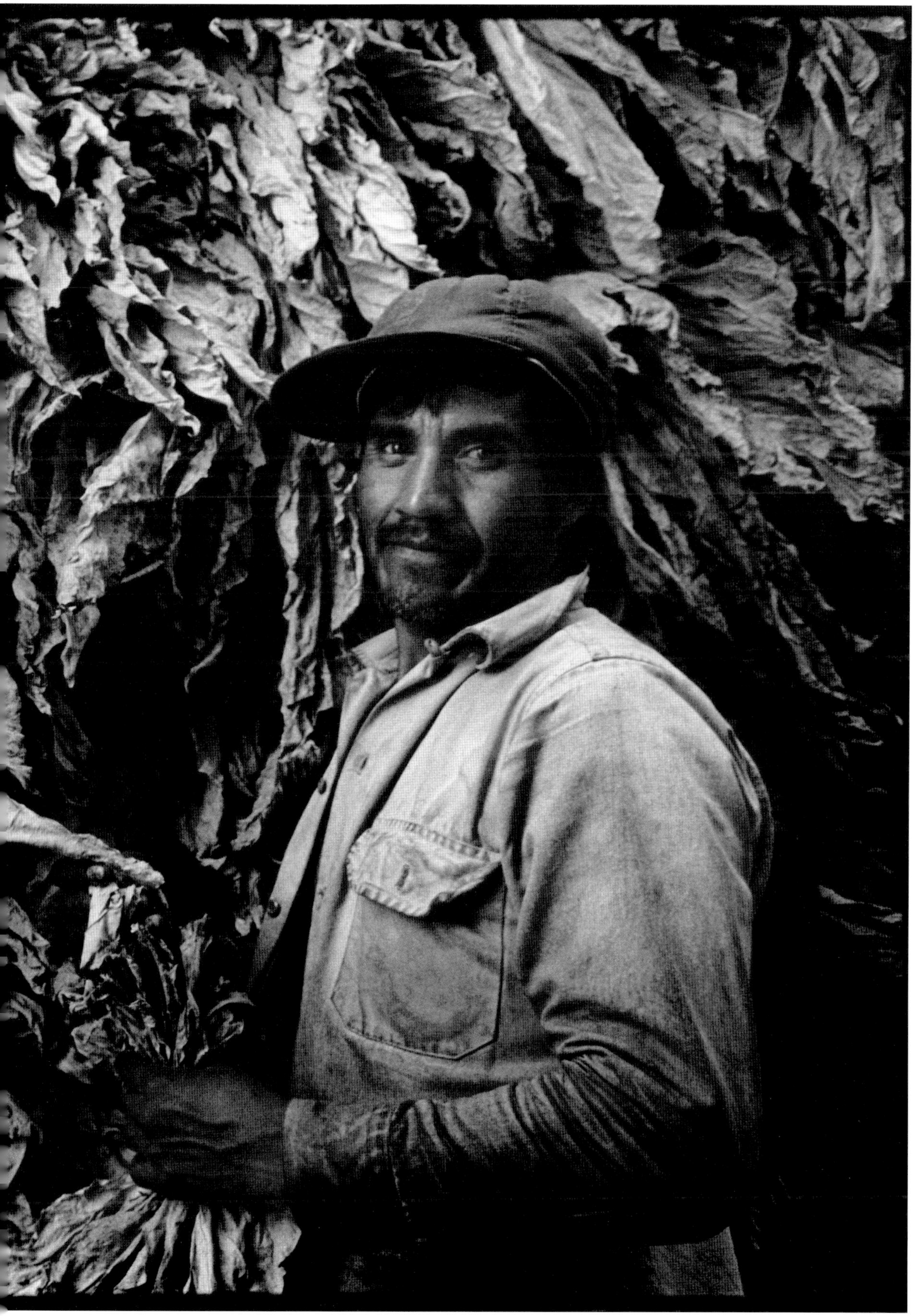

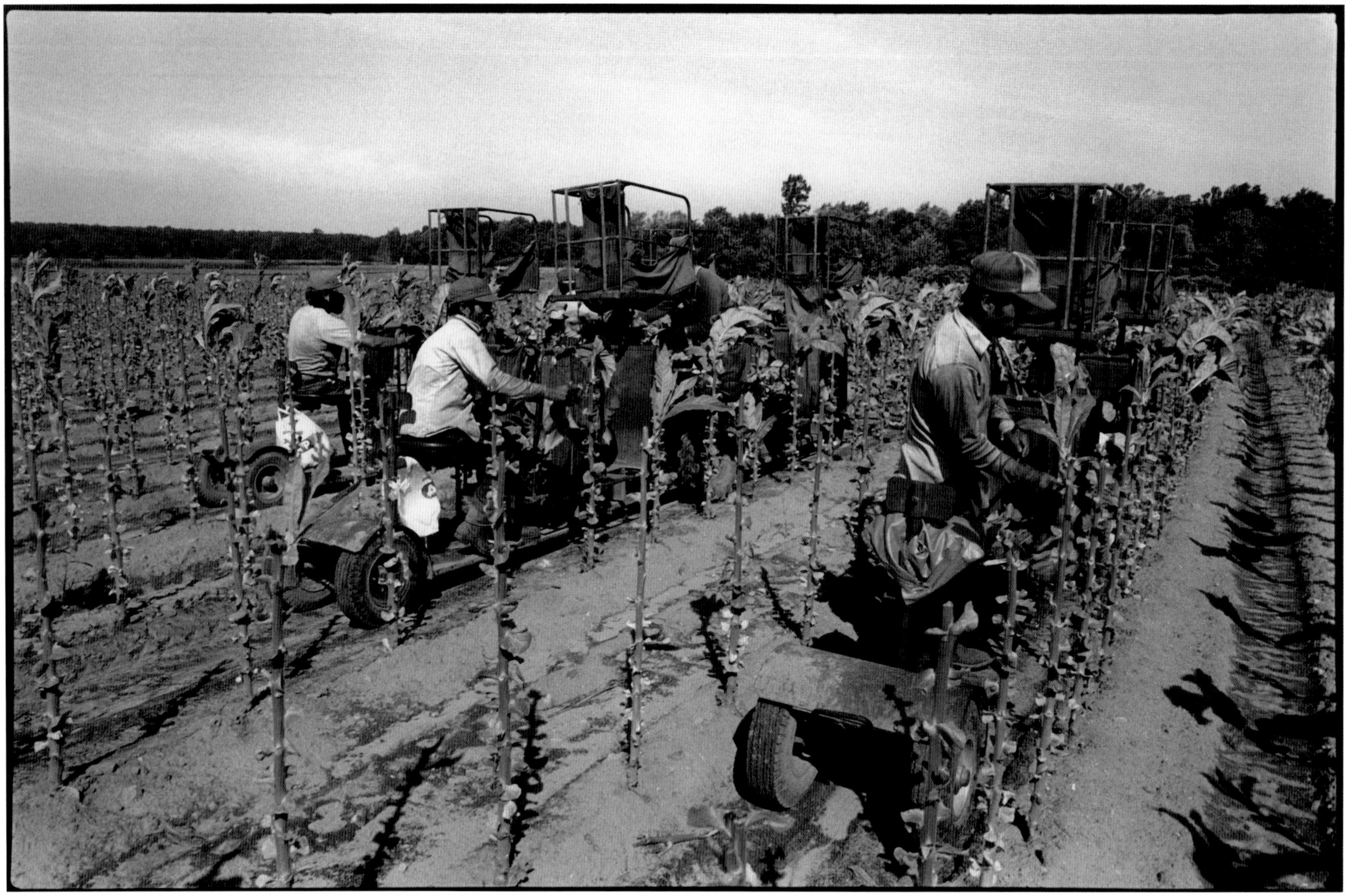

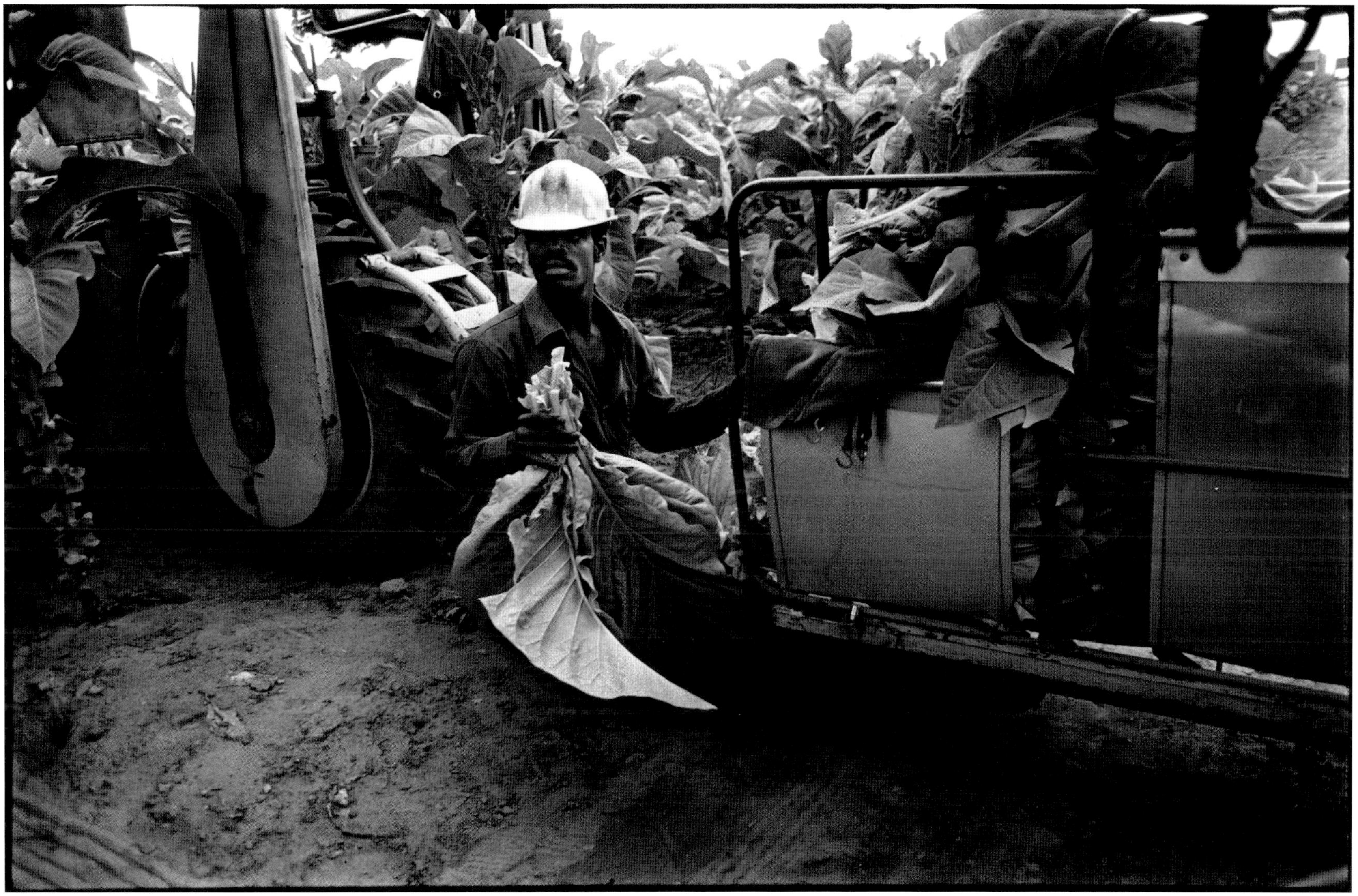

Tobacco is more constant. It's a crop that cannot stand waiting, and so you have to go every day no matter what the weather, rain or not. They spray it, and you have to work in that condition, and sometimes when you're picking tobacco that thing catches in your eye, so it burns a lot. After a while you feel the effects.

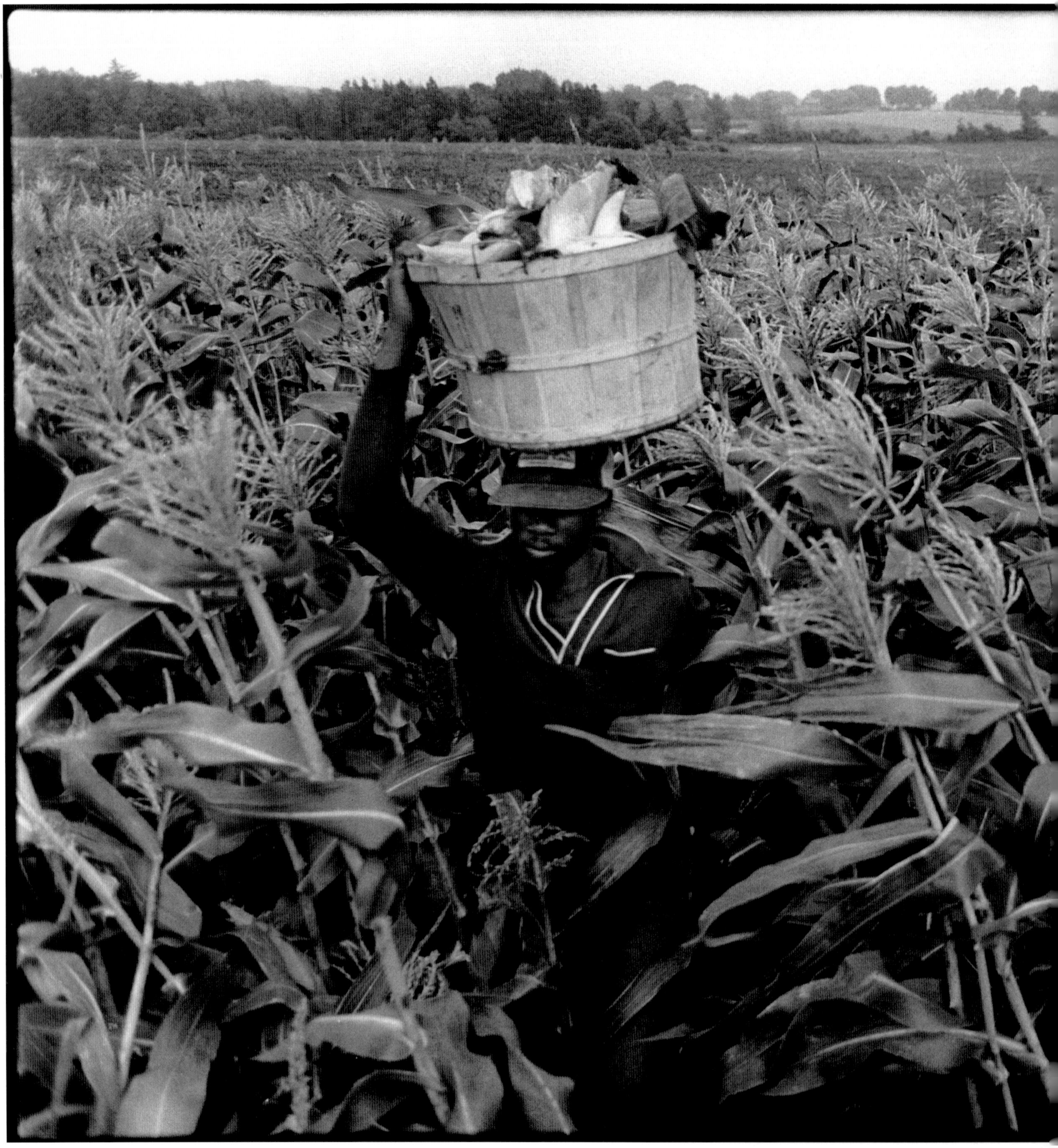

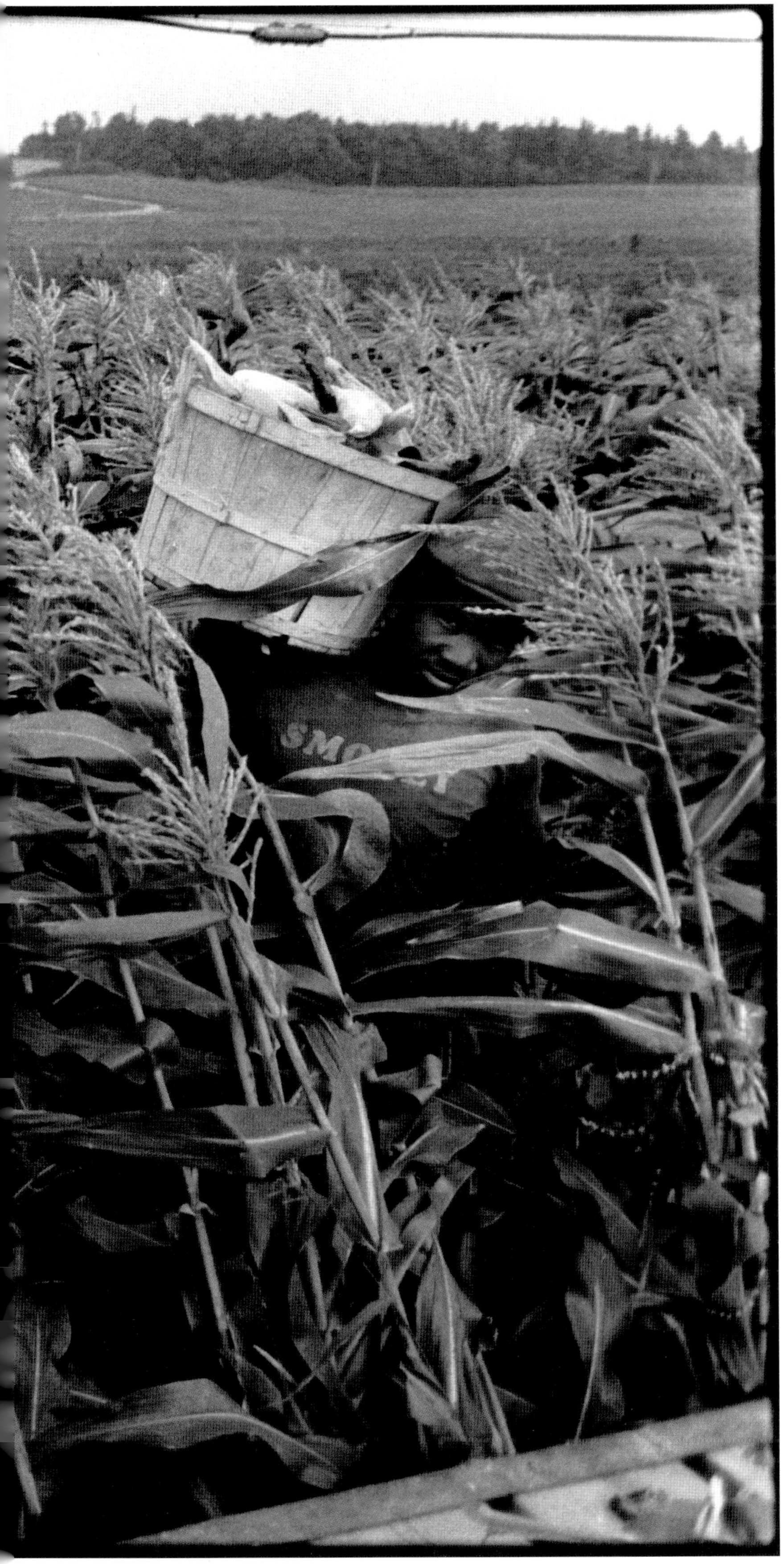

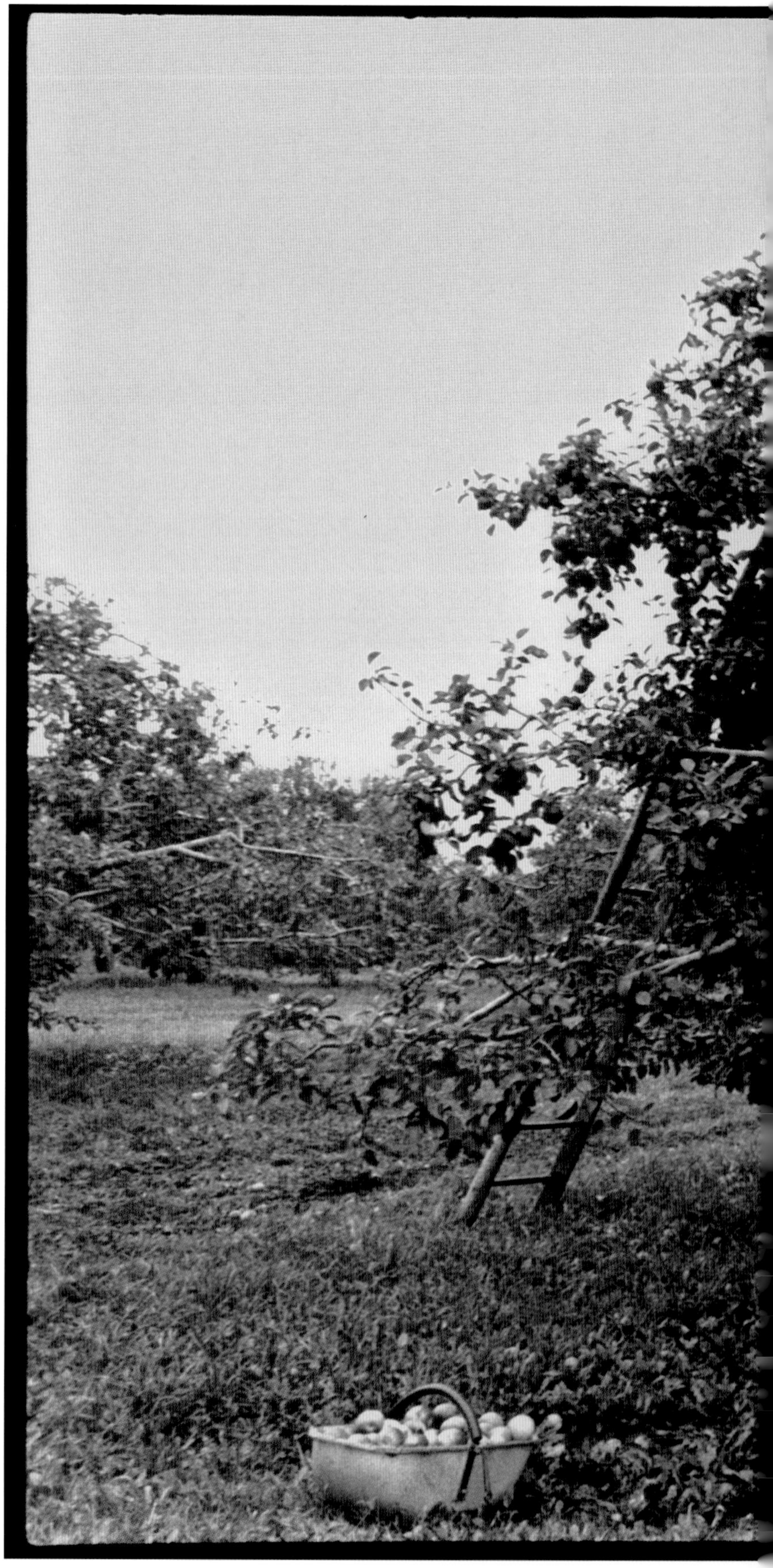

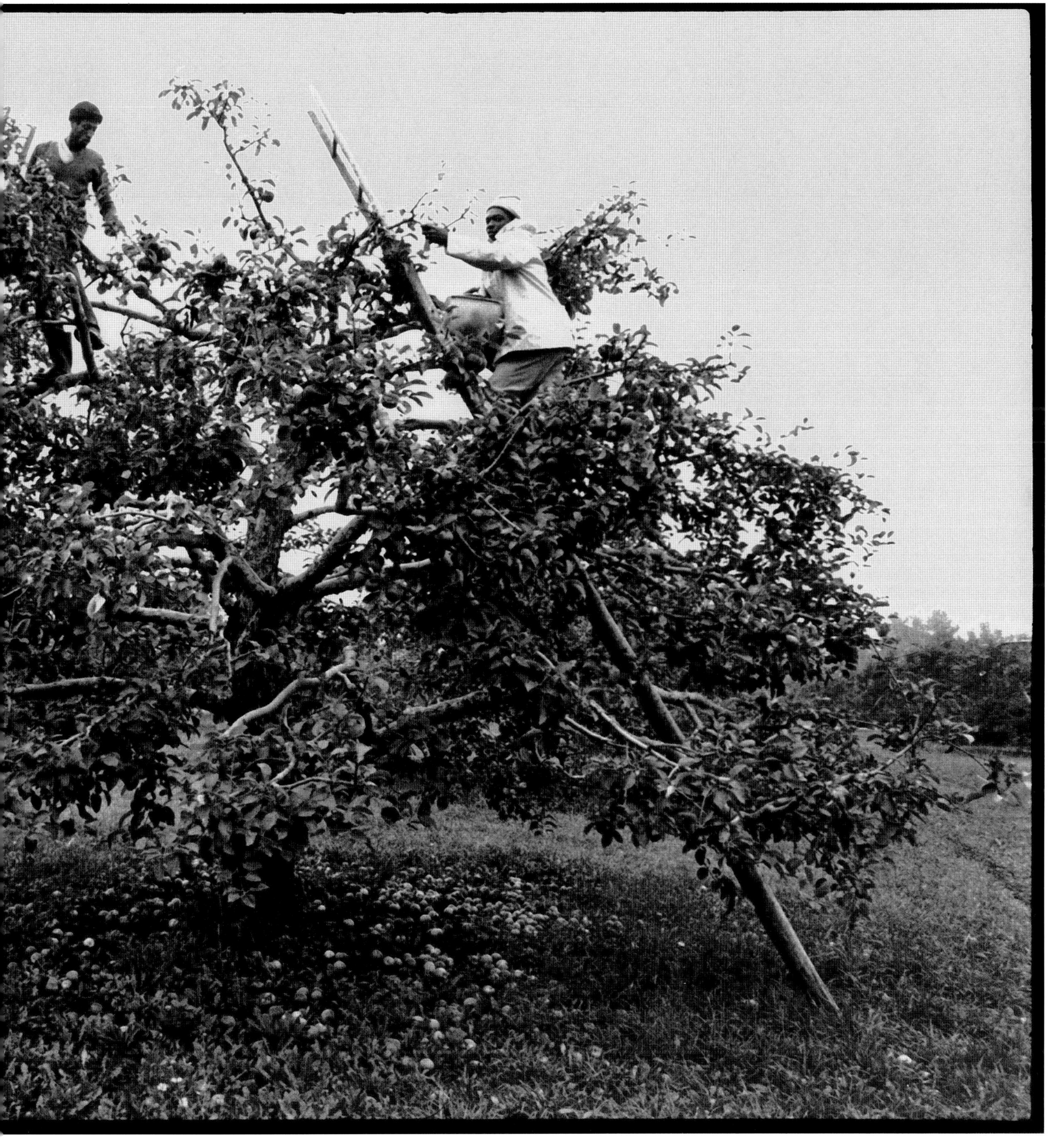

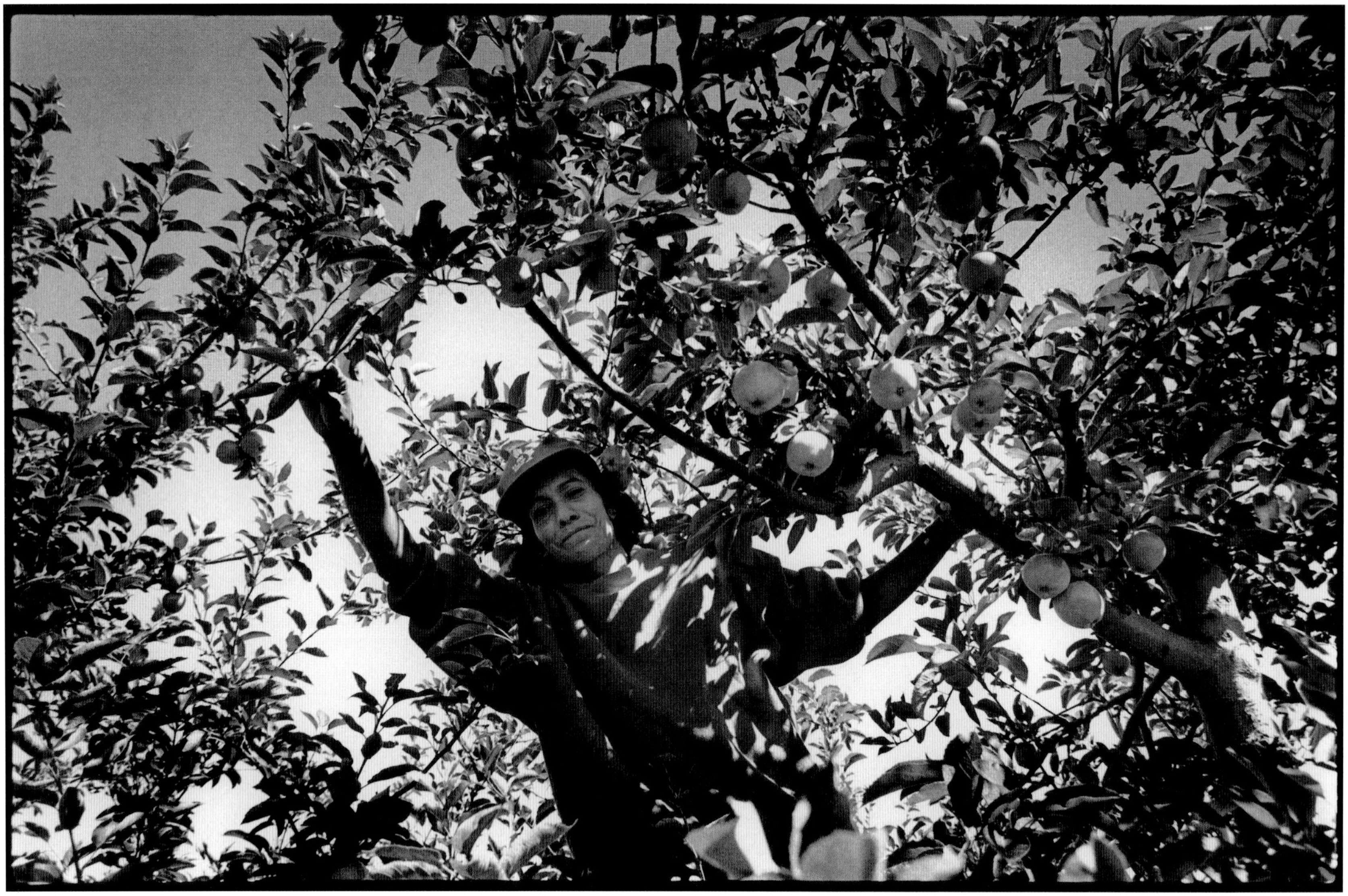

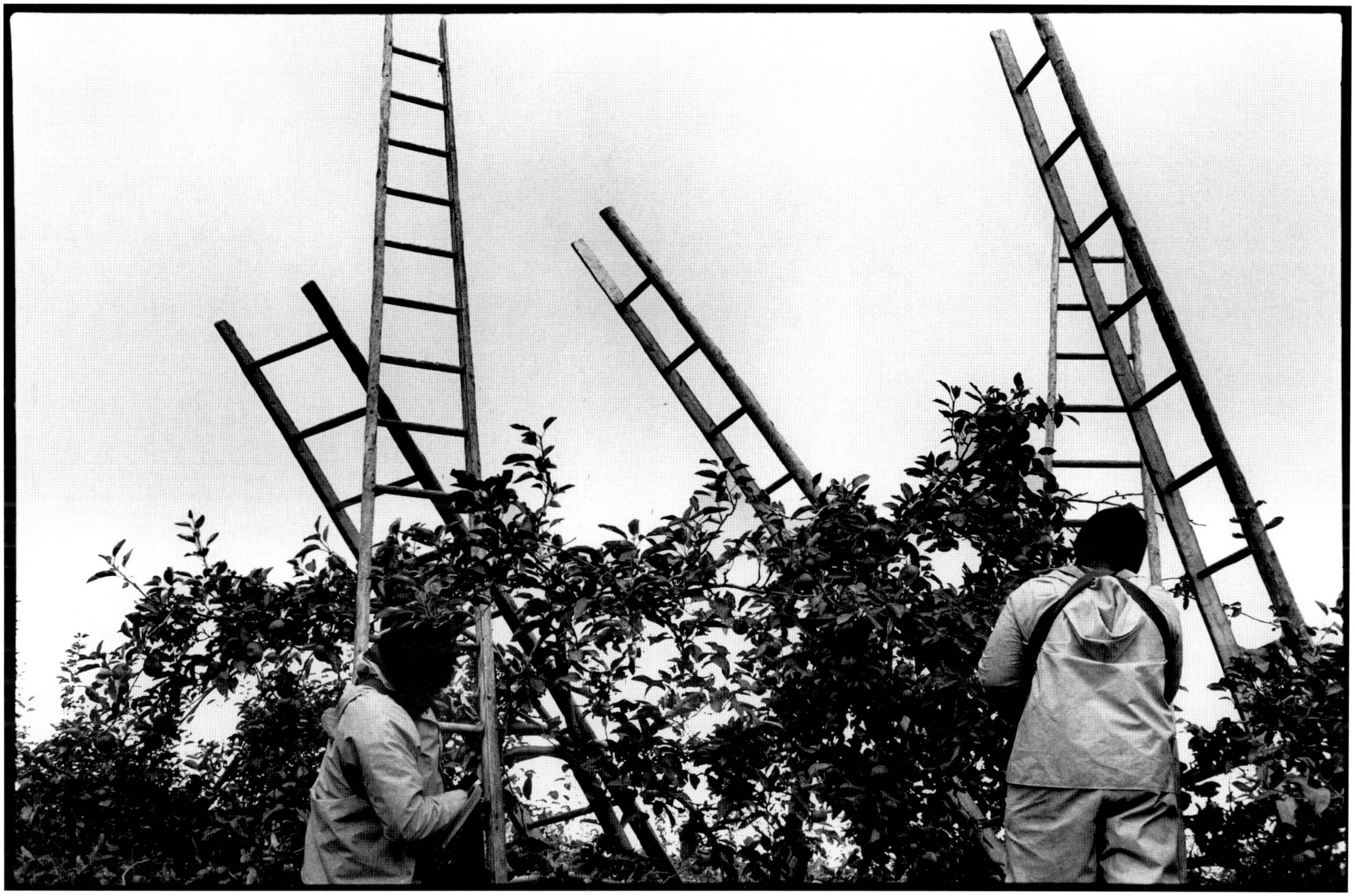

Is this interview going to be on television? Because if it gets on television or on the radio in my country, it could cause me problems, maybe even get me fired from my job. If the government rep comes to hear of it, he could say, "Why are you talking about these things with people?"

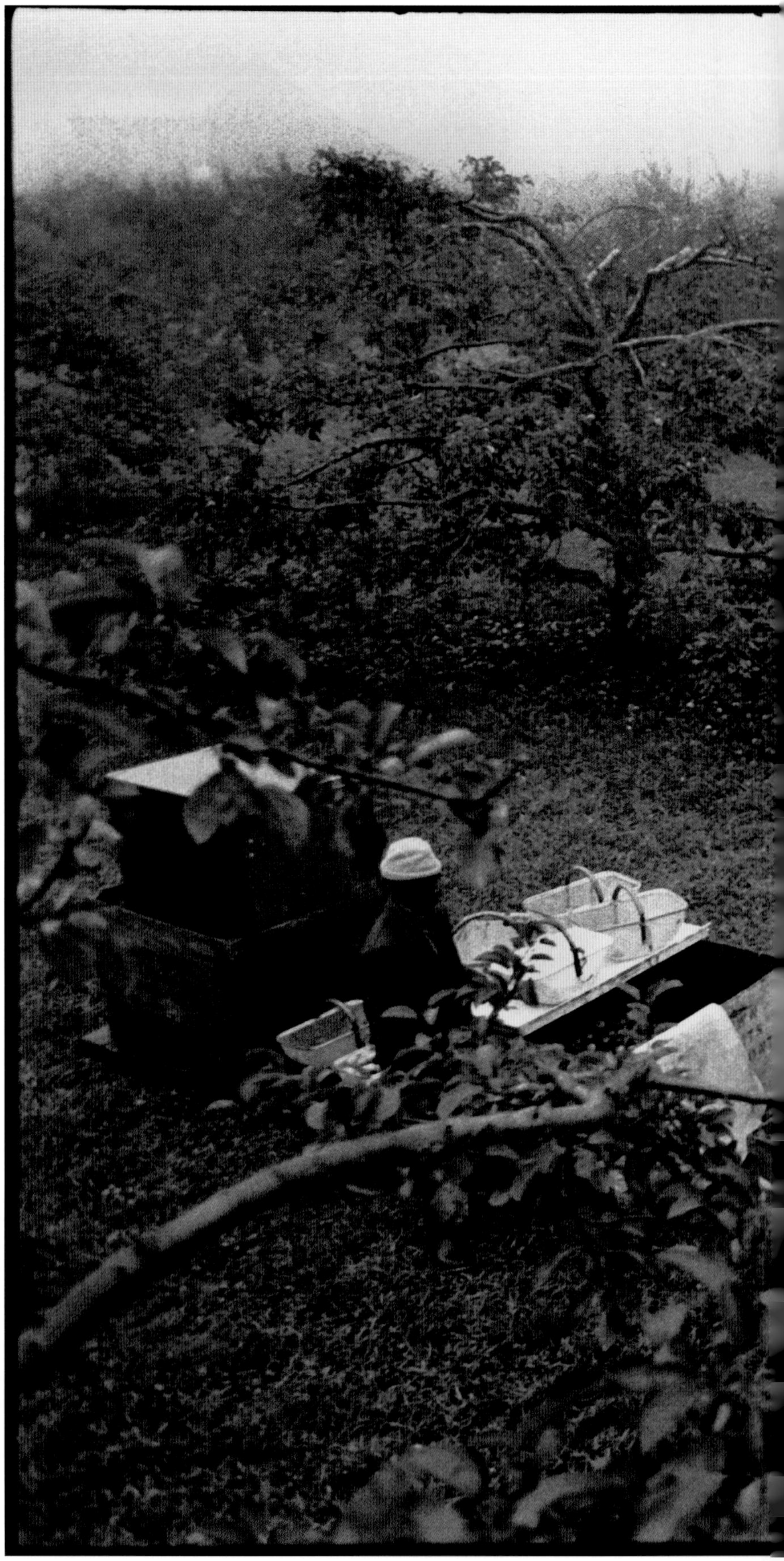

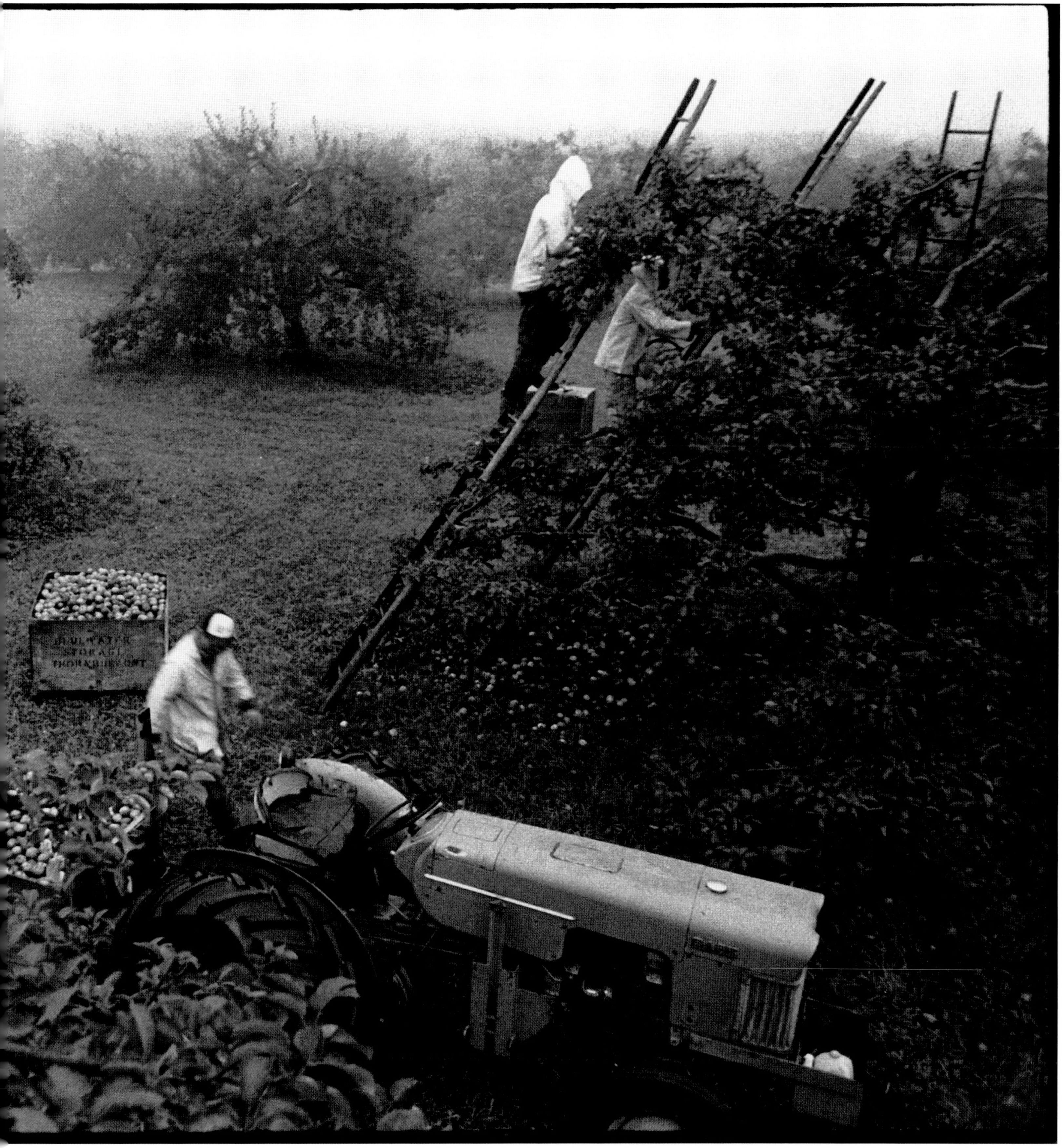

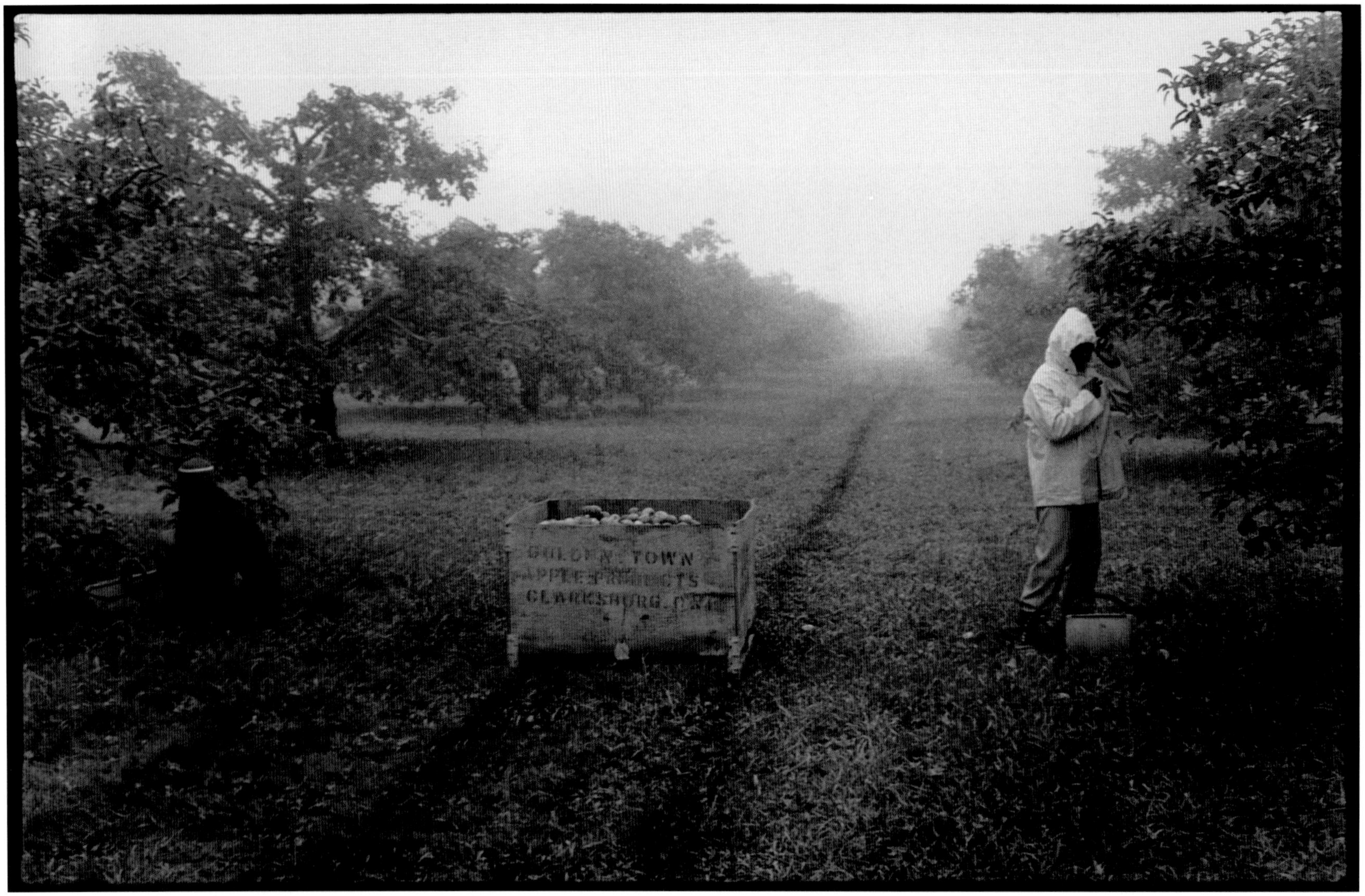

I don't like the cold. When I went to Canada, my first impression was, well, far different from here, in every way. More different, the cold is number one. She [his wife] doesn't believe it when I tell her. I tell her, when you put a bottle of beer in the window, it freezes. In November, outside the window.

And the work, again, it is different from here [Jamaica], so you got to work up there to pay yourself. We're doing the heavy tasks. Different style, and you don't see the hills like out here, no mountain, more flat. And just orchards.

My impression still was to go there and to gain some experience.

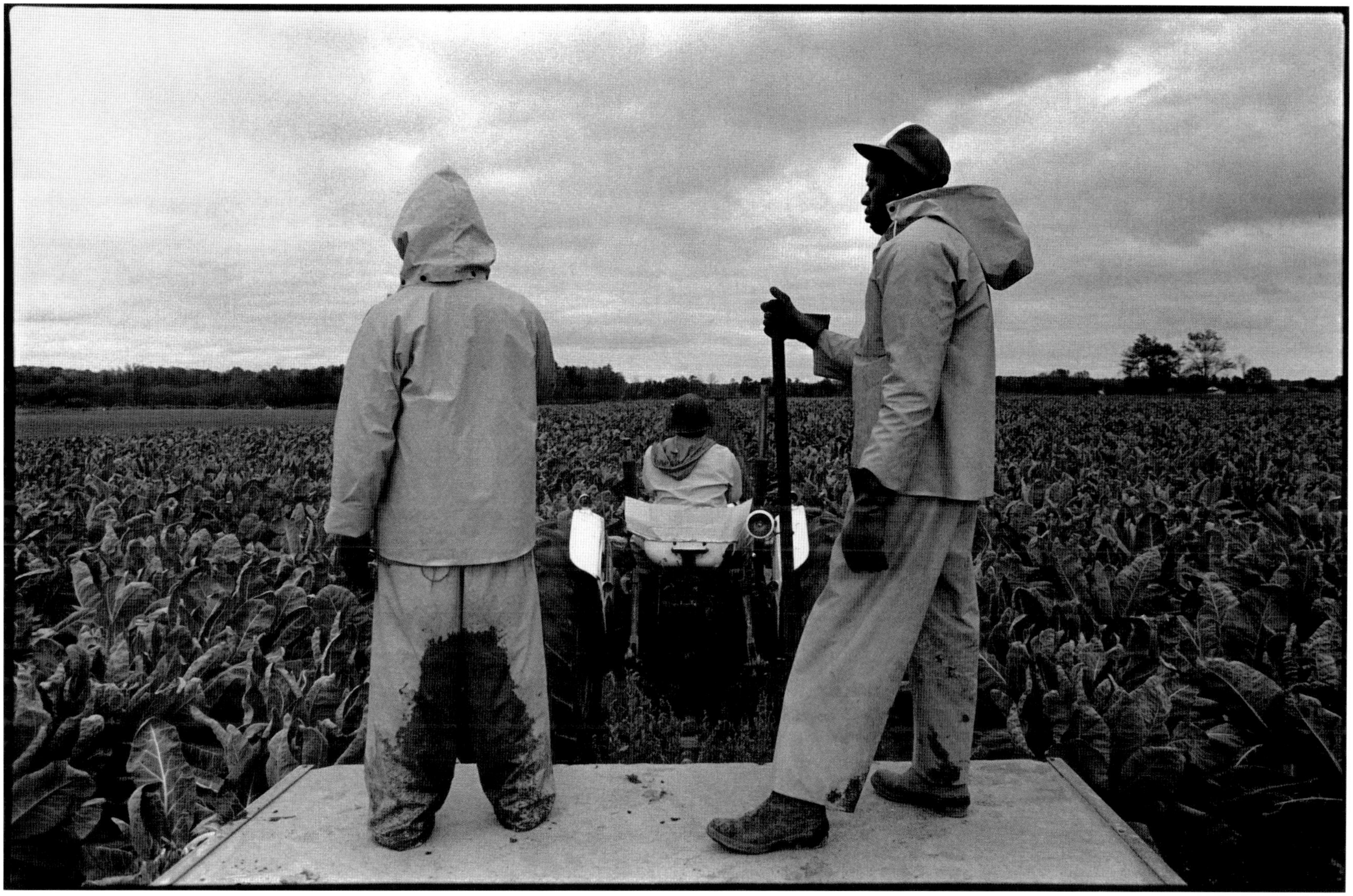

My experience in Canada was lots of hard work. Sometimes we worked seven days a week, depending on what you reap. But it was okay. I like the idea of going to a big country, travelling. I like the pace, you know. I went from Fort Barrington to Plymouth [Montserrat], then on to Antigua, and then straight to Toronto. We arrived in the night. From Toronto I went to Waterford. The boss-man picked us up [at the airport] at four in the morning. When we arrived at the farm, he woke us up. That's when I first saw the fields. I thought: lots of work to be done. That was my first impression. The fields were like a lawn.

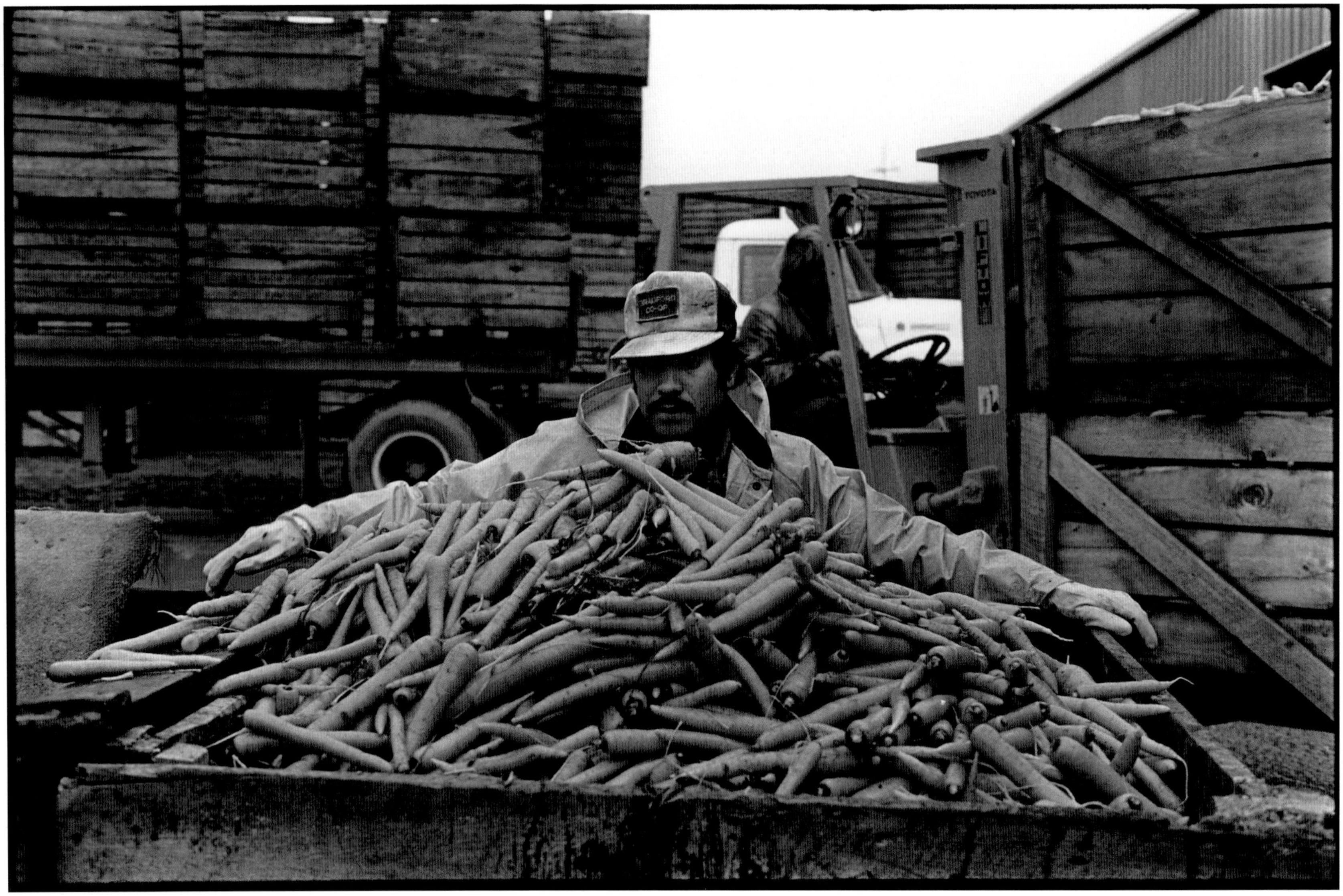

The cold. It would start in September, and for me it was unbearable, I just couldn't take it for long.

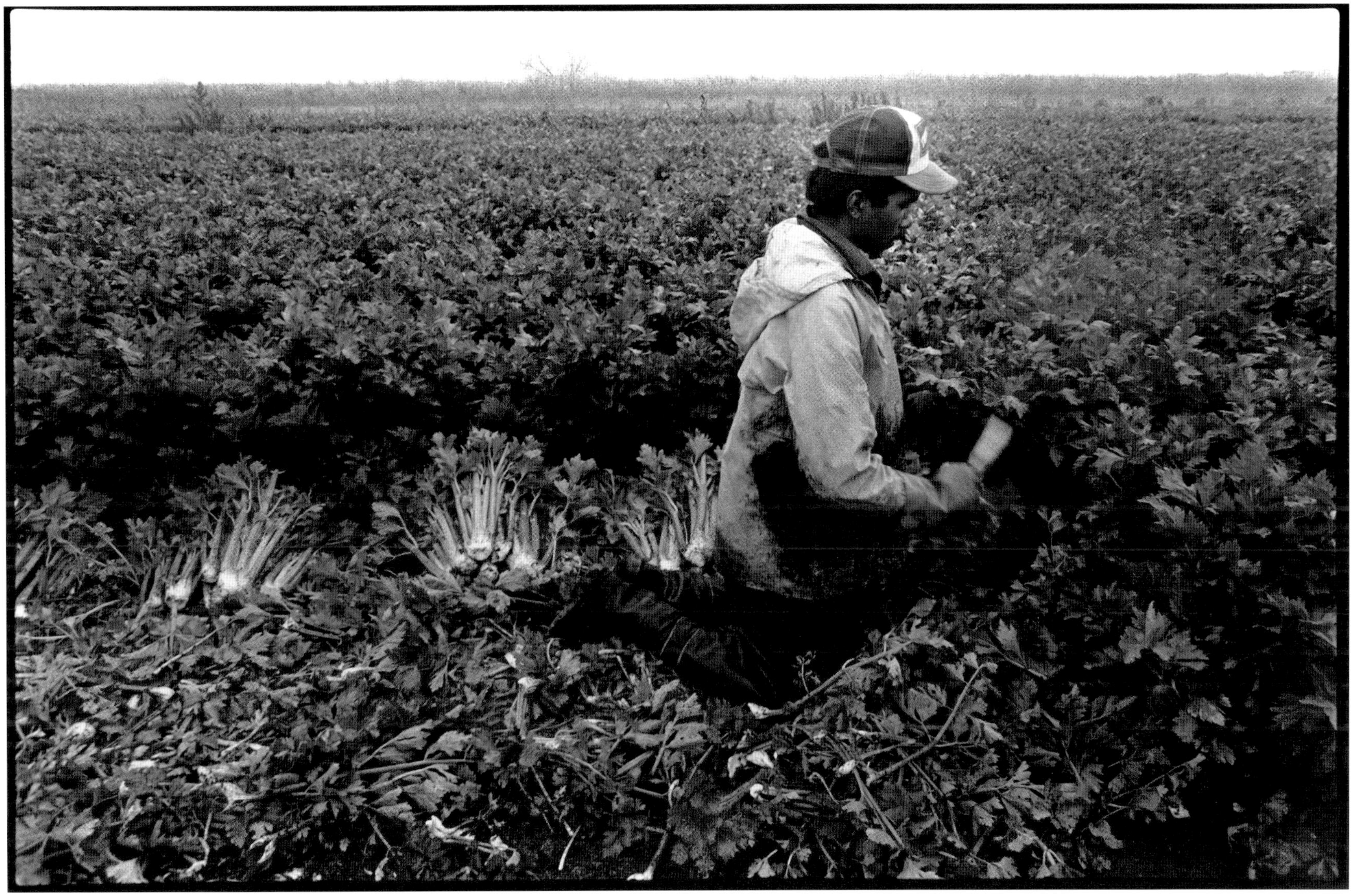

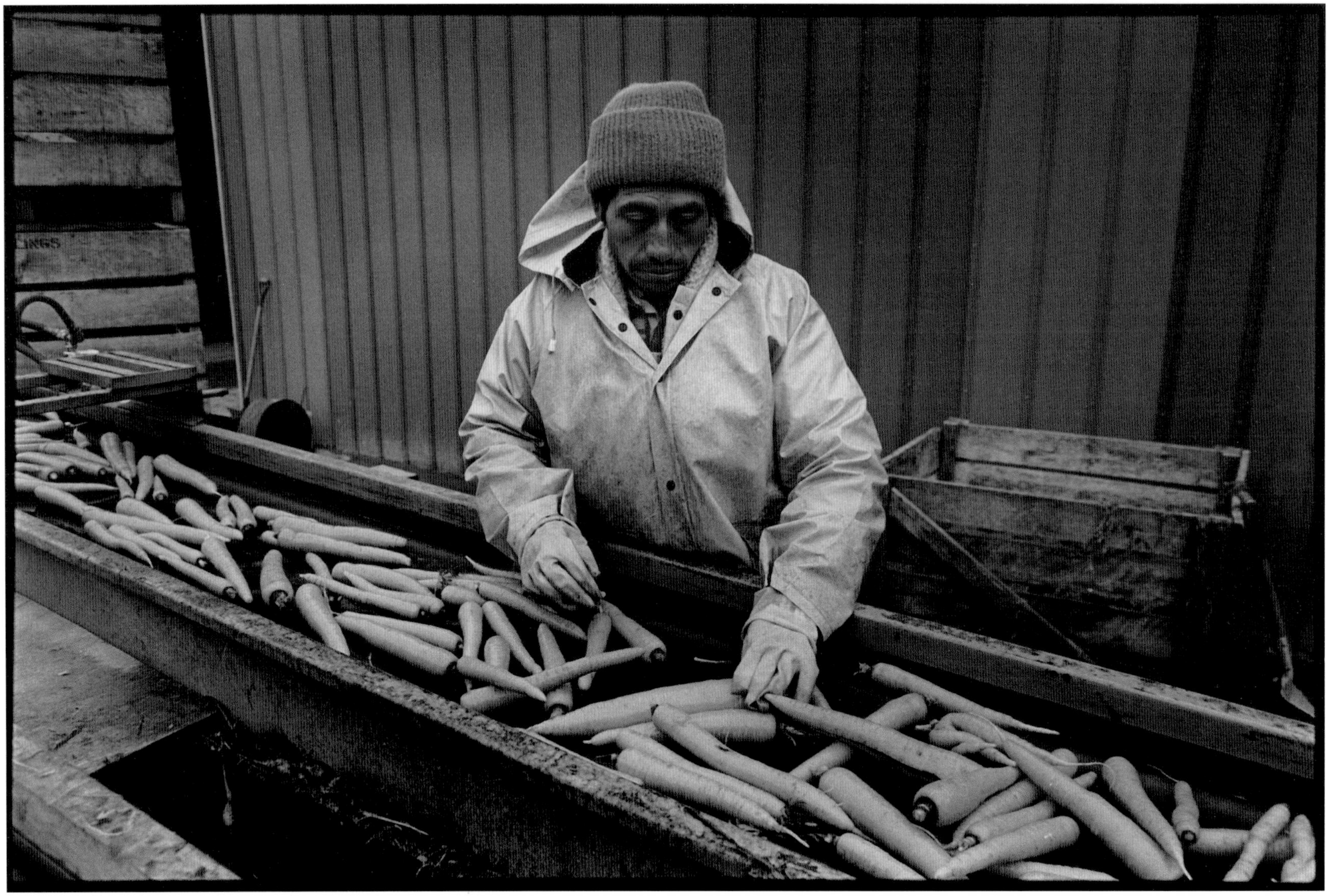

You have to work every day . . . No time to go to church, every day you have to work. Sometime in Canada, I have to ask them "today is what?" The only way you don't work is the rain. Unless the rain is falling very hard and if it holds up, you have to go. We have to stay at the camp, and if you're there for one week and you don't work, you don't get no pay.

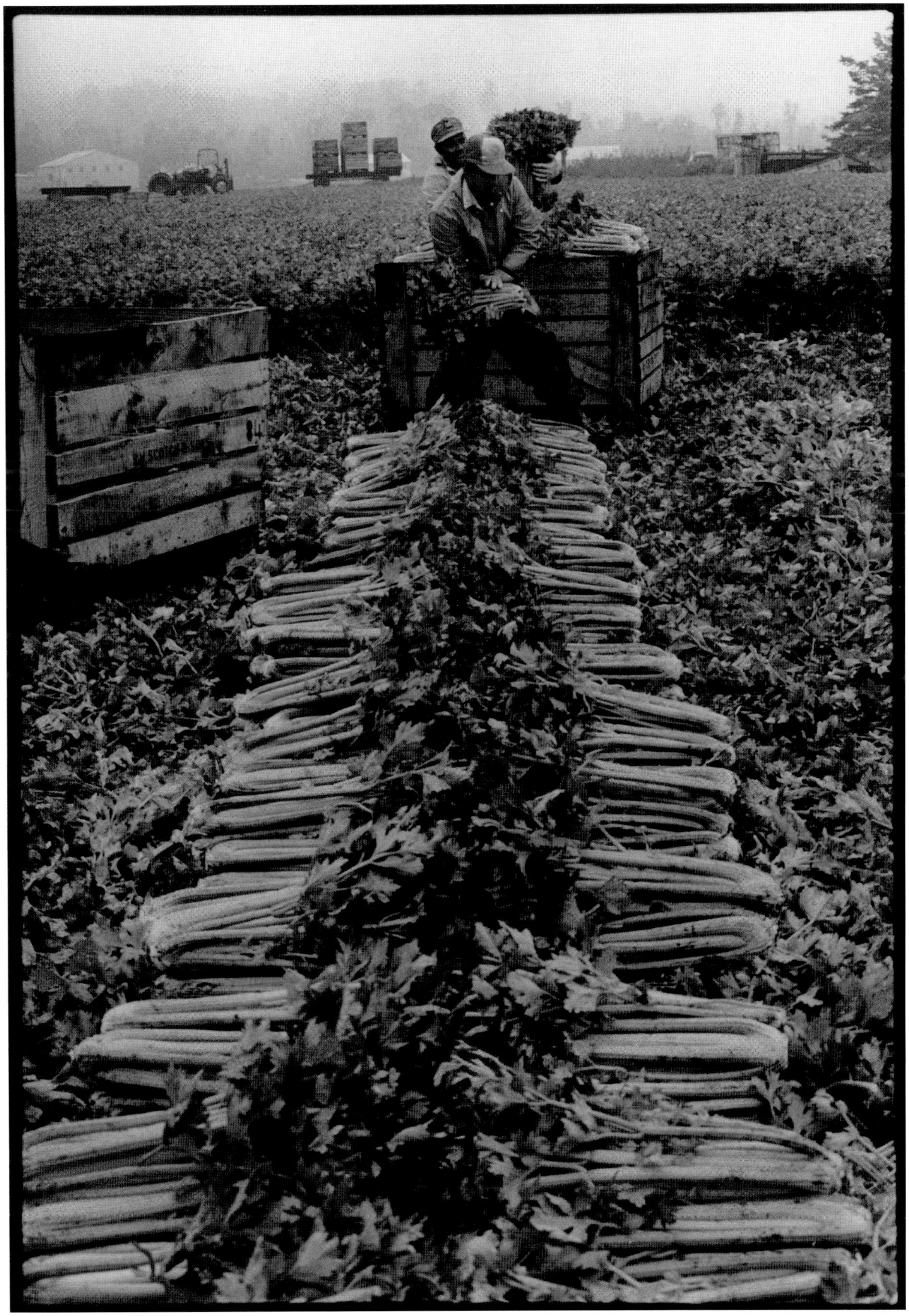

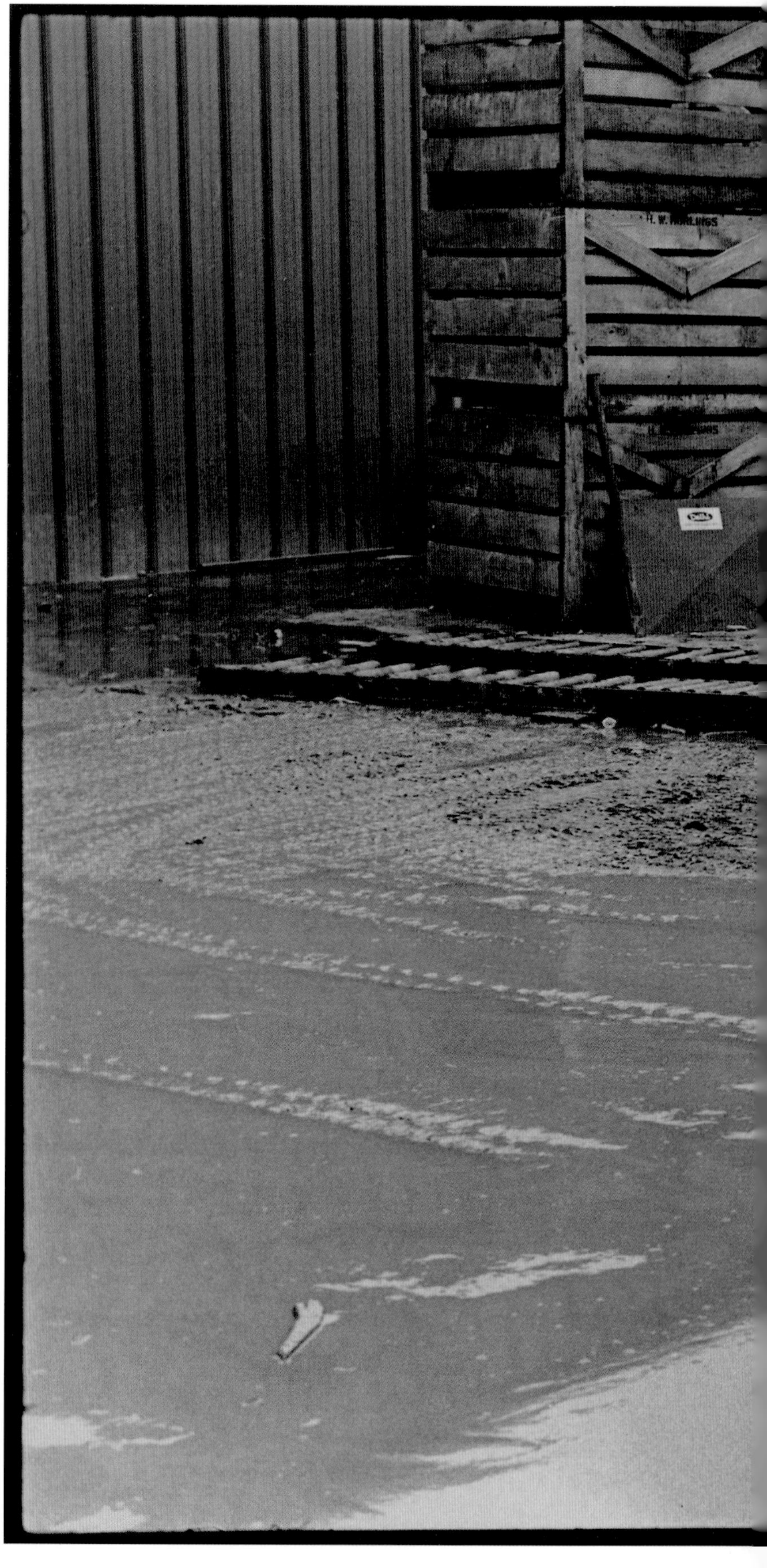

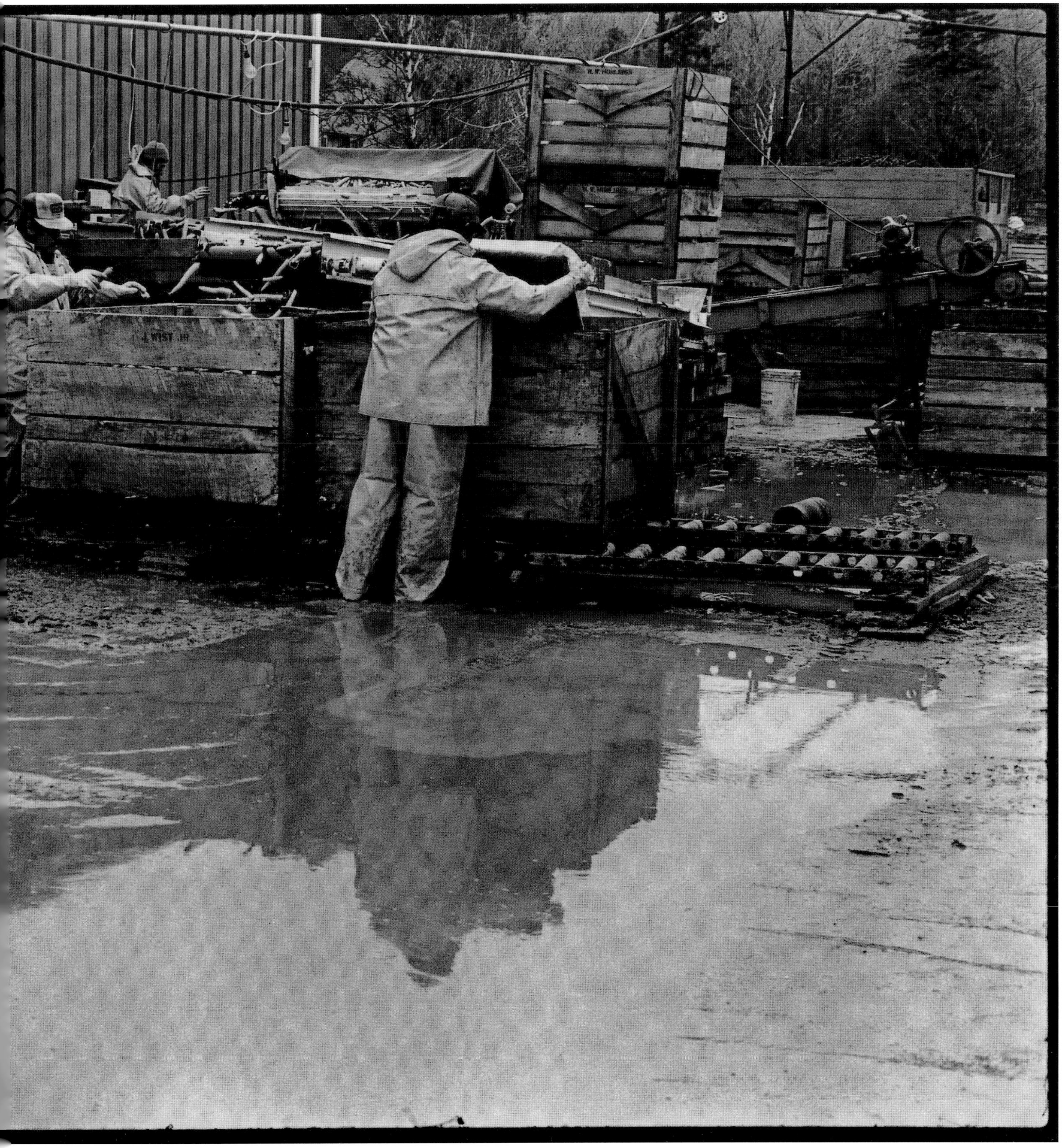

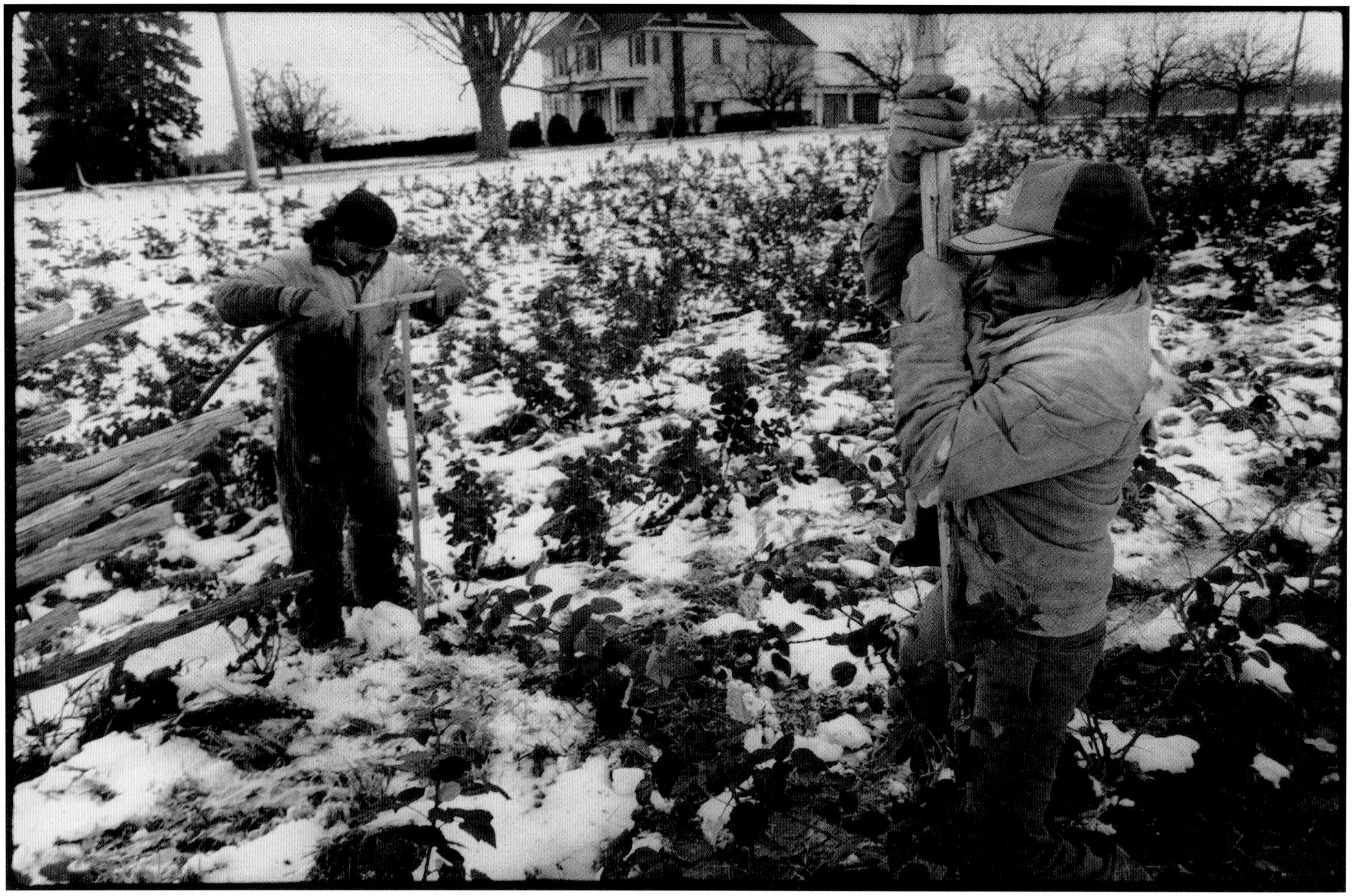

You have to pass a medical examination – blood pressure, a general examination, the whole body. And for the physical, which you obviously have to pass, you have to be completely healthy for them to give you a permit. If you are not healthy, you don't get a permit to go [to Canada]. If you're not sick, if you're in good health, it's okay … but if you're not in good health, and you really want to go there, you have to pay something under the table, so that they can say you're healthy, to make your health look good. But with my co-workers, there was no problem. They're all healthy, you see, since they're from deep in the rural parts of the country – me, I'm from the city – the countryside is more healthy for you, no? Life is better there, more tranquil …

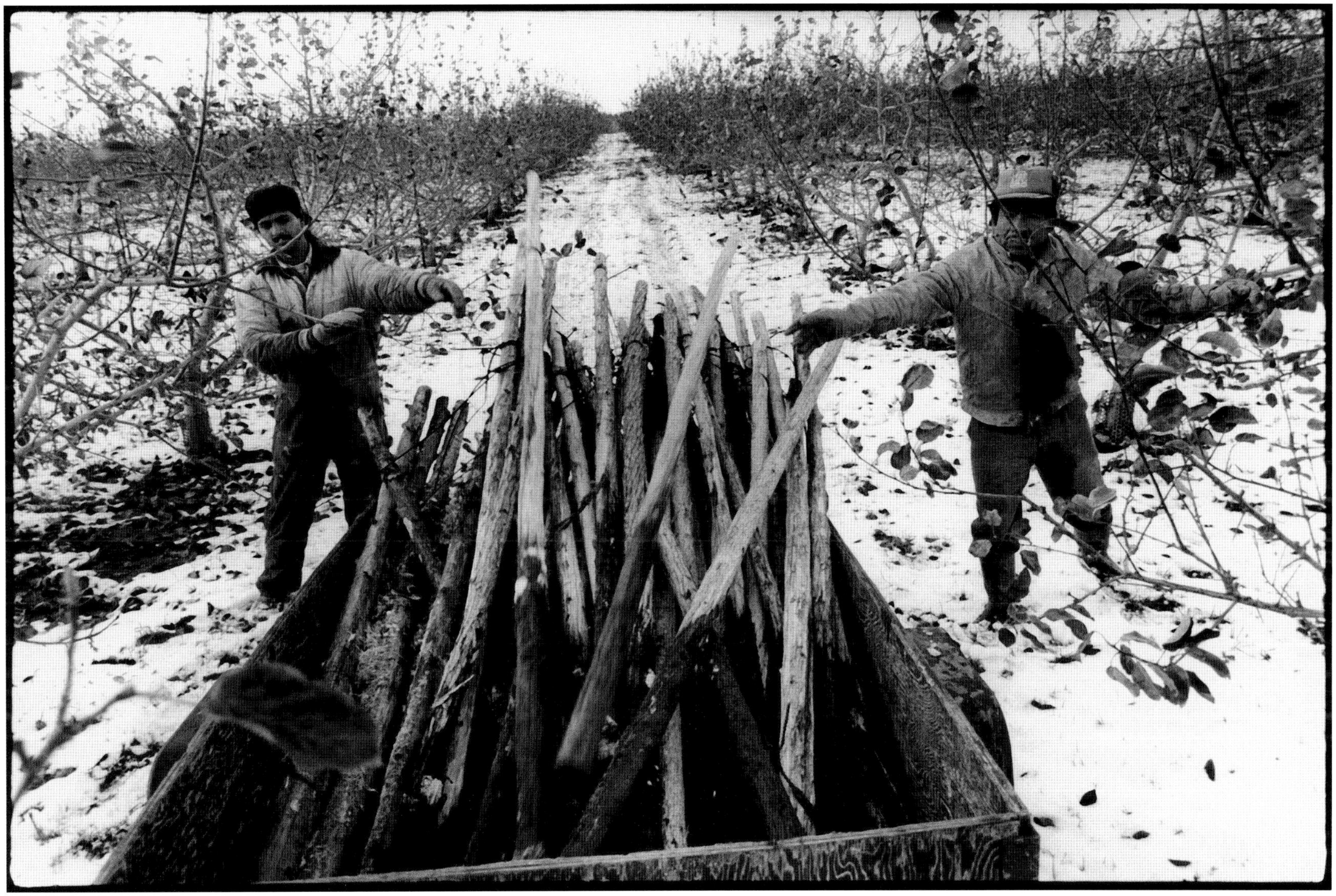

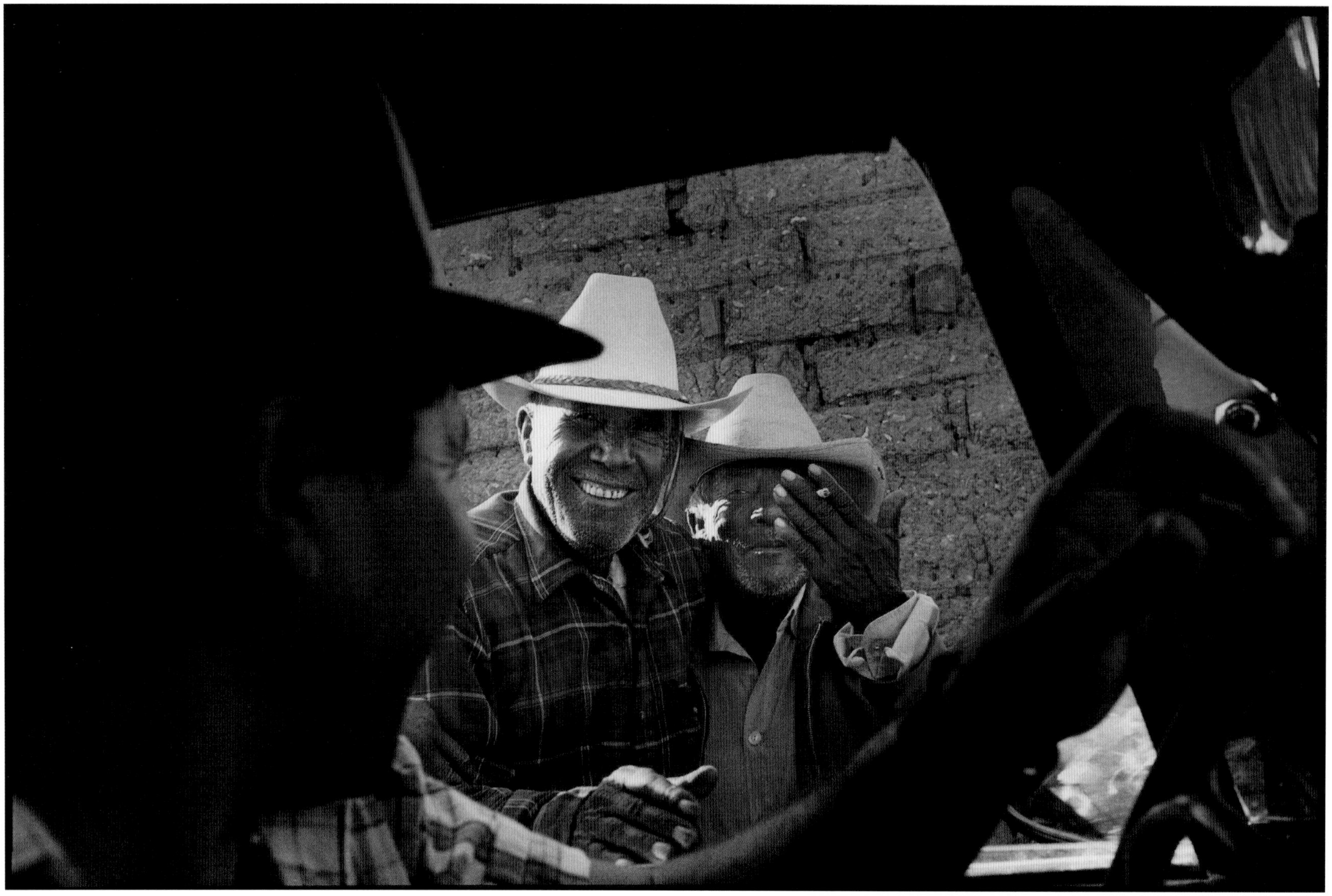

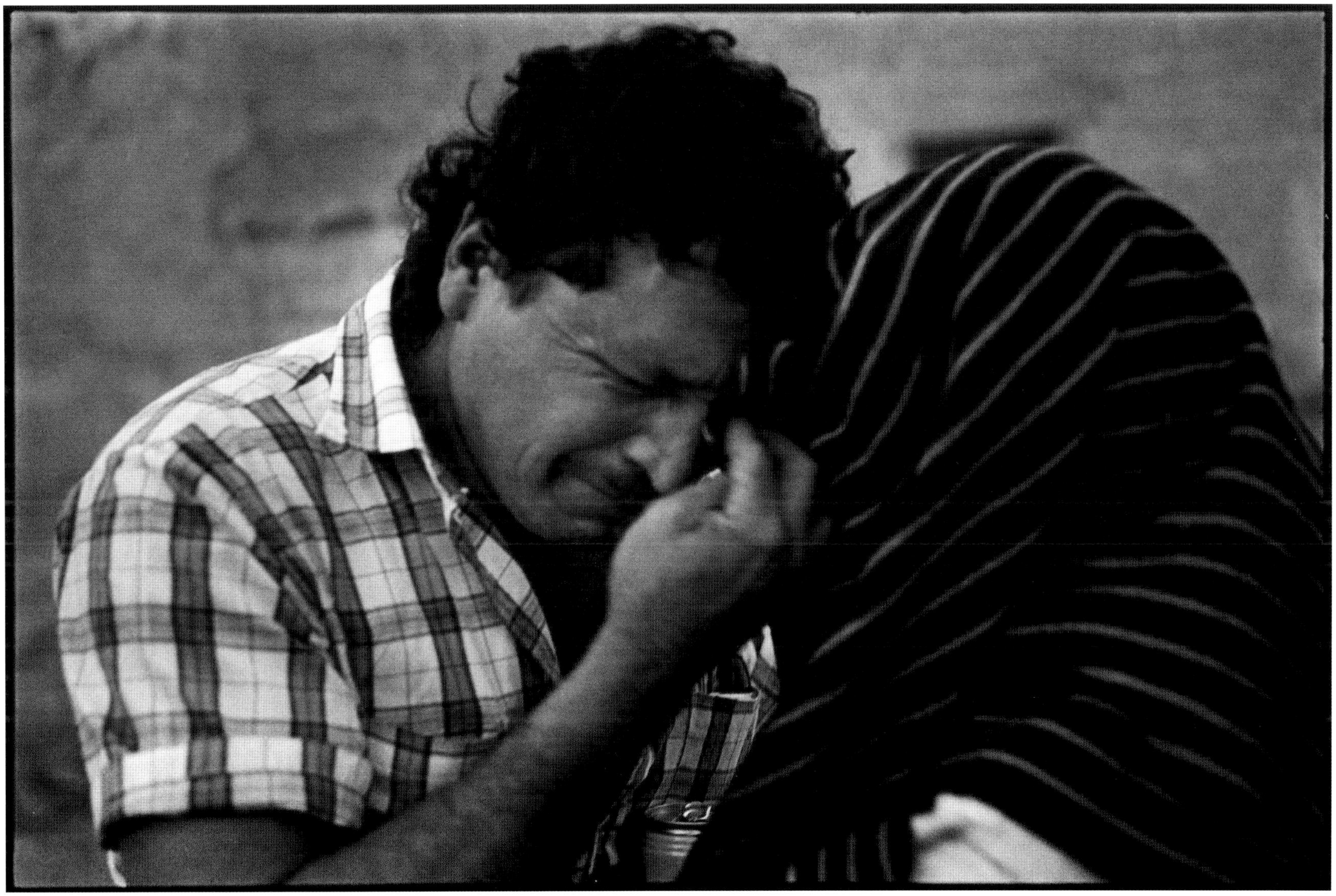

There is a saying in Mexico: "to learn, one has to suffer."

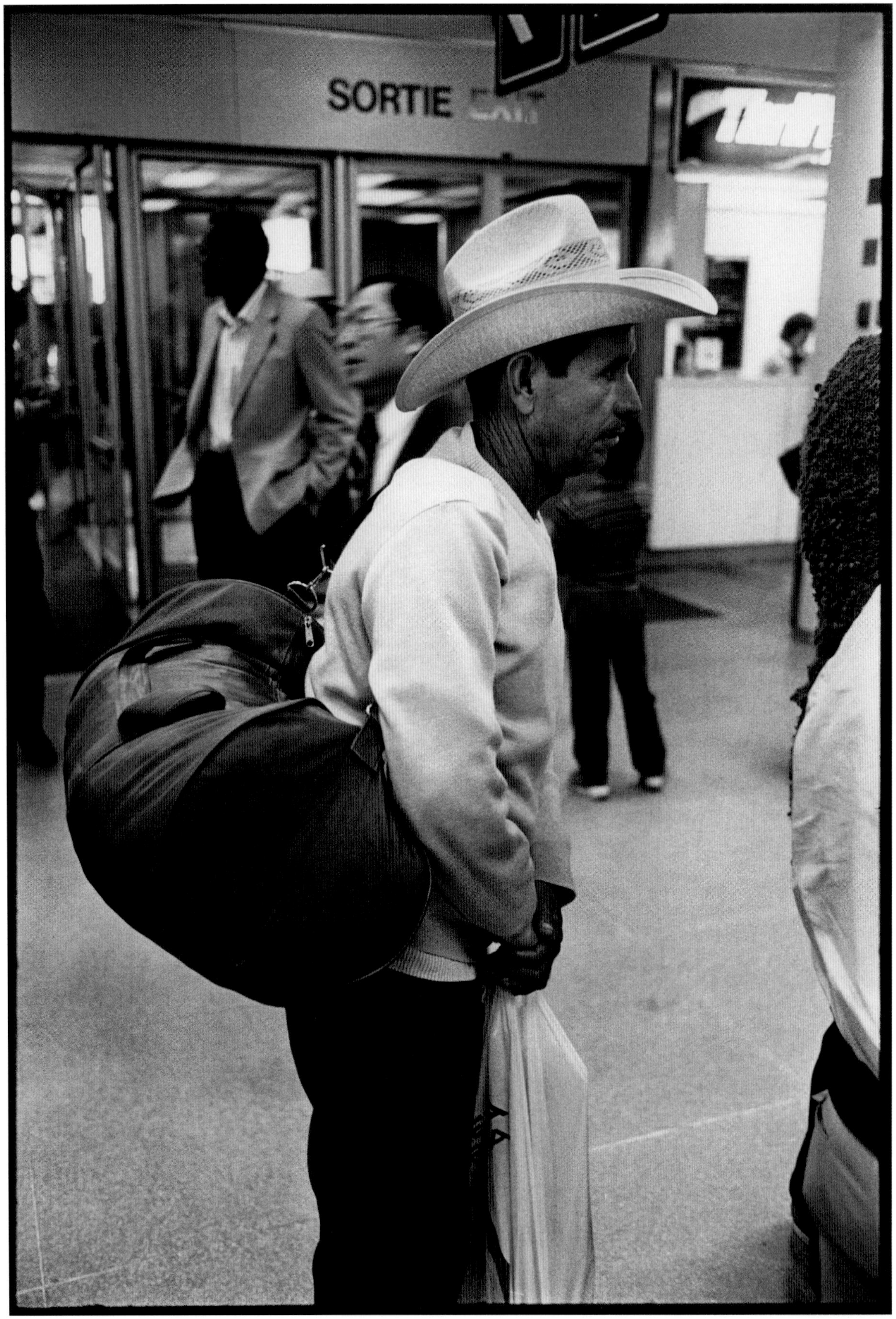
SORTIE

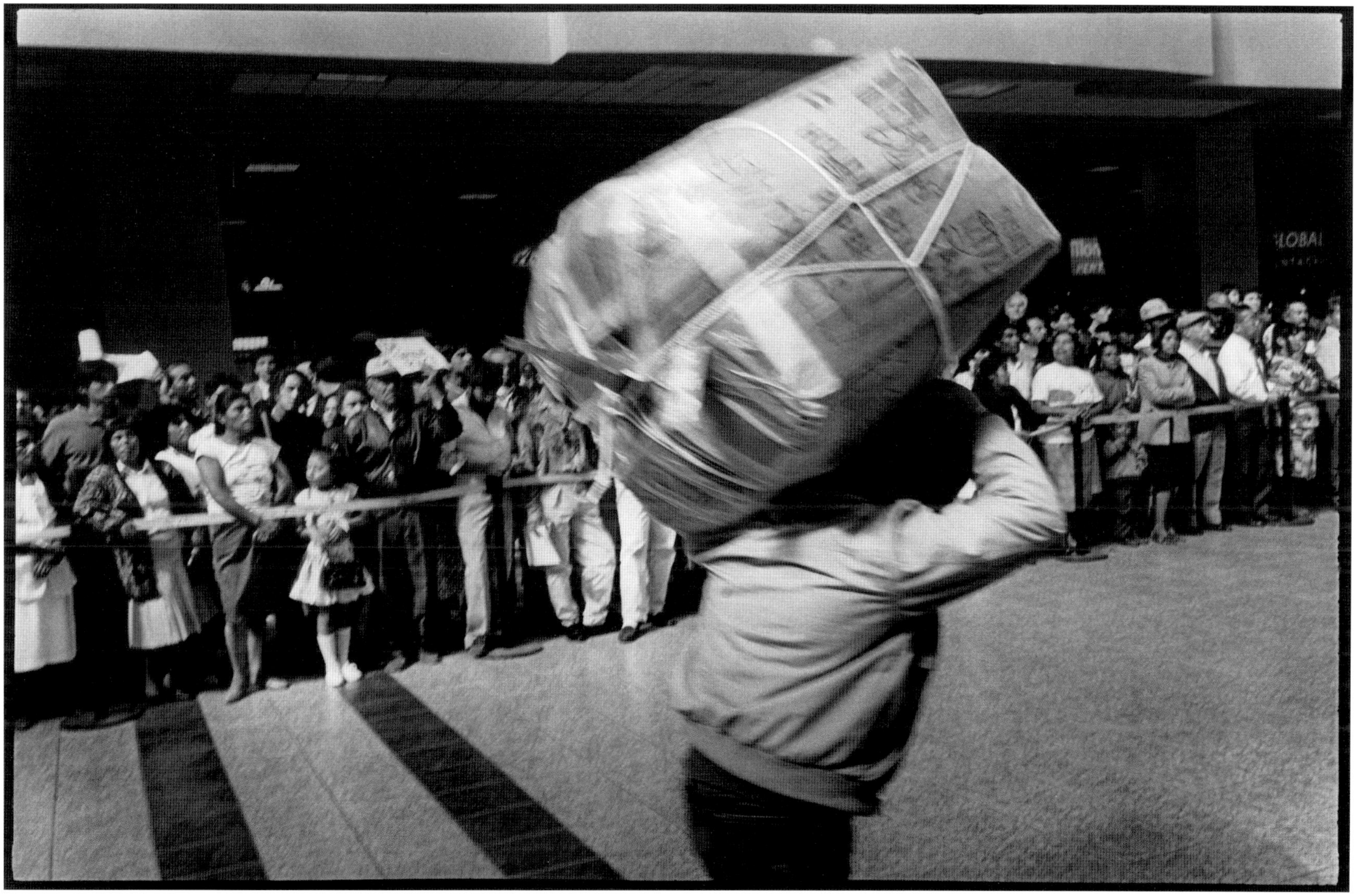

It was the fourth time that we were waiting there, at the airport. I came on the 19th, they requested that I go to the airport to see if it was possible for me to come [to Canada]. But there was no chance of that. Then they requested that we come back on the 27th, but the government representative did not show up. Nobody showed up, and so we stayed there overnight, waiting in case somebody showed up. That was on Friday. By Monday, some had left, and there were only seven of us, and so we went to the office and asked why no one came to see us, or if they were going to send us [to Canada]. The person in the office was very dismissive towards us, but then the government rep came, and when we told him our story, he said, "Come back tomorrow at 6:00 a.m., and if you can't leave on the 6:00 a.m. flight, you'll leave on the 10:30 a.m. flight." And so that's why we waited right there, to see if our luck was going to change, and yes, we did get lucky [by the 31st], and we were able to come, so we could start working.

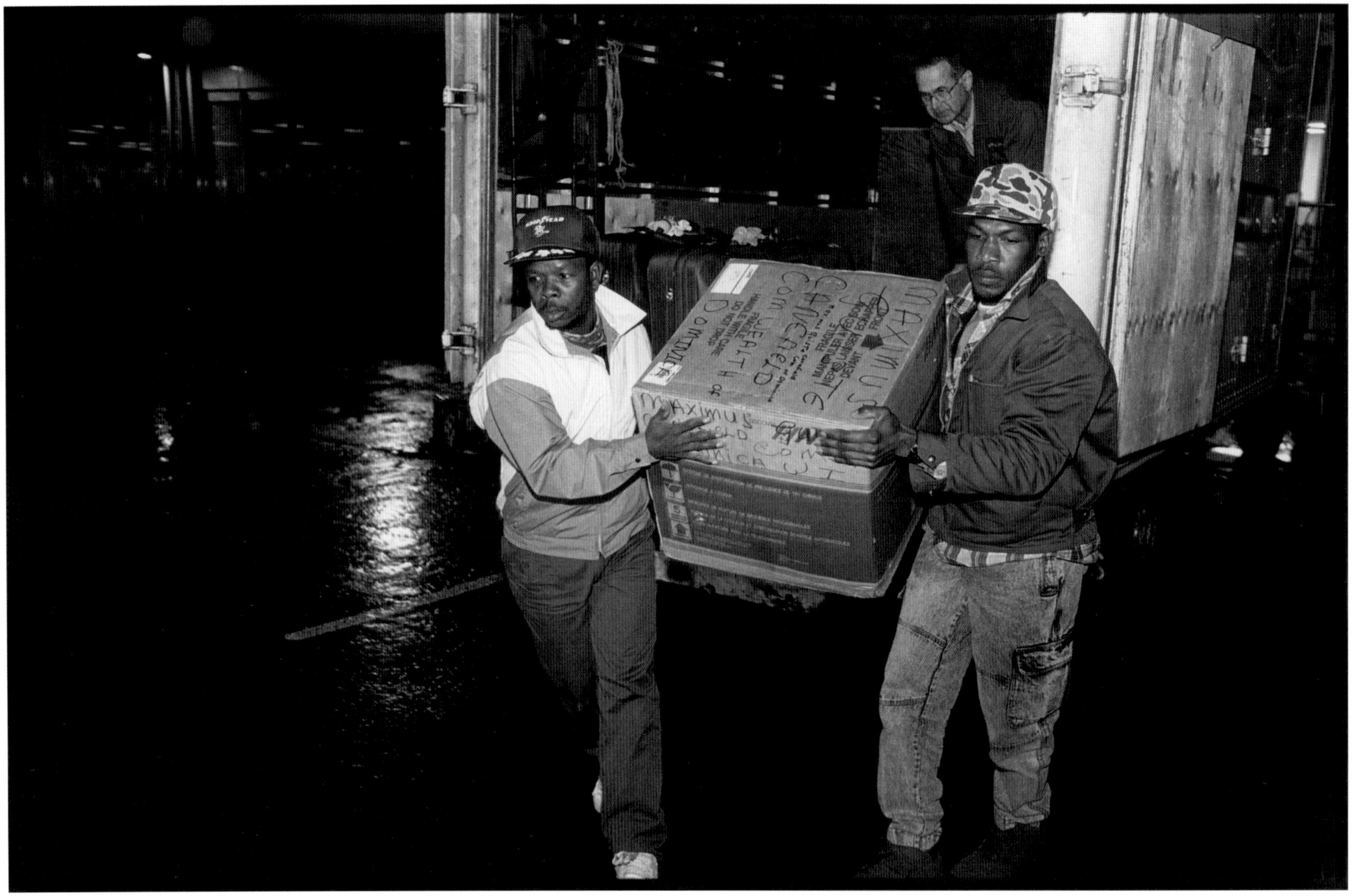

[An exchange on a plane from Mexico City to Toronto, as lunch was about to be served.]

– Thank you very much for this interview, and good luck. Now we're going to eat, right? When was it the last time that you ate?

– I haven't eaten since last night at 7:00 p.m.

– It's now 3:00 p.m.

– Well, yes …

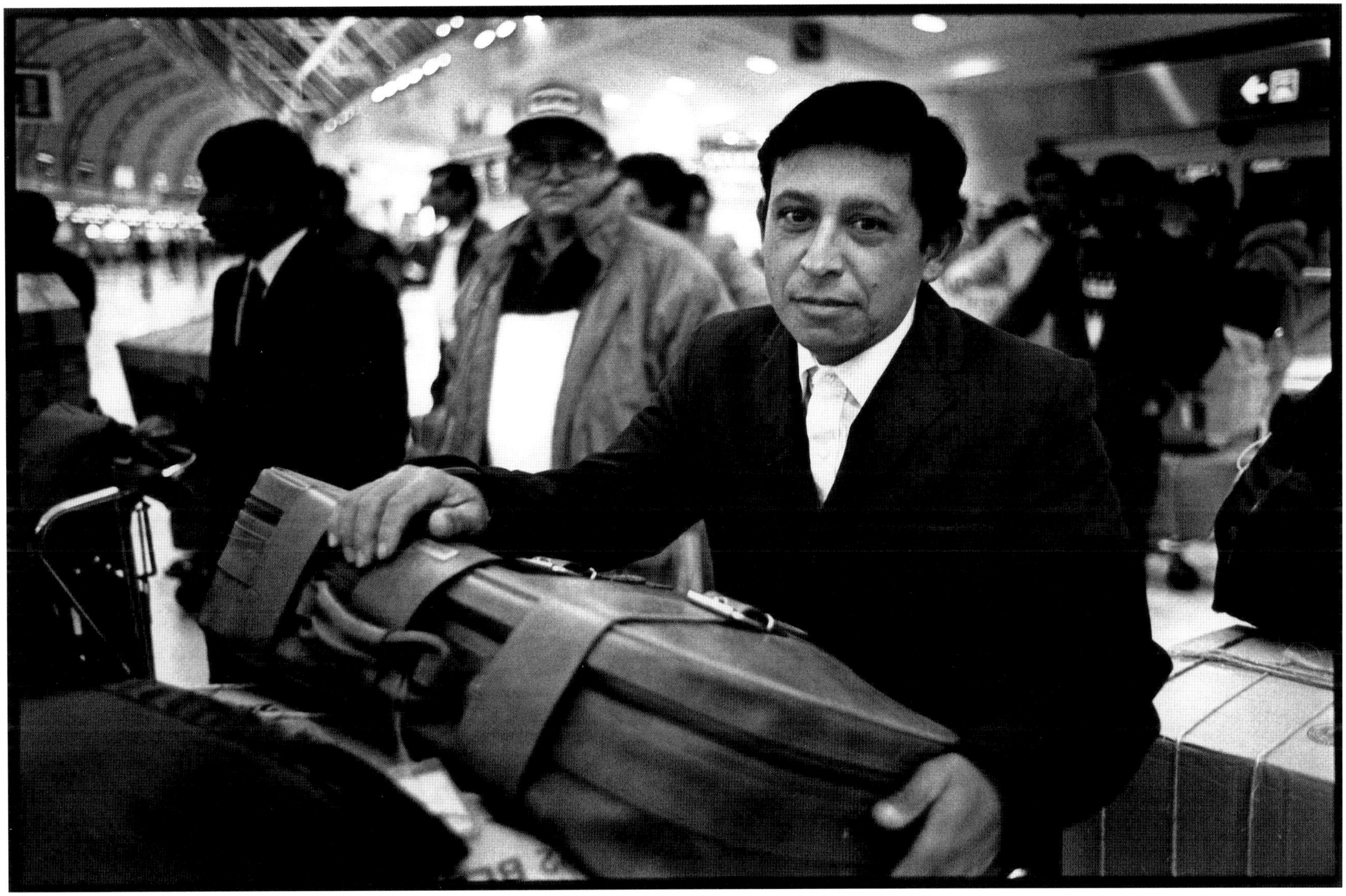

When I went to the airport I saw many owners who had accompanied the workers, and they said goodbye to them warmly, very warmly. But there are differences, some bosses are good, some are not so good ... some only have a few workers, and they take us to the airport in their own car, but those that have forty or more workers, it's a different story.

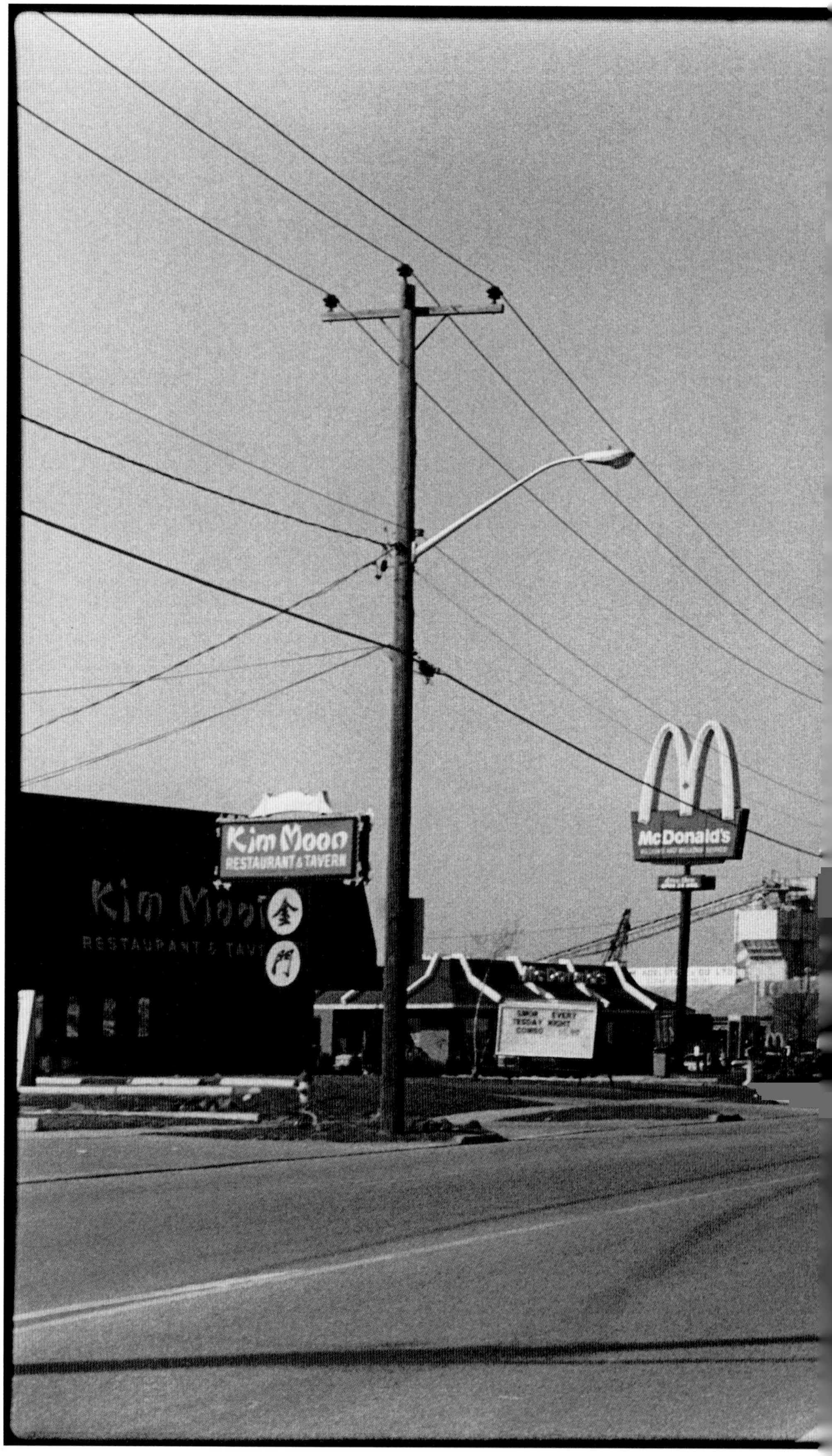
Kim Moon
RESTAURANT & TAVERN
McDonald's

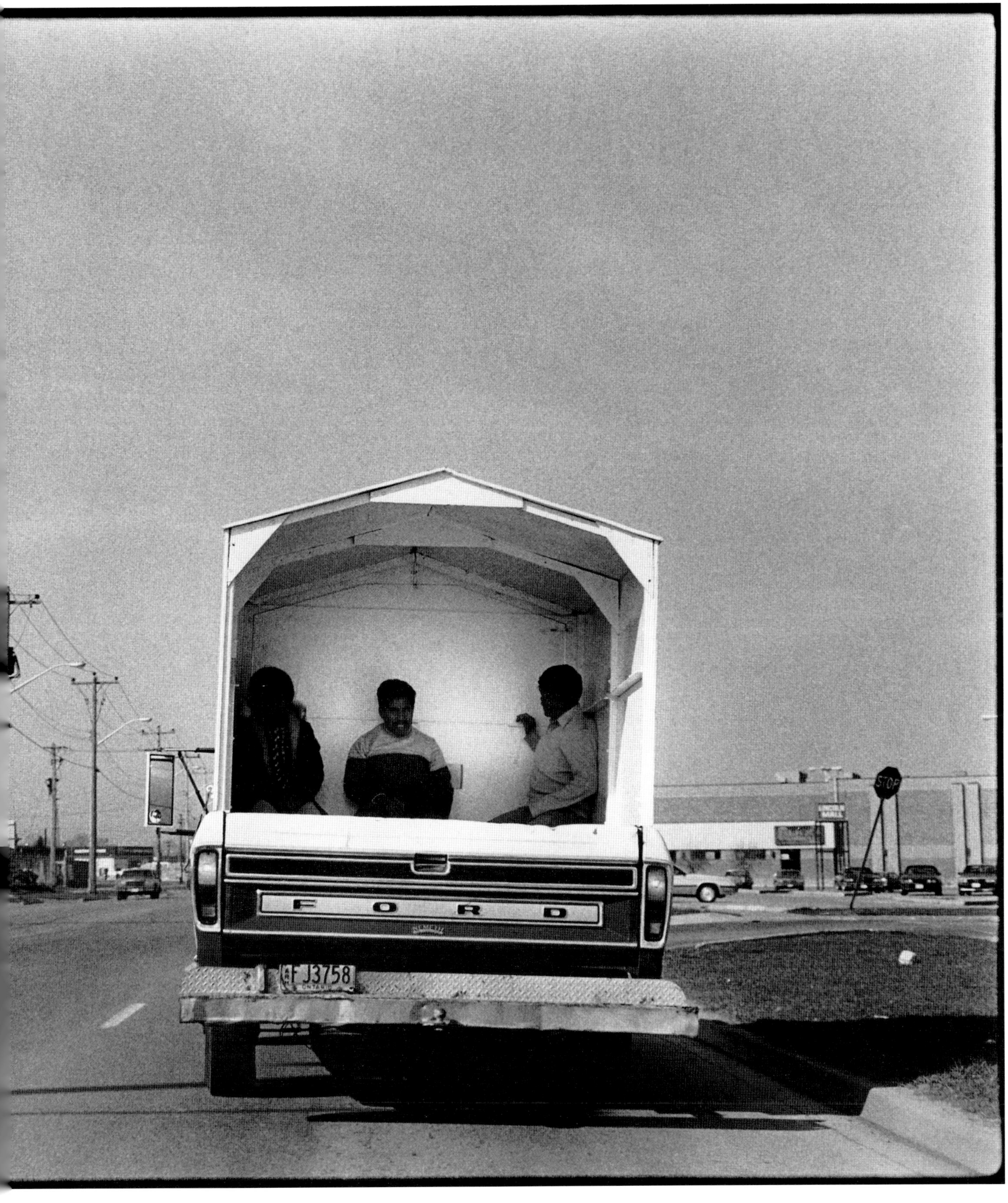
STOP
FORD

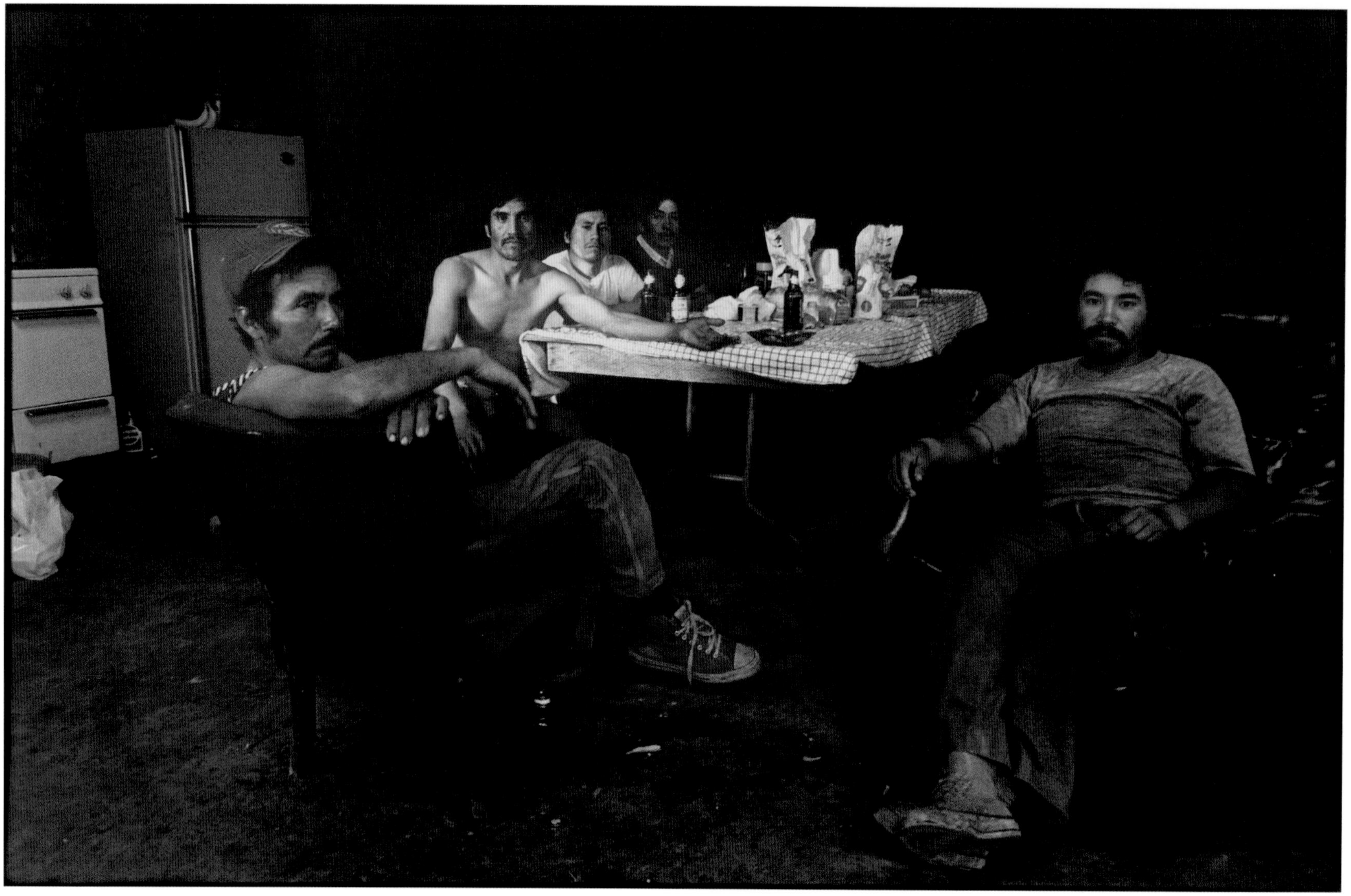

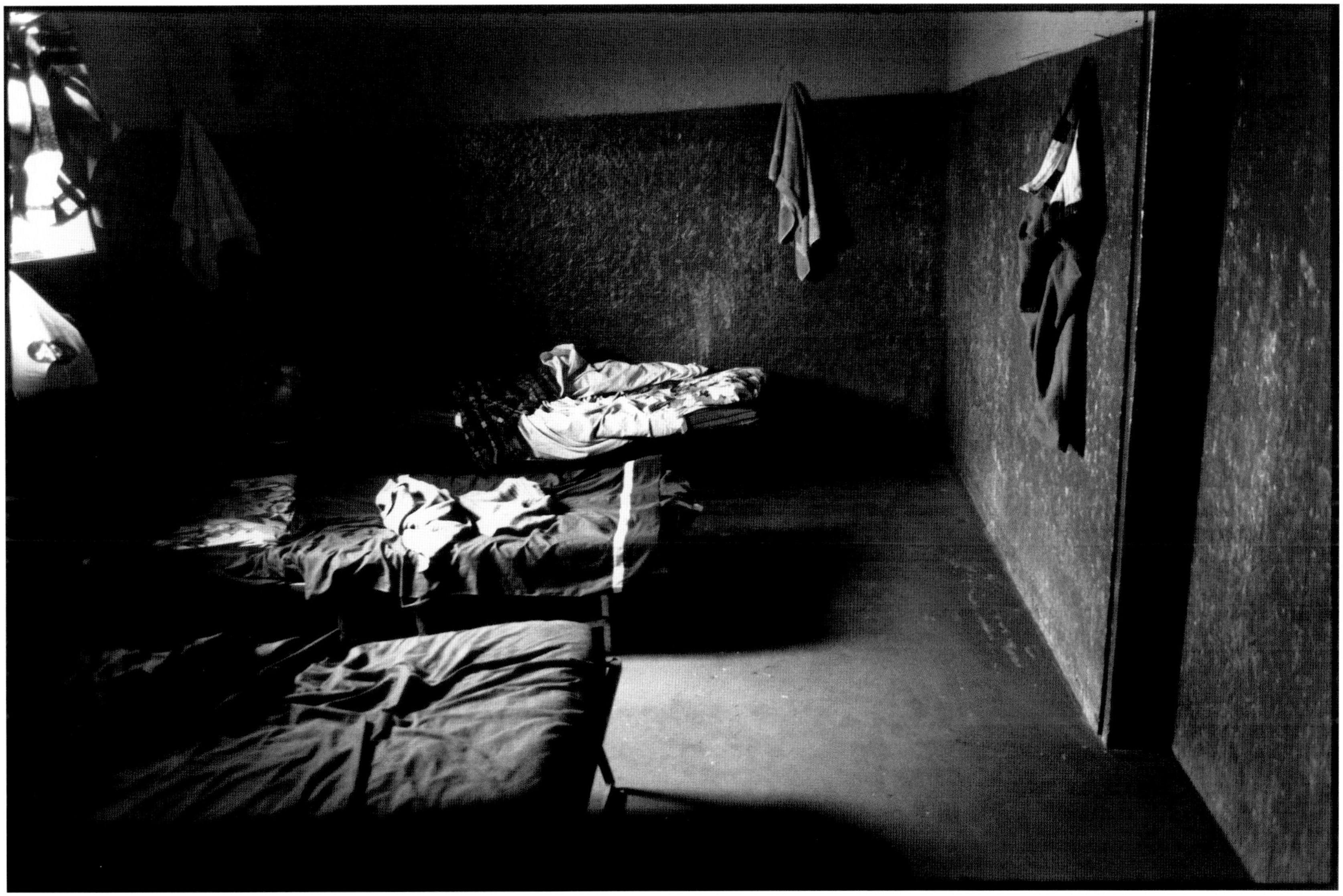

In 1984 it was a horrible situation for me. The conditions where we lived were terrible, and so was the owner. He treated us worse than animals, you could say. But I continued to work and put up with it for that year. I have pictures of myself looking very skinny, for the pressure that we were under. And I put up with it so that I wouldn't lose the opportunity of coming back to work in Canada. Why did I put up with it? For my children, that's why.

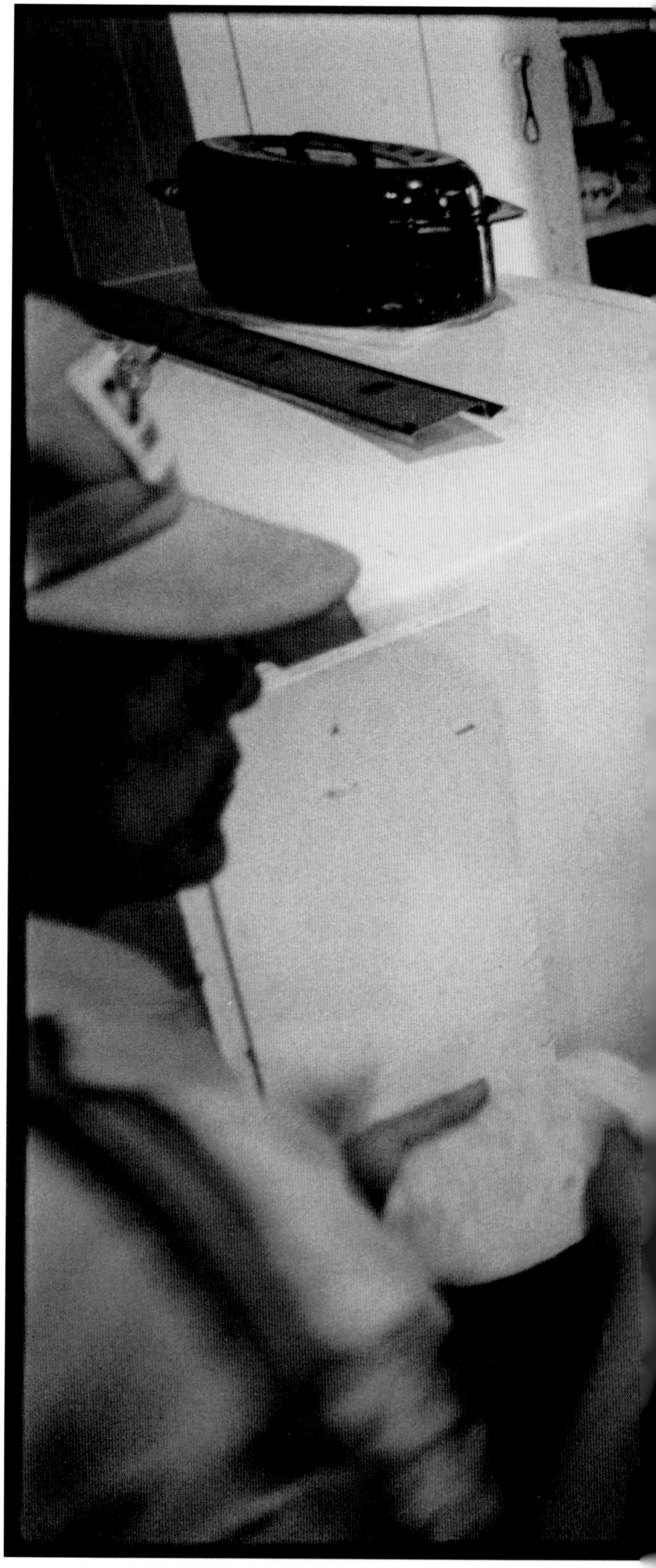

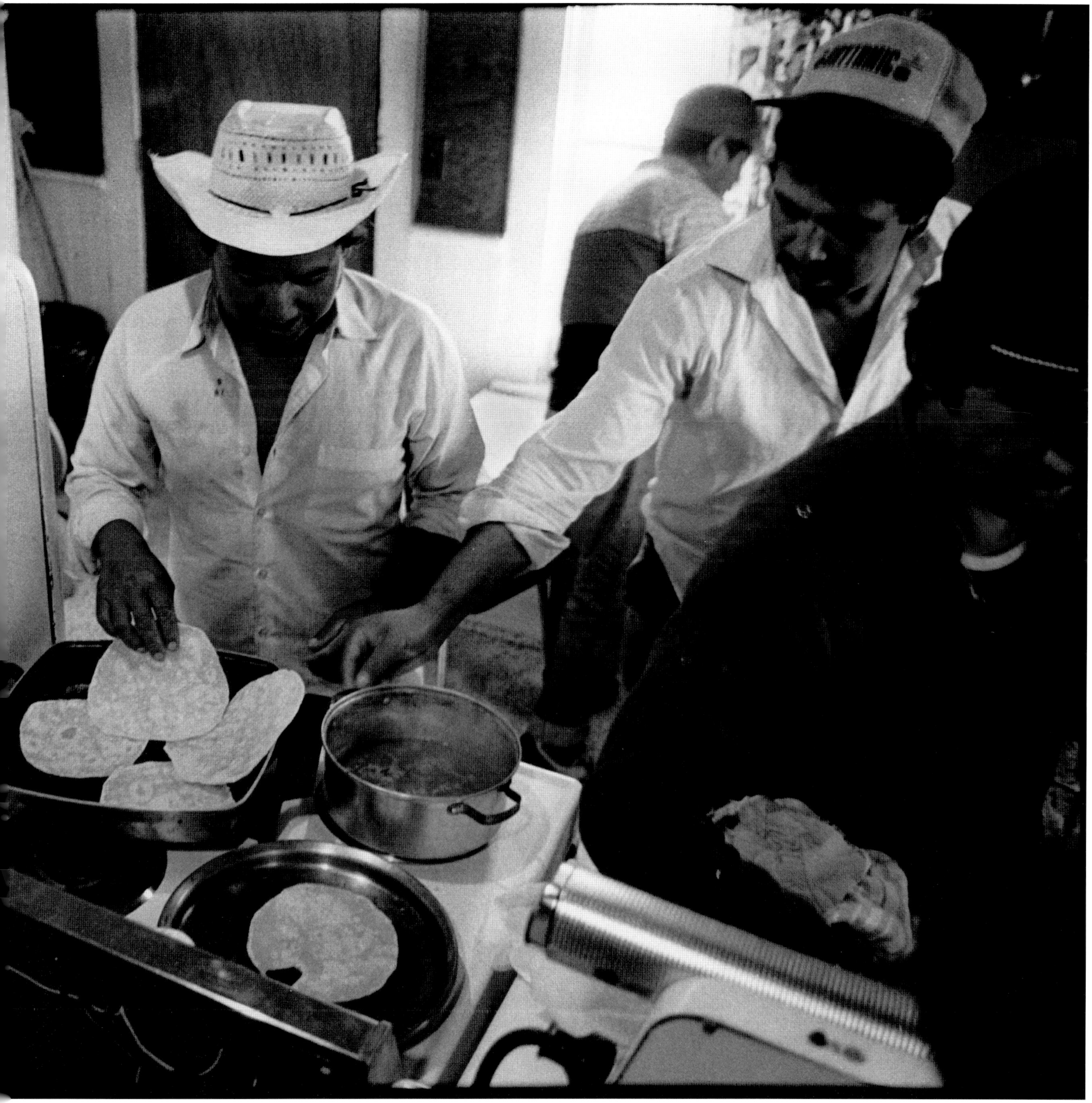

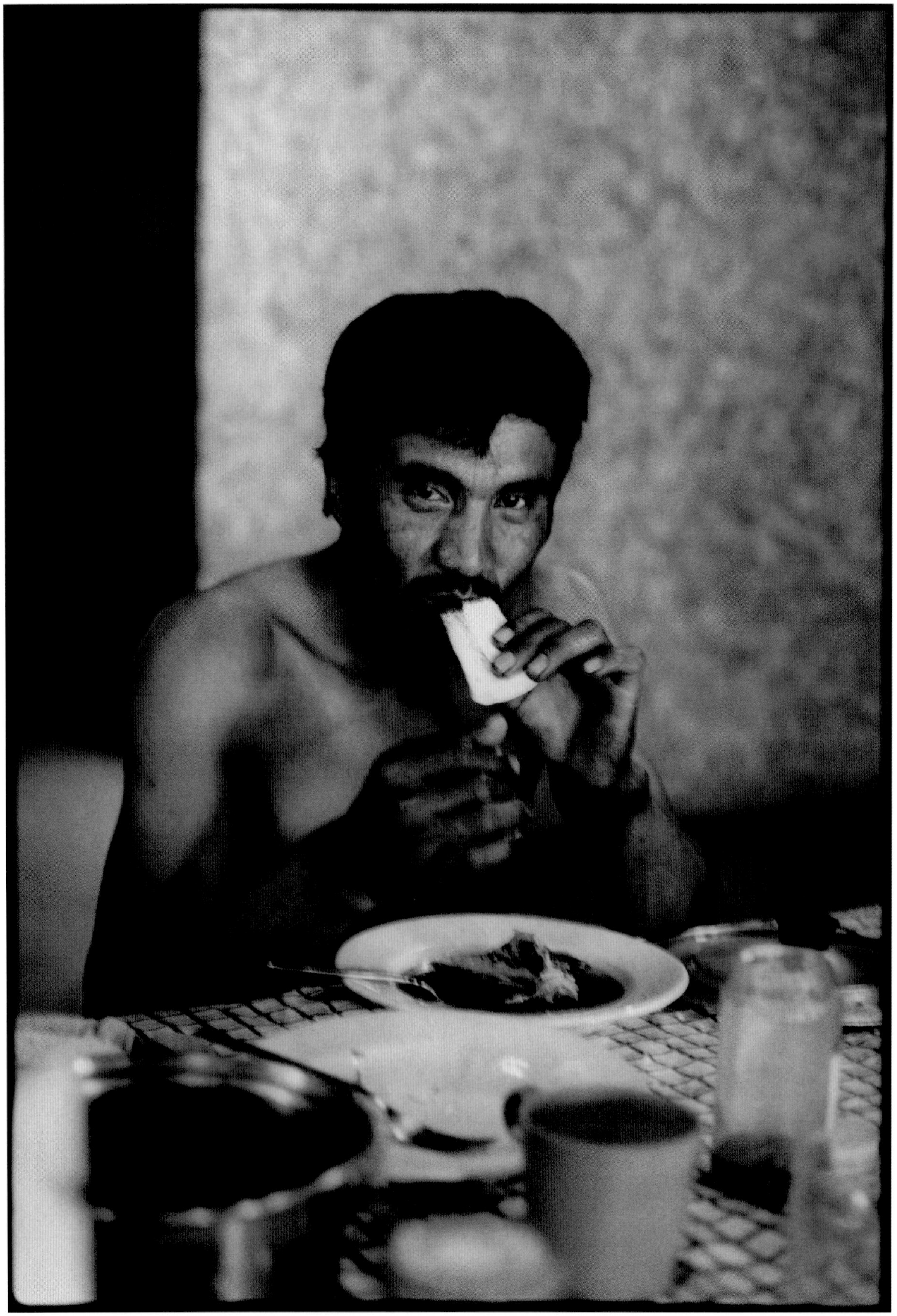

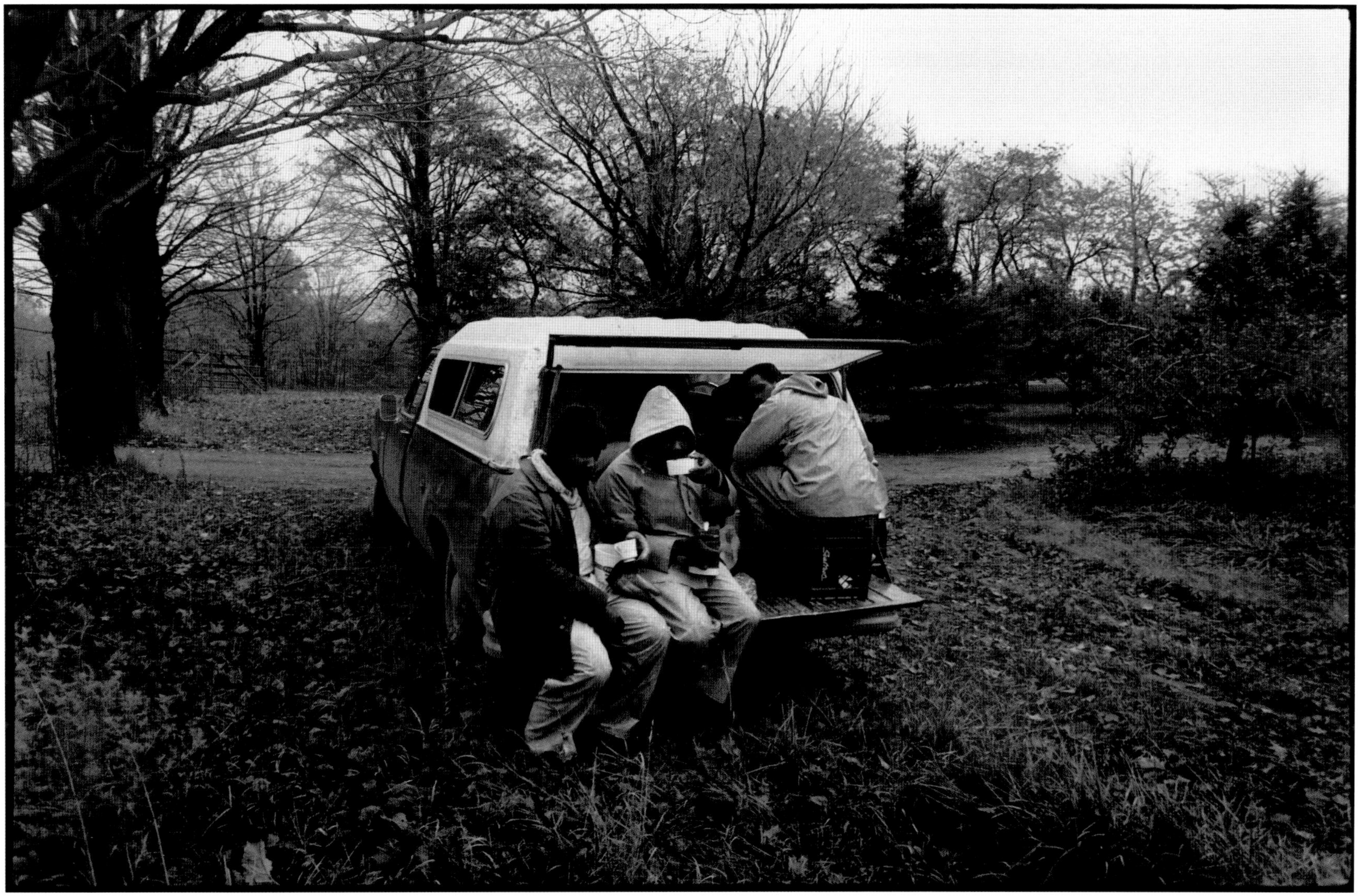

When you get the card [or notice of work being available], you can't say for sure you will get to go there. When you first get the card, still you have to go and get two or three tests.

Say four hundred men may reach St. Ann's Bay [Jamaica] and they are gathered on a playfield ground. So say this year, they say that they need four hundred new men to carry them to Canada. They may send out six hundred cards, so when the six hundred go, now you have a selection. They stand up and watch you as you line up, call your name and you go up to them, just stand there, and they look at your hands. They look at your hands and they say, "Your hands are soft," and they turn you down.

And if you pass that selection there, then in time they call you to go to town for a medical. If you go to a medical now and you fail that with a blood test, [blood] pressure or your teeth [are bad], you still can't go. If your pressure is too high, you're not going, and if you fail the blood, you're not going. They call it "process."

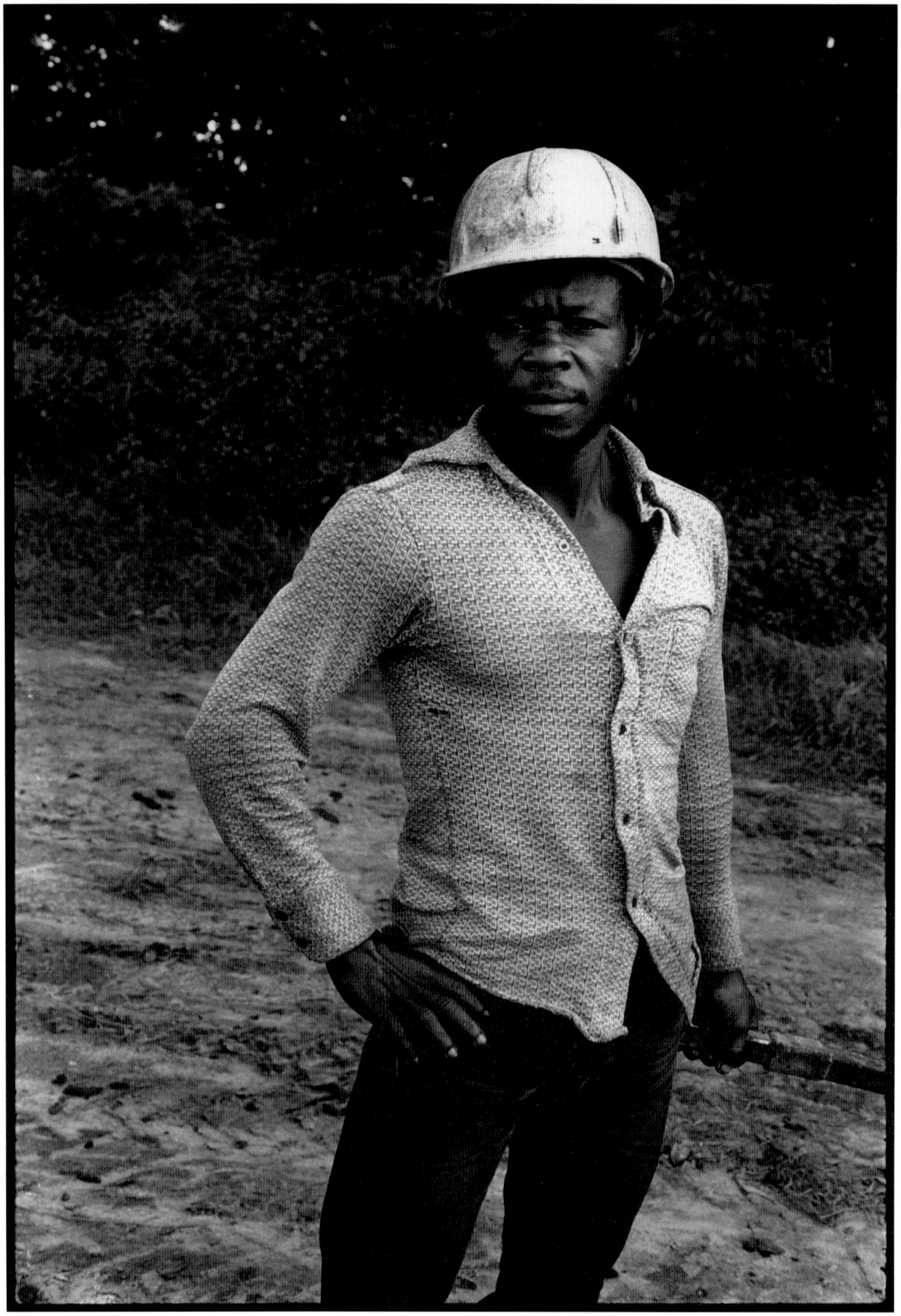

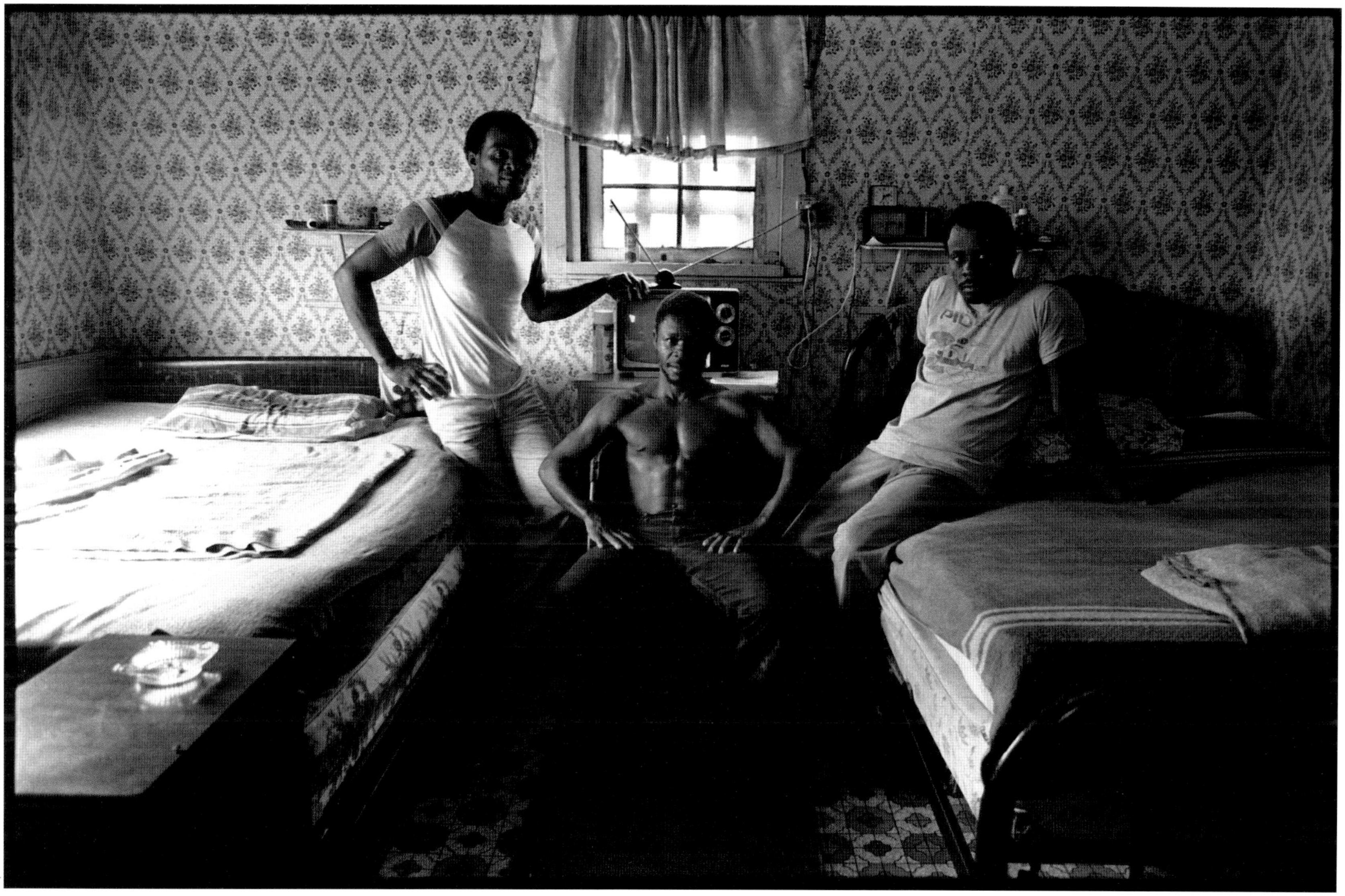

I've been to Canada six times. Canada is nice. But you have to make up your mind to work hard. Money is always a problem. I'm a very hard worker, all the bosses liked me. But some were rough in the cold months. After a few years I decided to stay home [in Montserrat] and do my own cultivation, and grow my own beans, lettuce, tomatoes, and so on. What I would like to have is some of the variety of seeds they have in Canada.

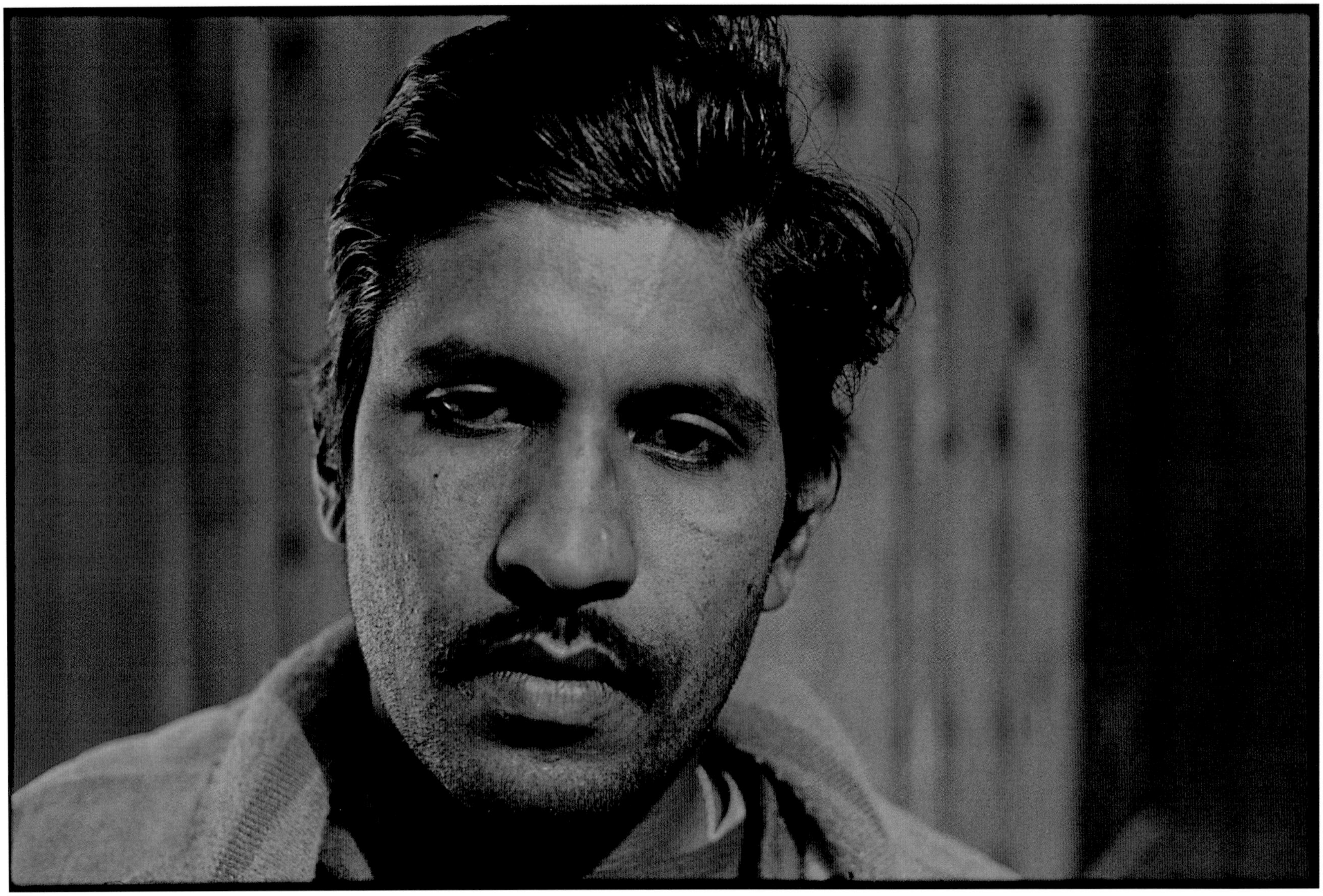

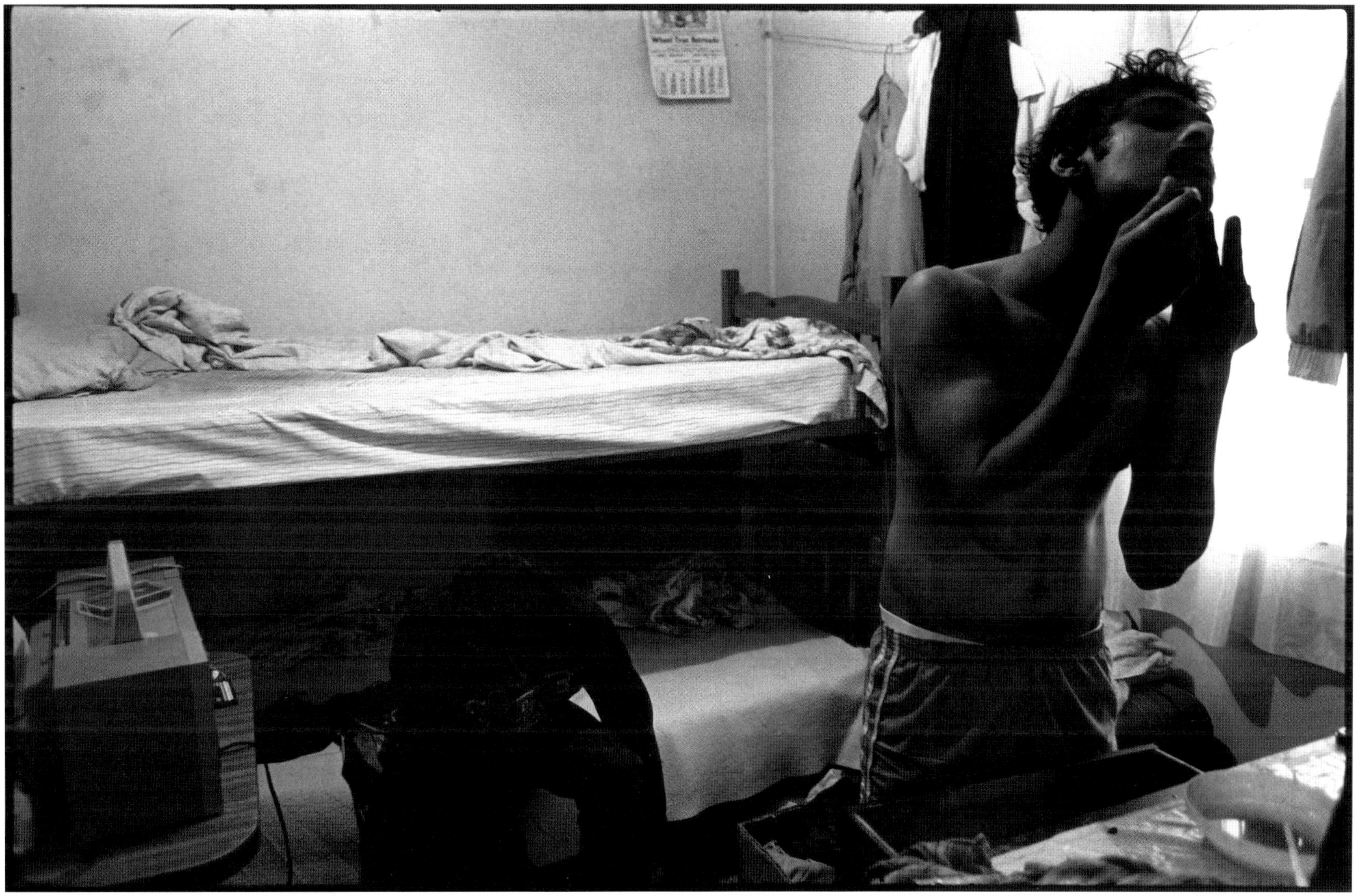

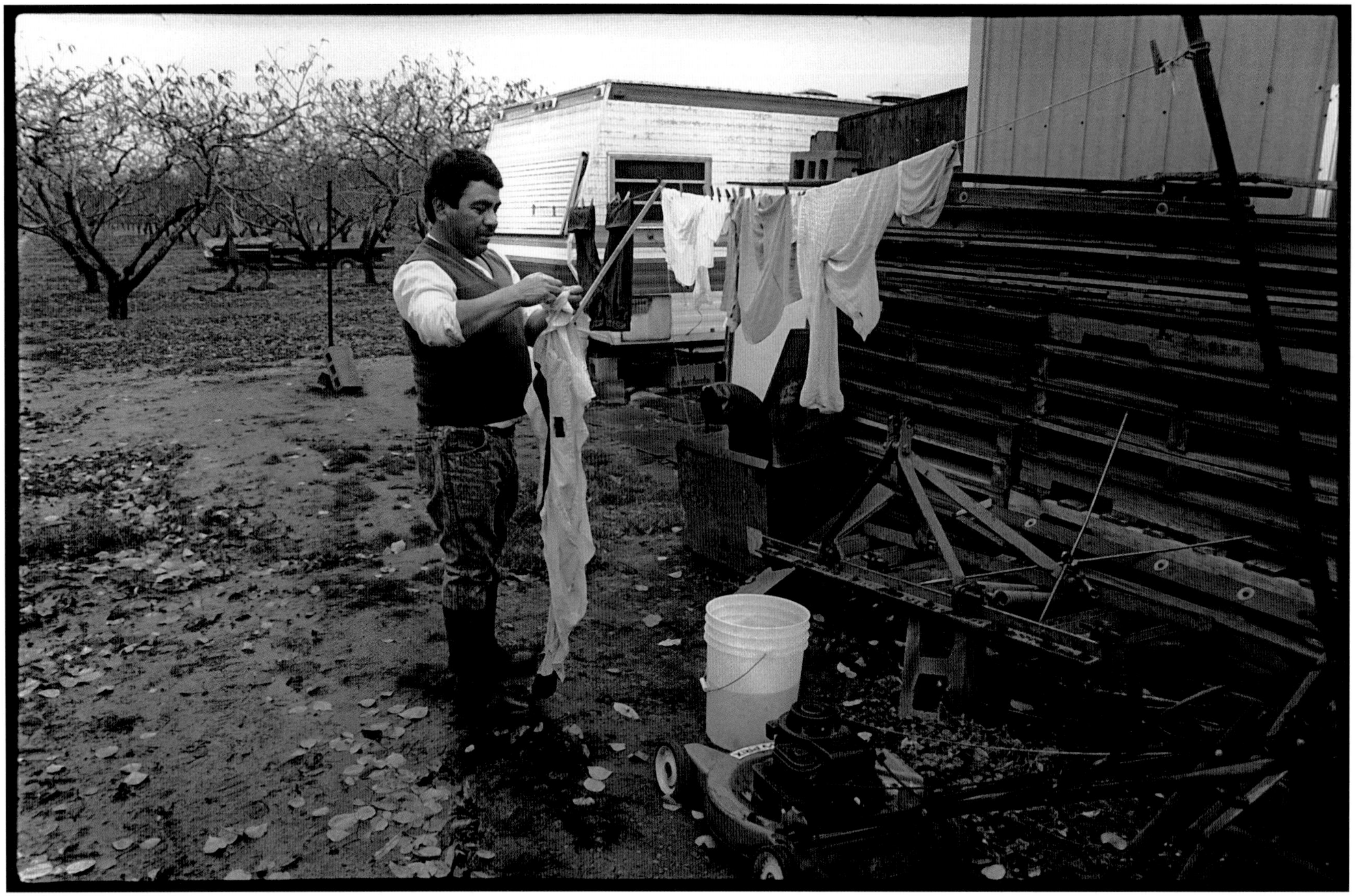

A man with no money – what can he hope to get with love if he doesn't have enough money to live on? Instead, a man who has both love and money – can you imagine? – one could live well.... Love isn't everything in life. Money is important, too, especially here in Mexico, where even when you're trying hard to get ahead, the work is badly paid.

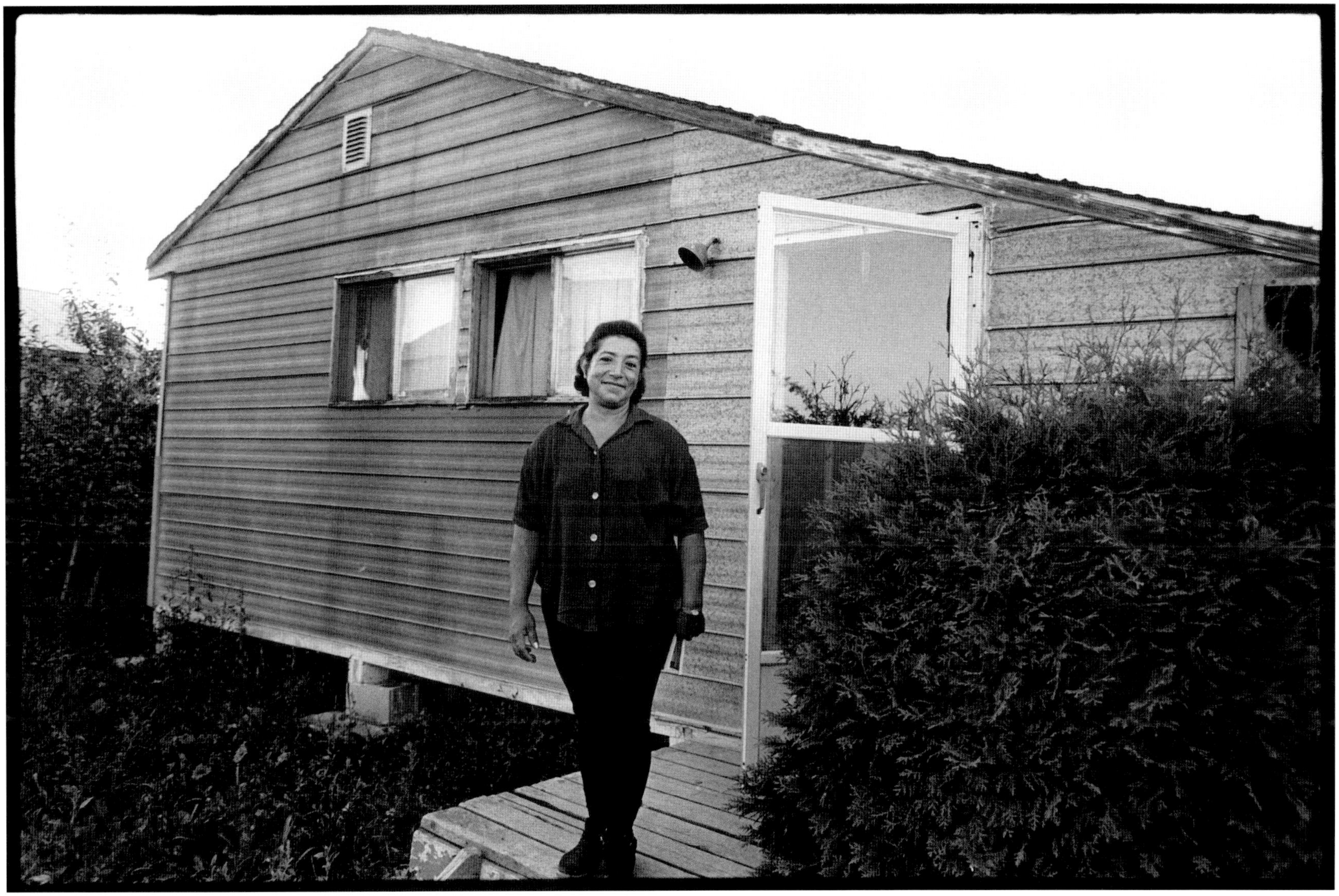

For me, my family is very important. Yes, you are full of sadness when you leave, but full of joy when you return.

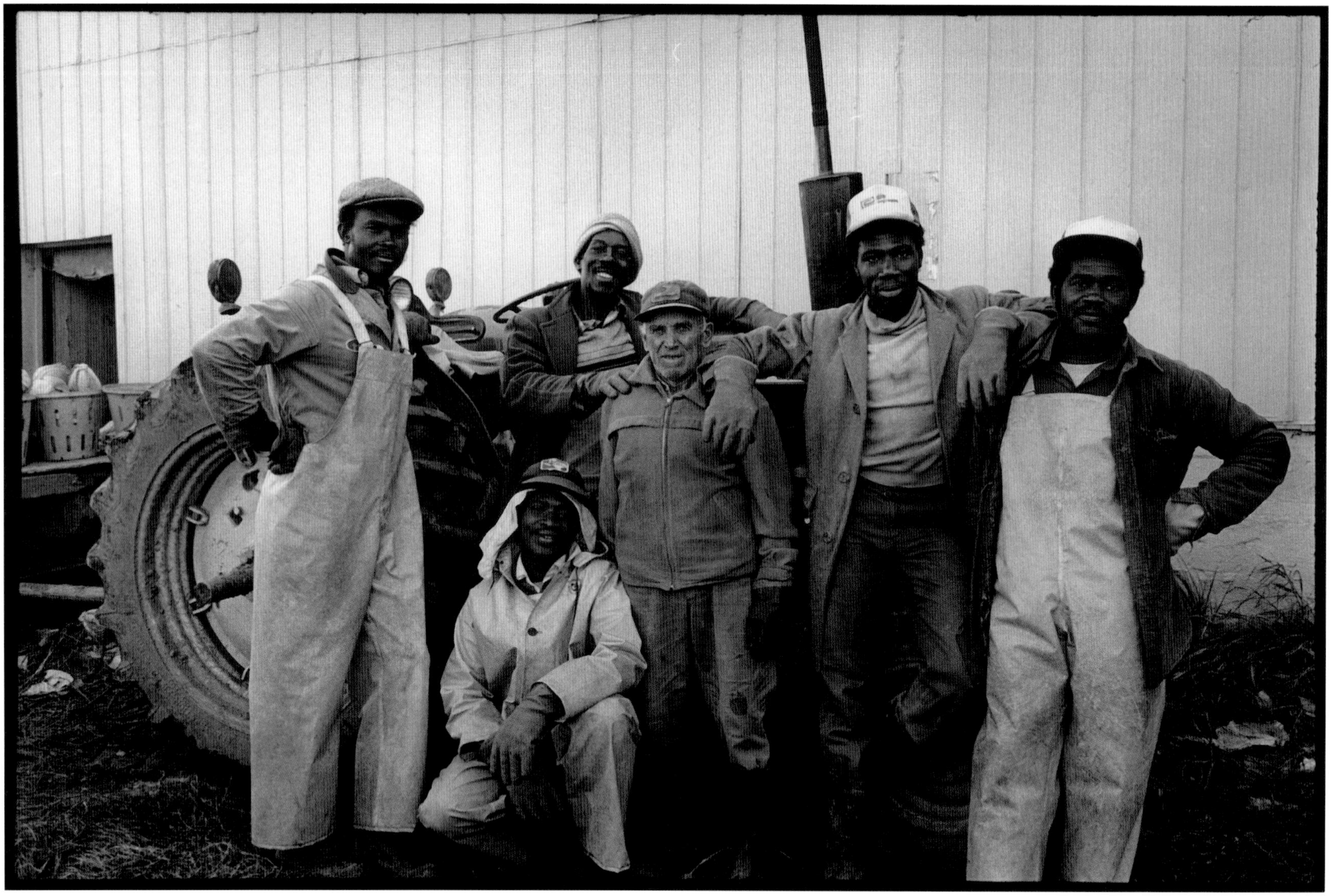

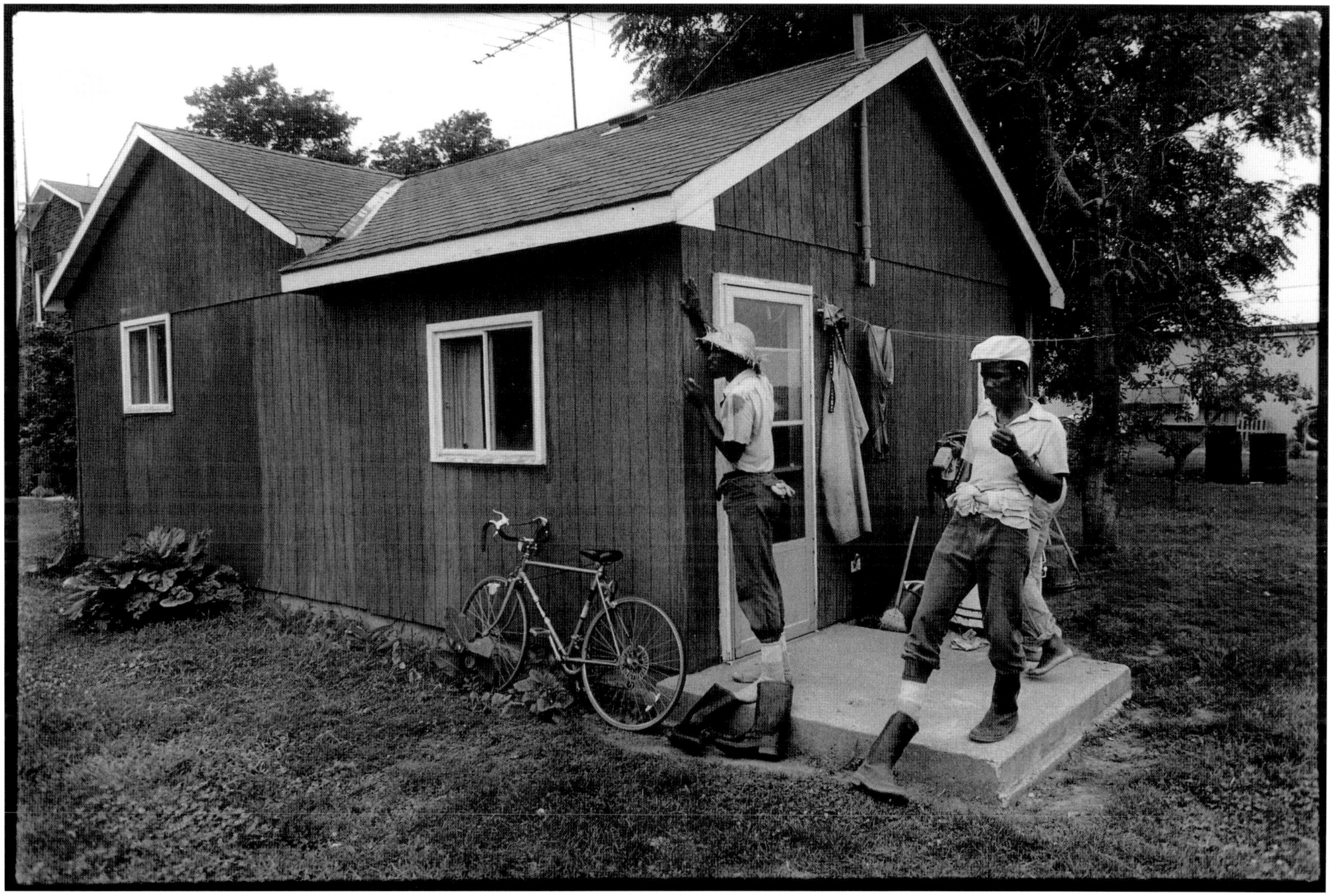

Most of the time, why we come is because you are in season here [on the farm], and we are not in season. We come up for your harvest, and when we go back home [St. Vincent] our harvest is just progressing [getting underway] … It's a help, you know – it's a help, really, coming here, because a lot of things, clothing and shoes, the most important things for your children, are a lot cheaper than back home. We save a lot of money that way. We spend at least 60 per cent of our money here [in 1984]. The majority of what we make … well, all the work up here is hard, it is not easy. I really come out to work. But sometime you need a better boss. That fellow, George, he's the best boss I have ever had. I've been through a few of them. Everybody's not the same.

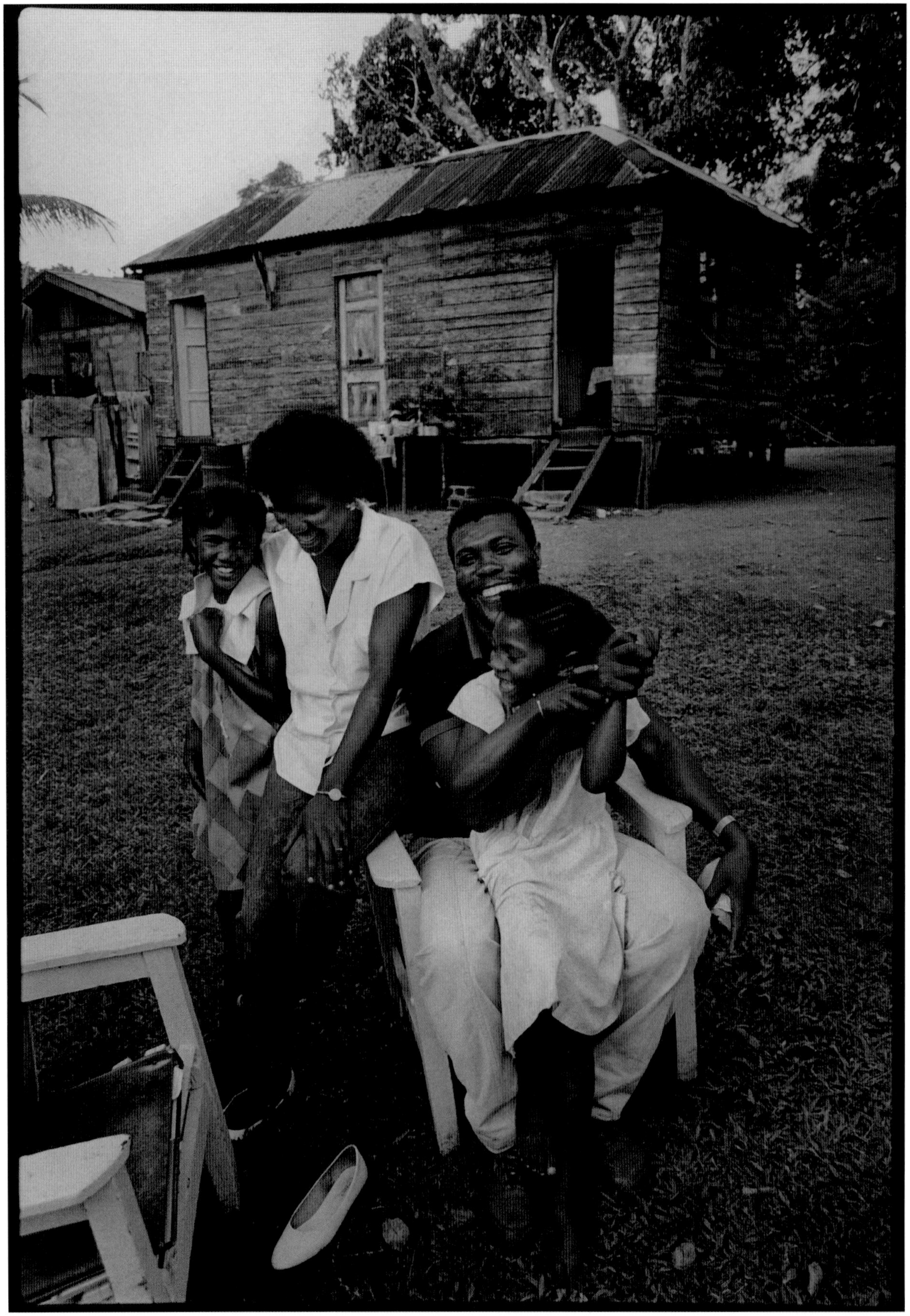

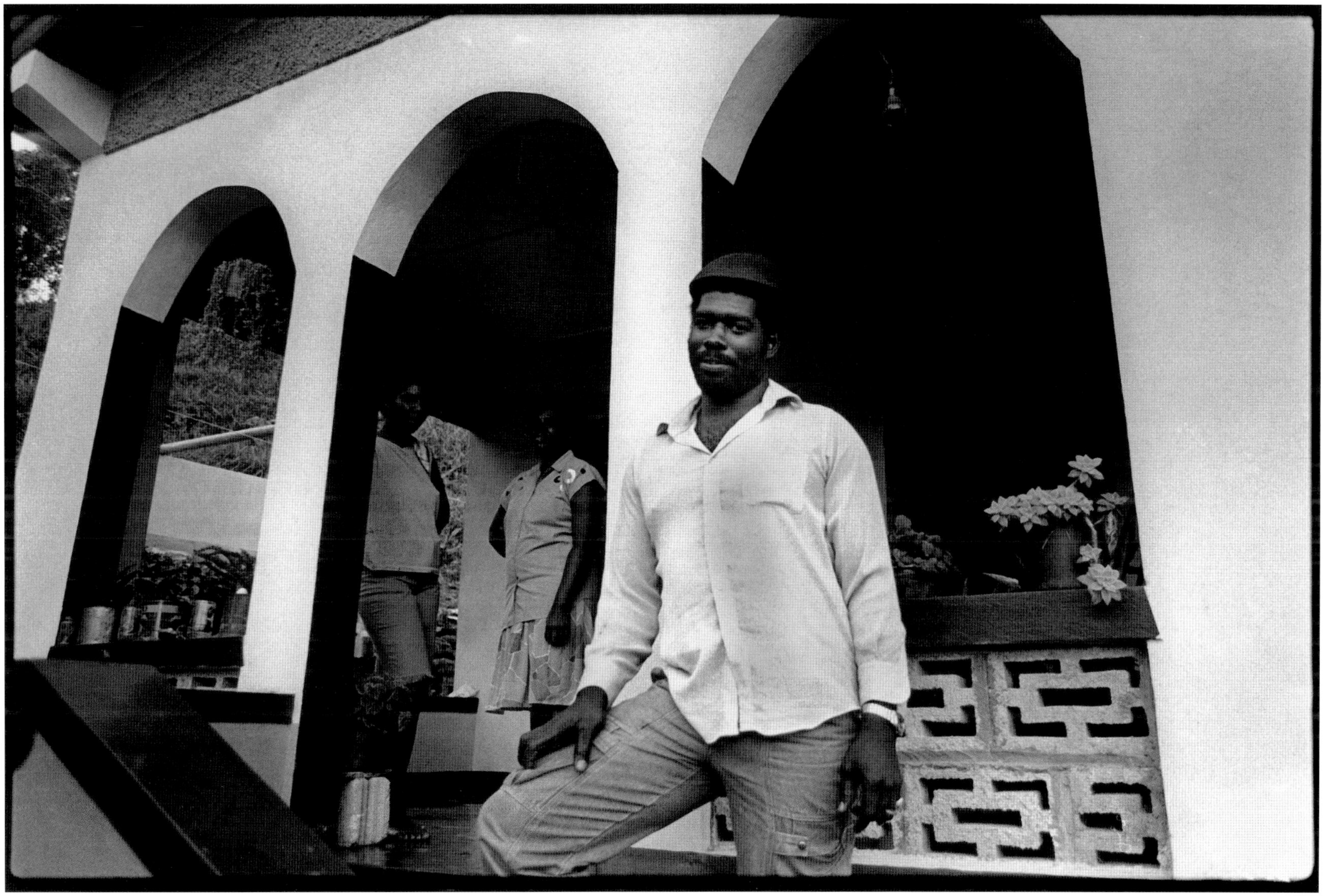

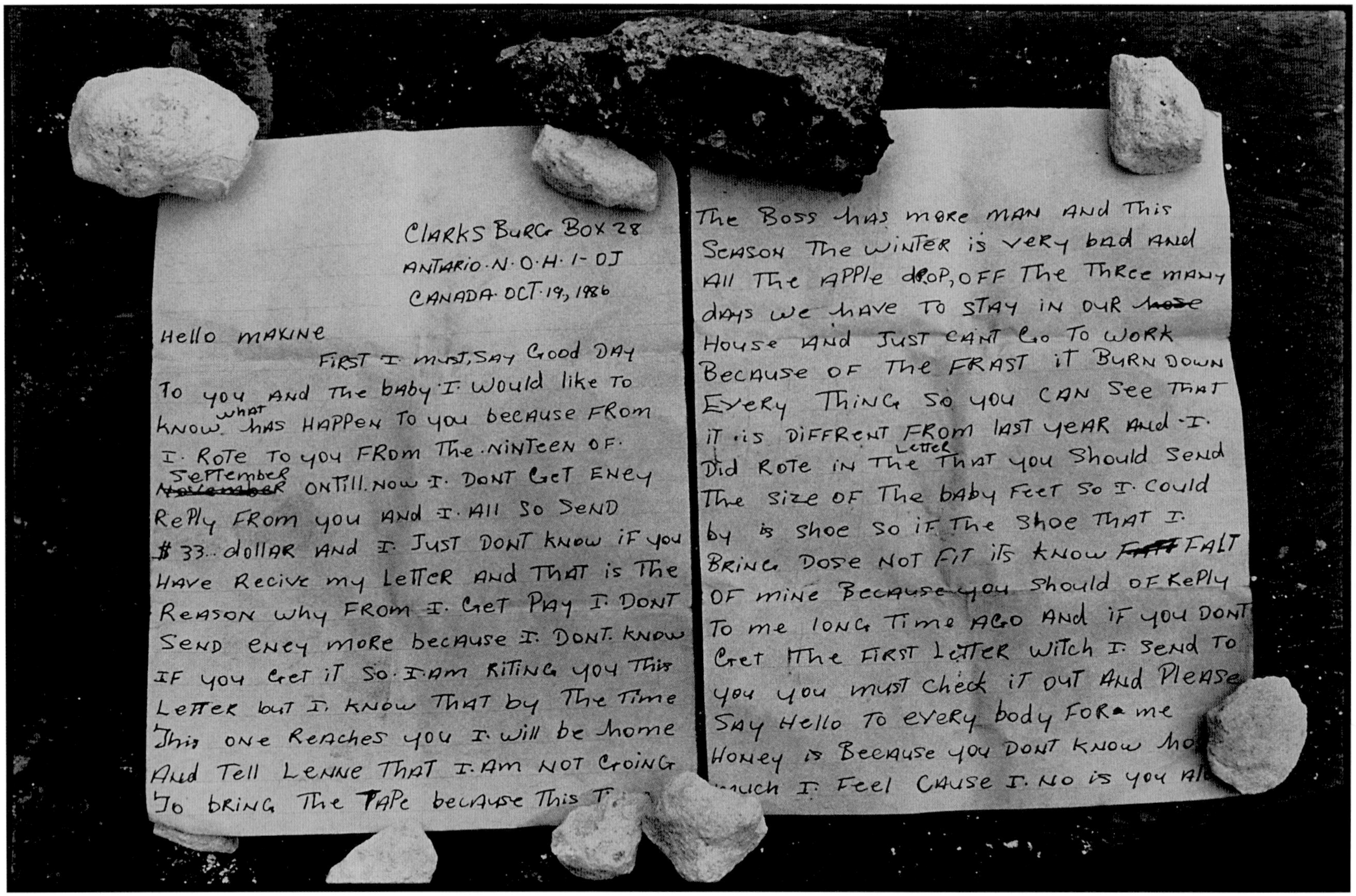

CLARKS BURG BOX 28
ANTARIO. N.O.H. 1-OJ
CANADA. OCT. 19, 1986

Hello MAXINE
FIRST I. MUST, SAY Good DAY
To you AND The baby I. would like To
know what has HAPPEN To you because FROM
I. ROTE To you FROM The NINTEEN OF
~~November~~ September ONTill. now I. DONT GET ENEY
REPLY FROM you AND I. All So SEND
$33.. dollAR AND I. JUST DONT know if you
Have Recive my LETTER AND THAT is The
REASON why FROM I. GET PAY I. DONT
SEND eney more because I. DONT. know
IF you GET iT So. I. AM RITING you This
LETTER but I. KNOW THAT by The Time
This one Reaches you I. will be home
And Tell LENNE THAT I. AM NOT GOING
To BRING The TAPE because This T…

The Boss has more MAN AND This
SEASON The WINTER is very bad AND
All The APPLE dROP, OFF The Three many
days we have To STAY IN OUR ~~hose~~
House AND JUST CANT GO To WORK
Because OF The FRAST iT BURN DOWN
EVERY THING So you CAN See THAT
iT is DIFFRENT FROM last year And I.
Did ROTE iN The Letter THAT you Should Send
The size OF The baby FEET So I. Could
by is shoe So iF The Shoe THAT I.
BRING DOSE NOT FIT its KNOW ~~FAFF~~ FALT
OF mine Because you should OF REPLY
To me LONG Time AGO And iF you DONT
GET The FIRST LETTER witch I. SEND To
you you must Check iT OUT And Please
SAY Hello To EVERY body FOR me
Honey is Because you DONT KNOW ho…
…uch I. Feel CAUSE I. No is you Al…

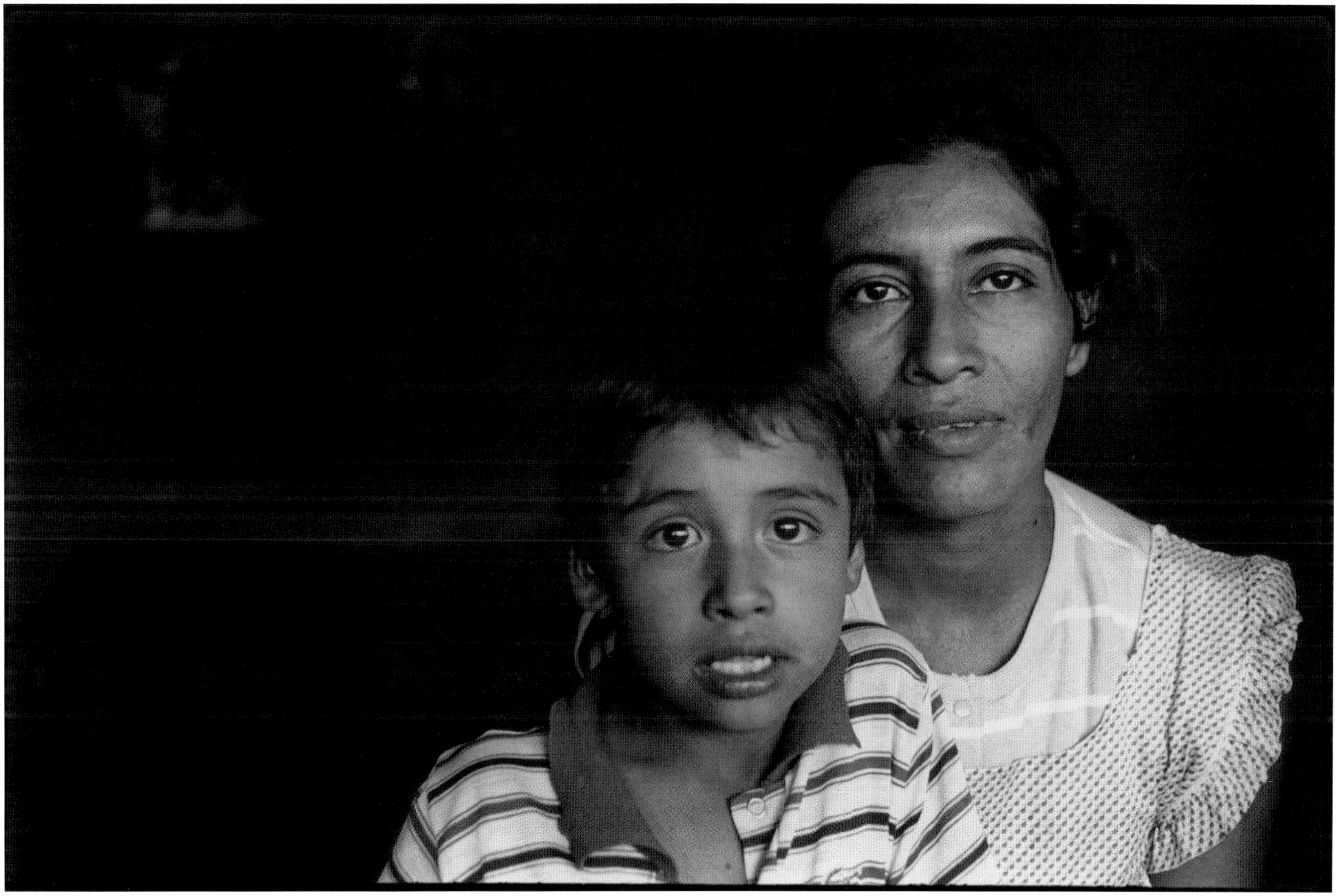

Some of the men return back home, and they're different ... they're more responsible family men. Maybe it's because they also suffer up there. Just like my brother, before going up to Canada, he didn't really like to work, he didn't care so much about providing food for the family, or anything like that. Before, he used to go out with his friends all the time. He almost didn't care about his children. He used to just hang around and drink a lot. And afterwards he'd cry and cry and carry on about it all the time. Not anymore. Since going to Canada, my brother is a different guy, has even stopped crying about things.

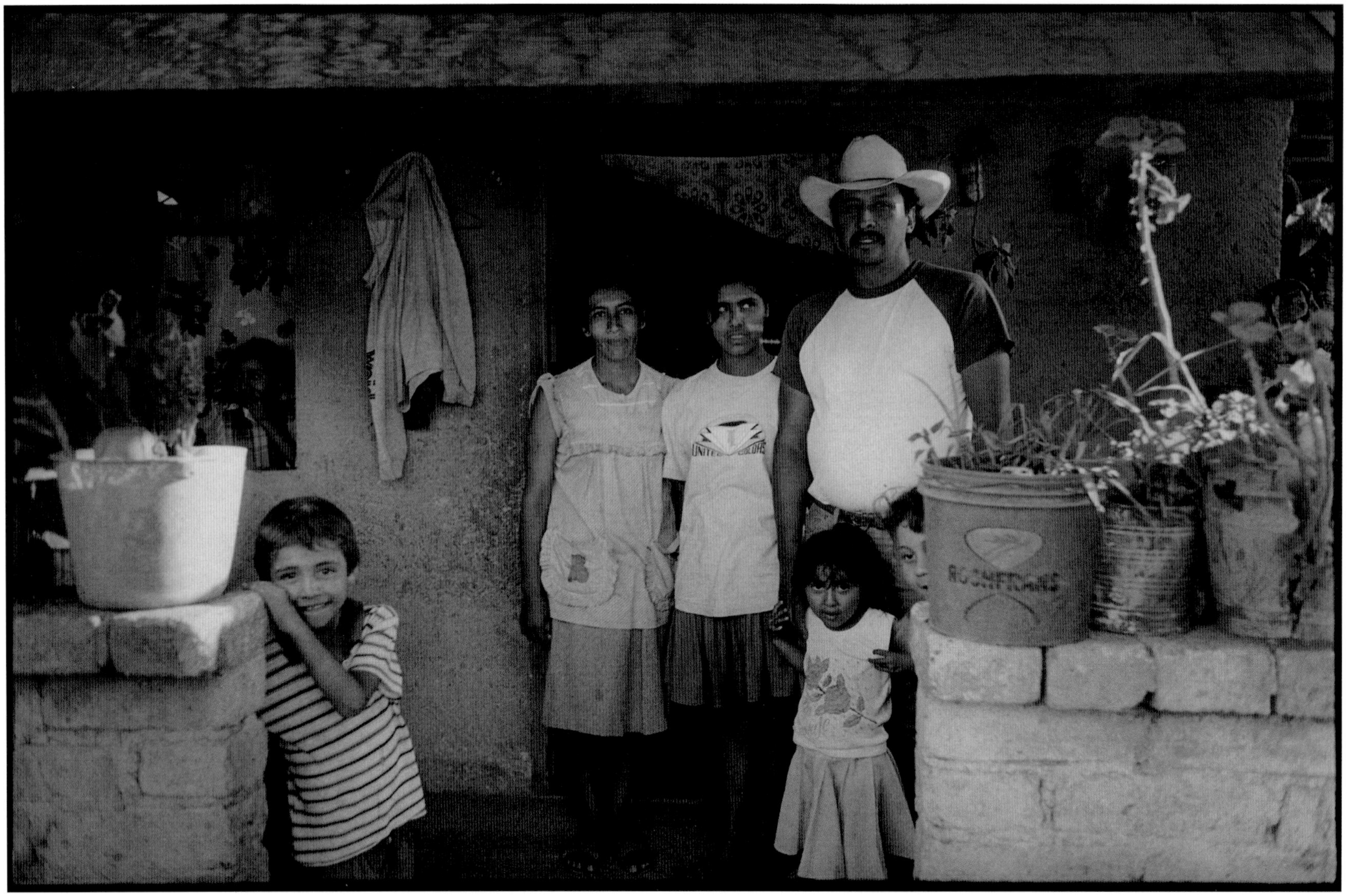

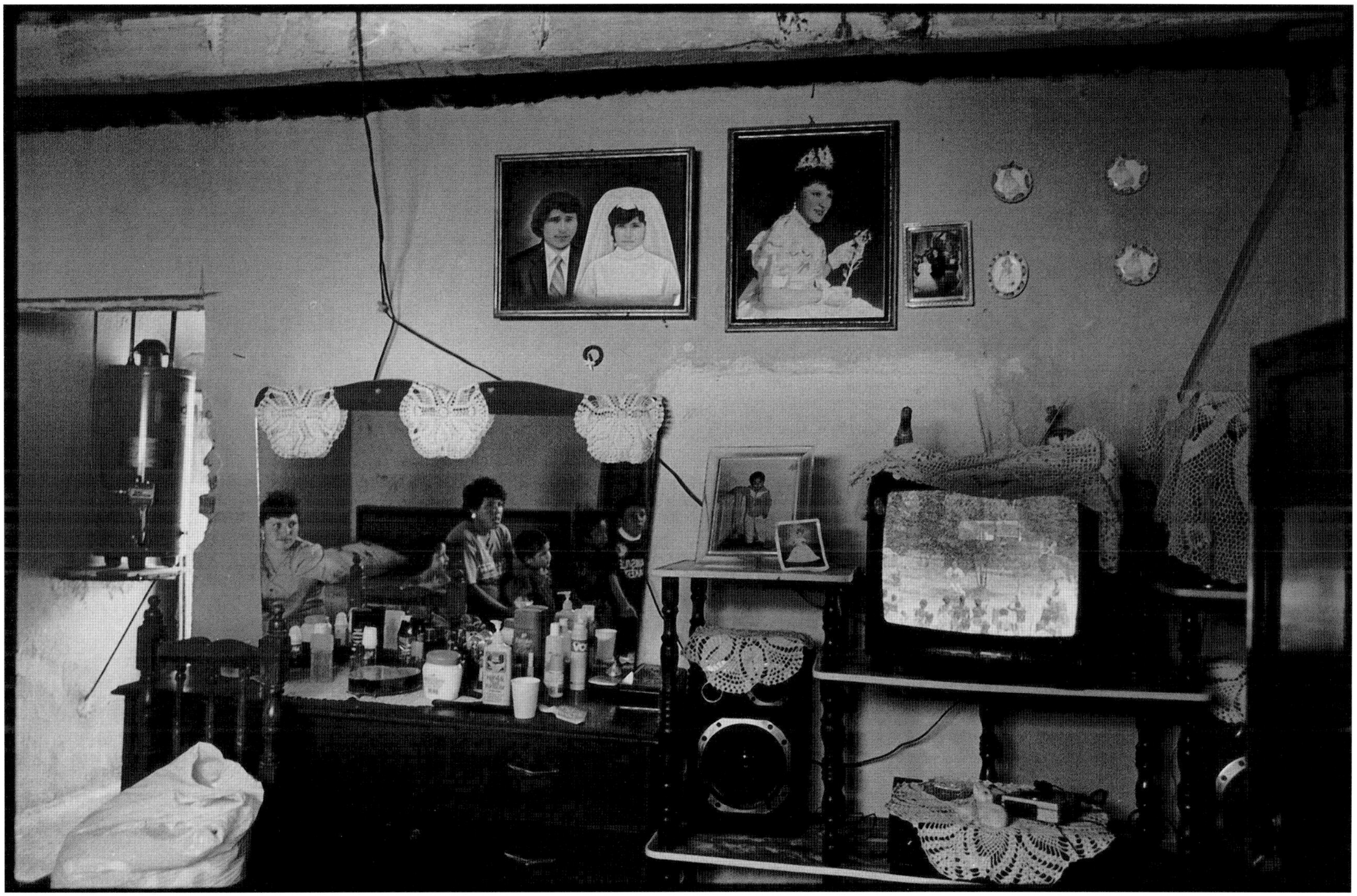

This house that you see is the result of my work in Canada, for which I am grateful to the Mexican and Canadian governments. As you can see, my house is not finished, but one day I will finish it, that is my dream. After twelve years [of going to Canada] there has never been a complaint against me, and most years I worked eight full months. As you can see, I spend more time living in Canada than in Mexico.

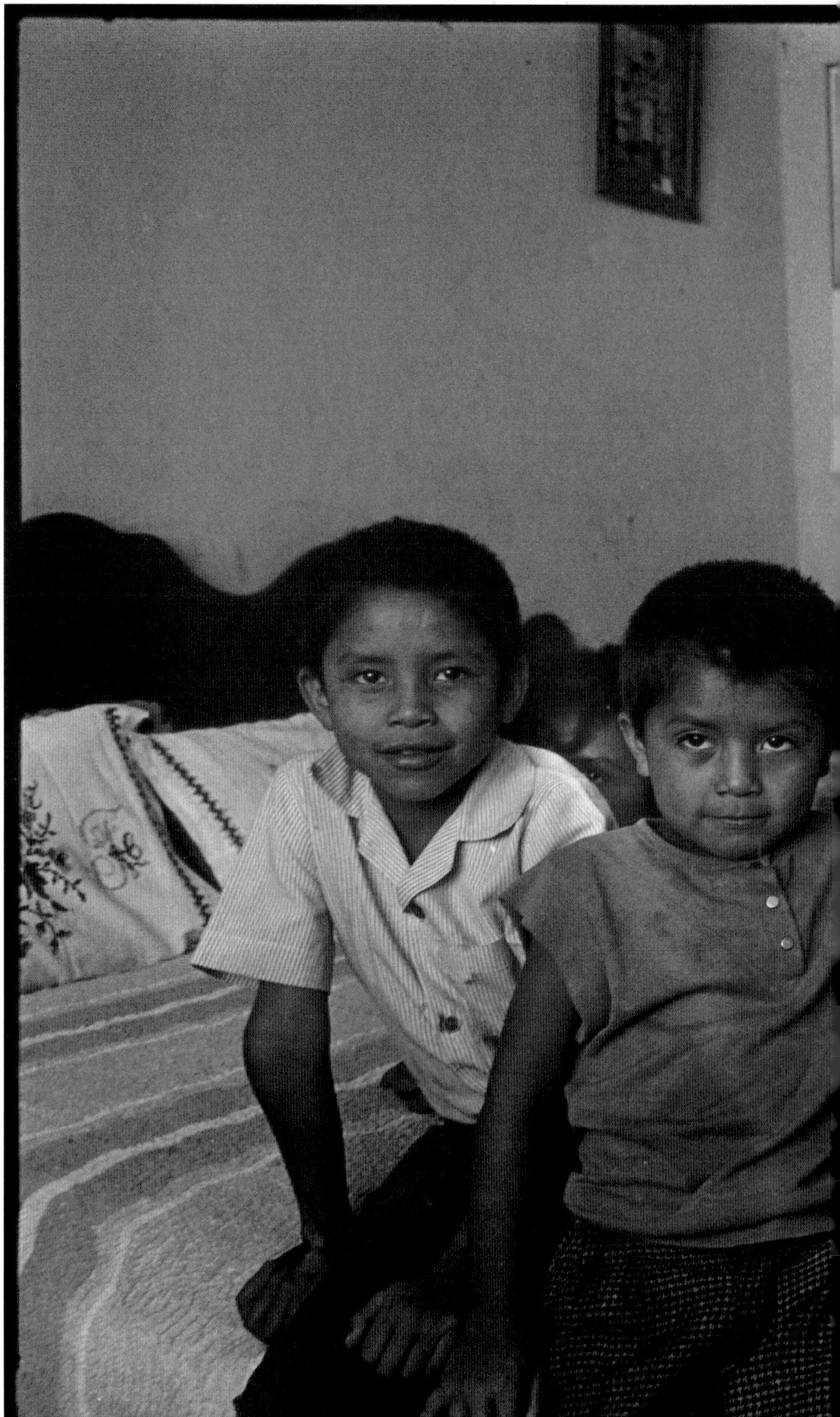

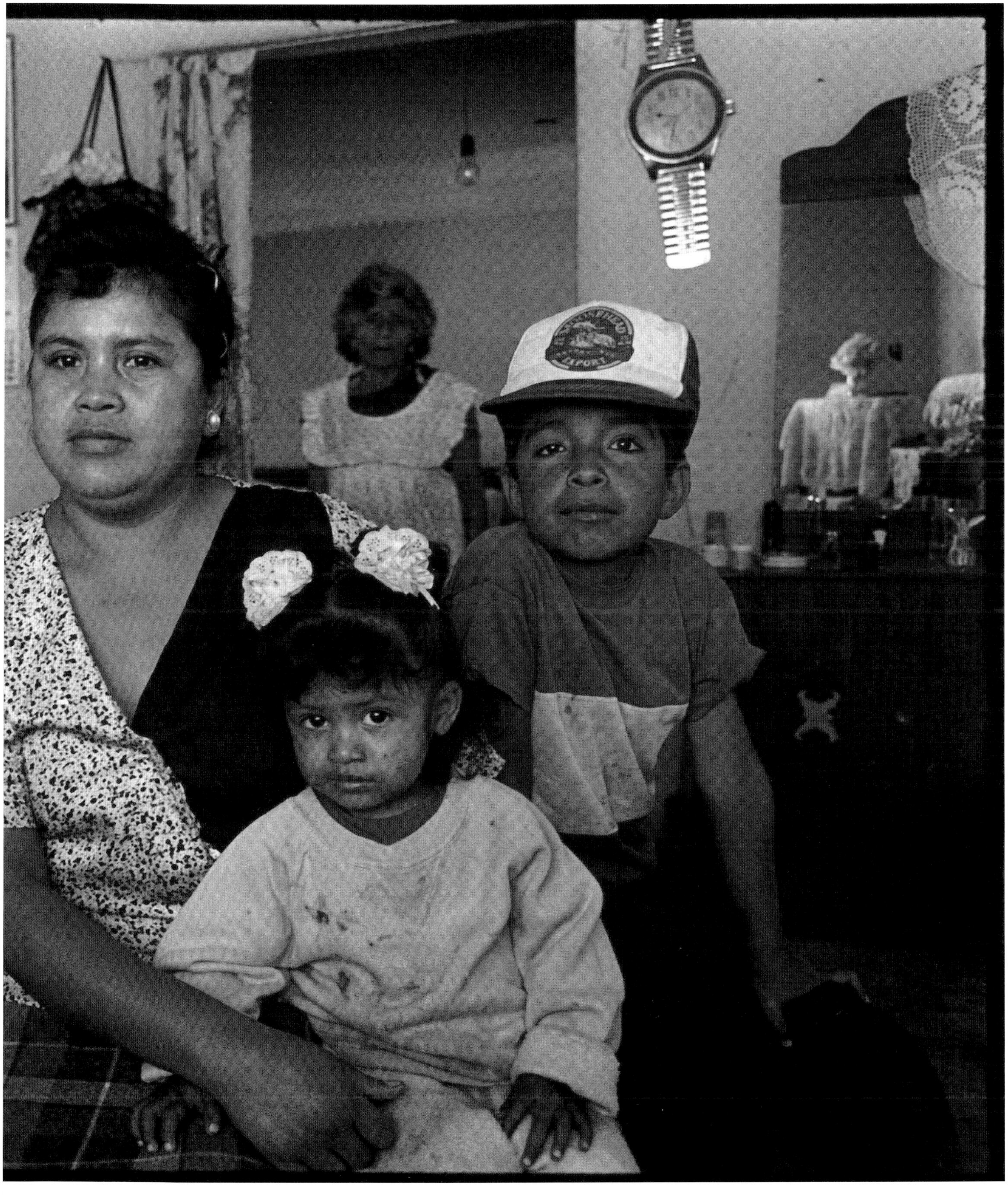

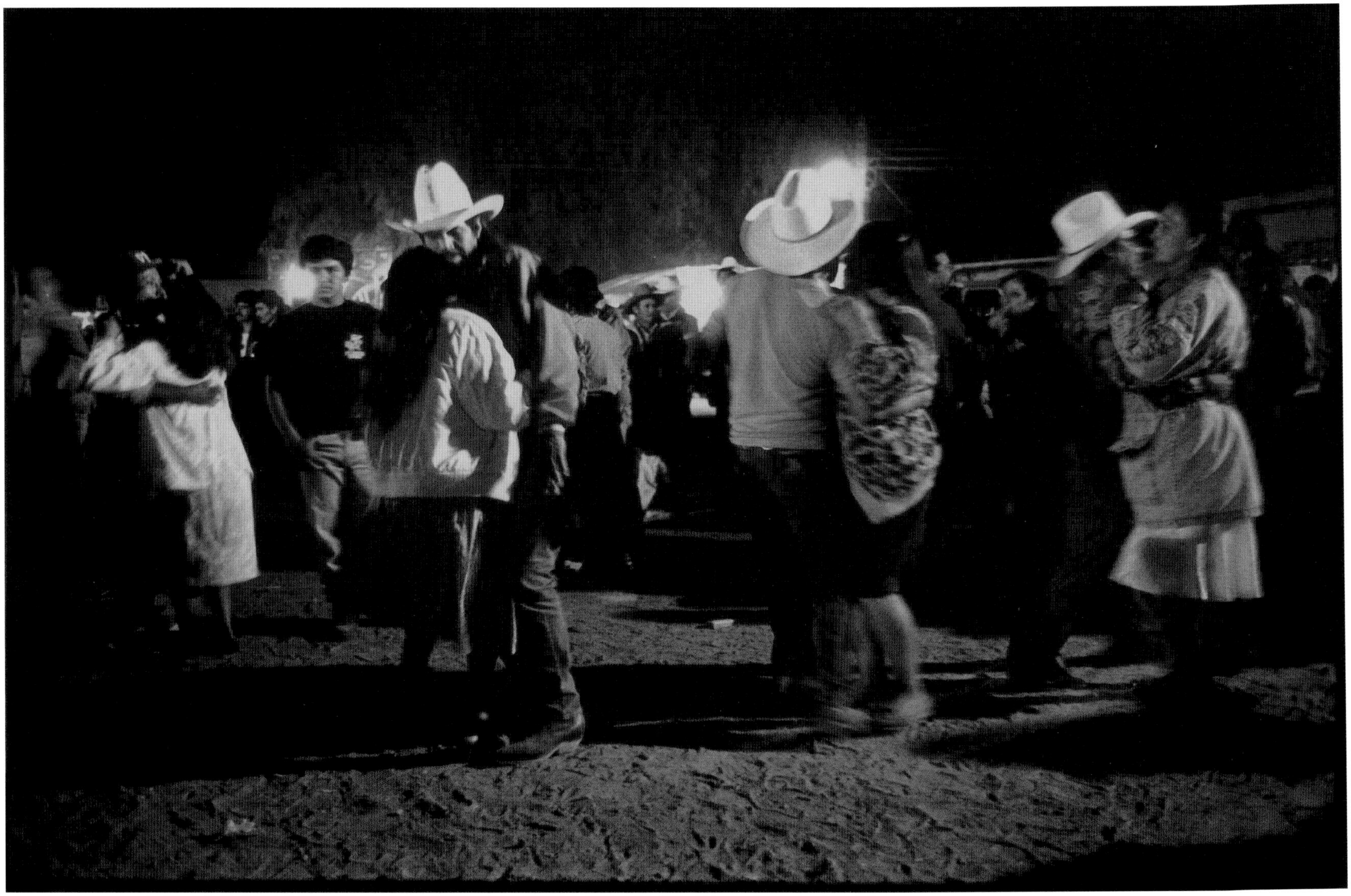

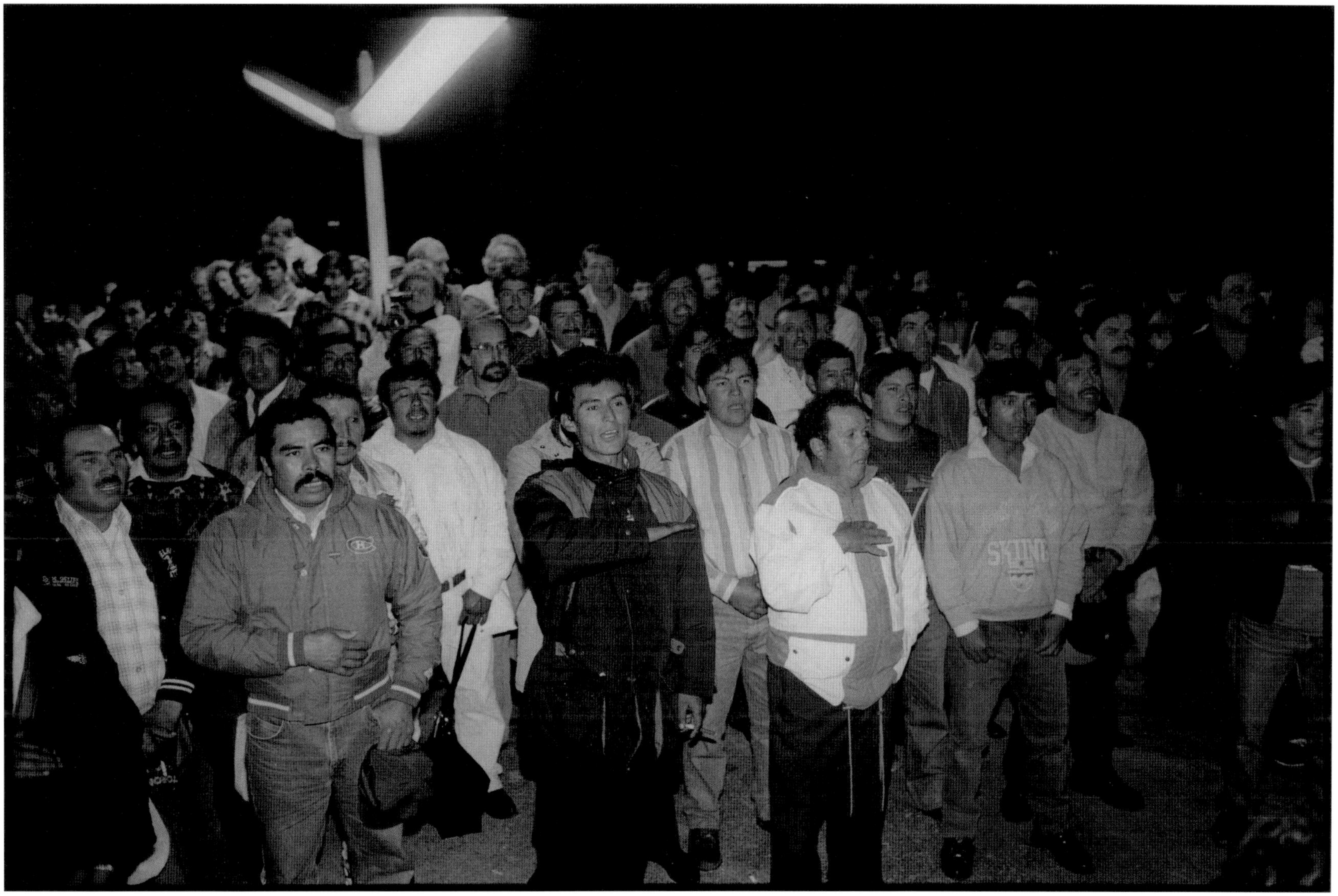

Yes, of course, when you go to Canada, you know ahead of time for whom and where you'll be working, but when you go to the United States, you don't know. Not who you'll work for, and not where you'll end up. Everything is more certain up there [Canada]. And you're not an illegal worker either. You can go out whenever, and go wherever you want. You don't have to be watching over your back for the *migra* [immigration authorities].

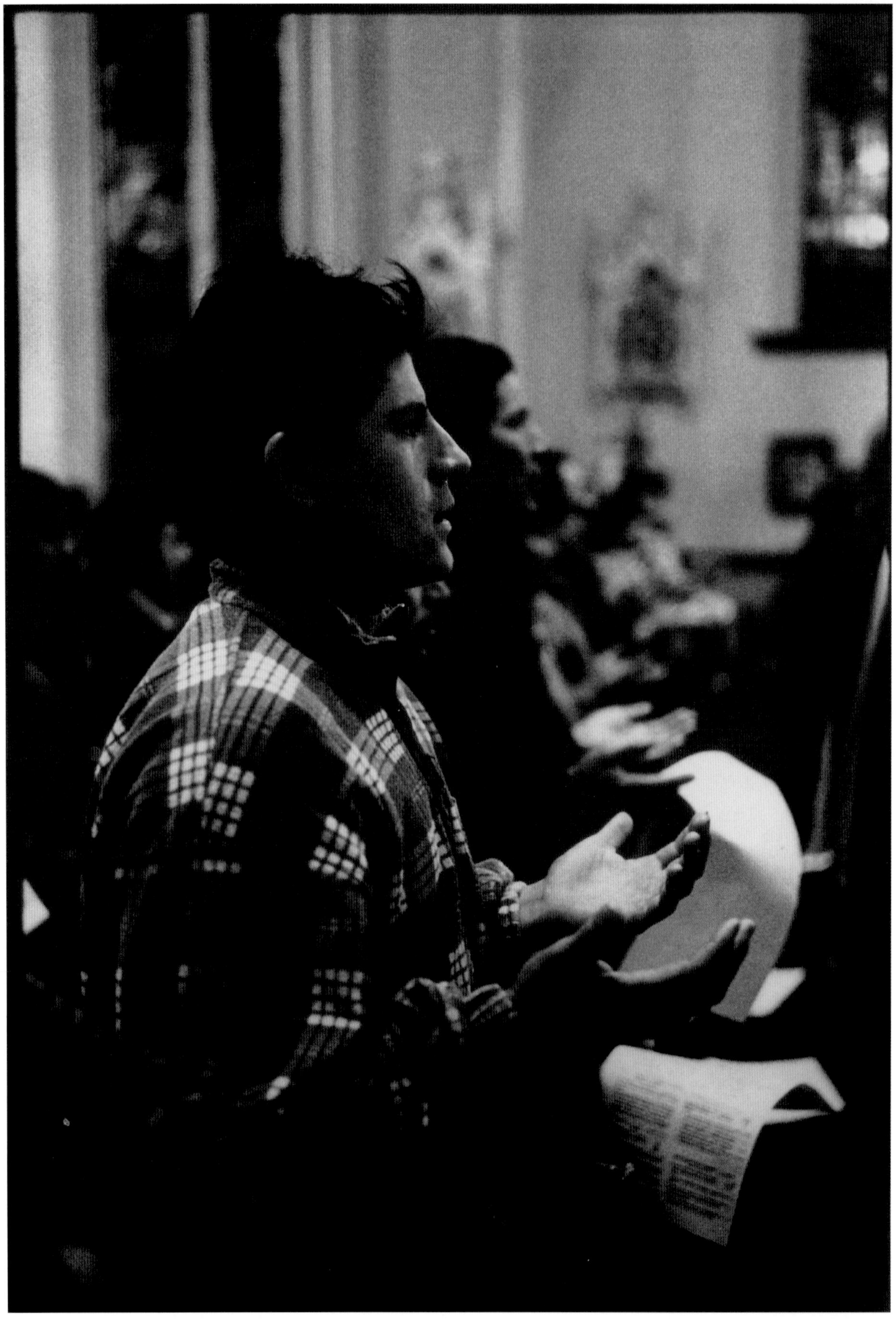

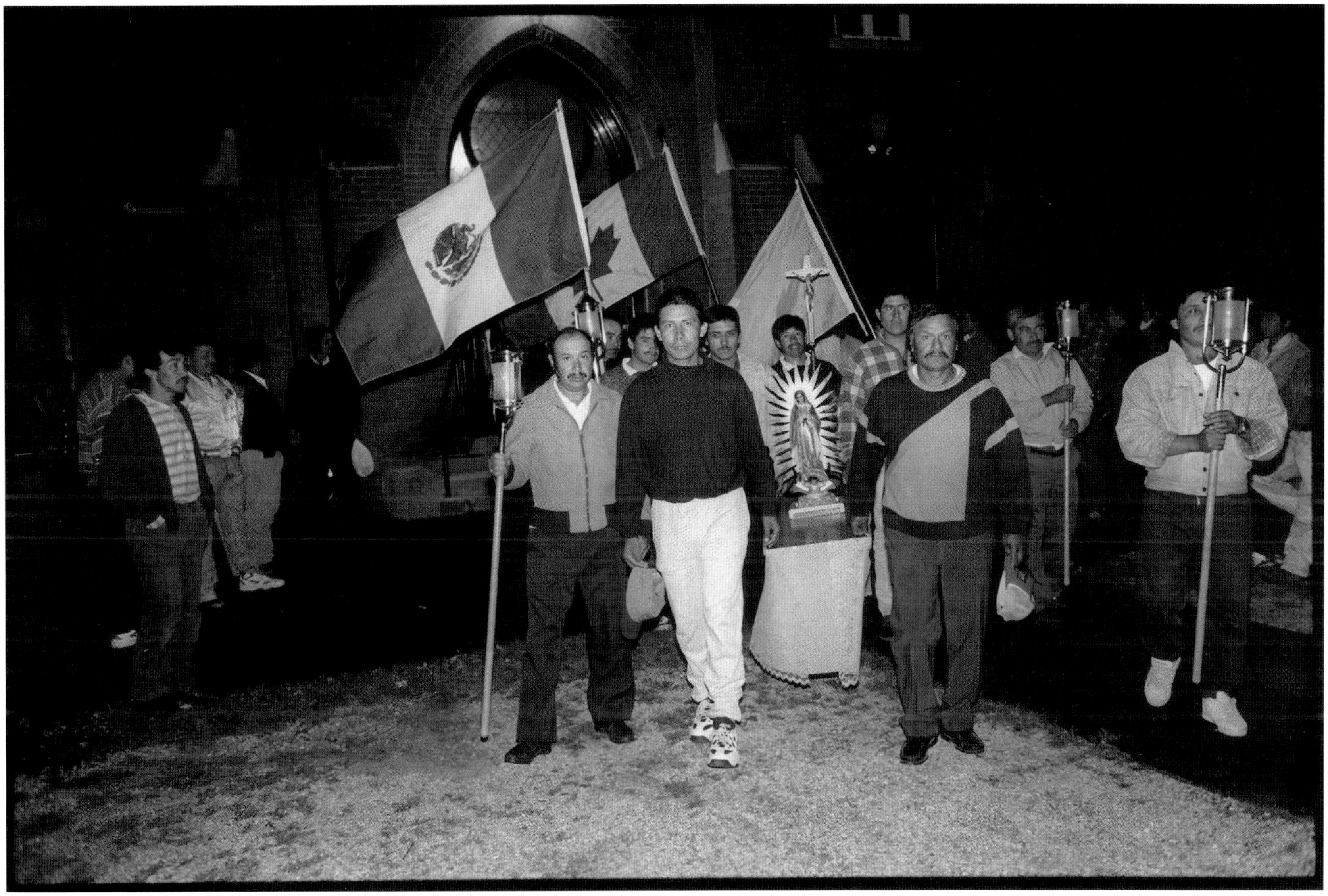

Yes, it's sad and even more sad when you're so poor. I don't know why God created us to be so poor, no matter how hard you try. Why is it that some people cannot even become well-off, and others end up rich very quickly? I have been going [to Canada] for twelve years, and I can barely hold my head above water. I can't understand it. That's why I'm saying that God should have made us all equal ... you understand what I mean? Then we could go to Canada or anyplace in the world, not to work, but for enjoyment. That would be great, wouldn't it?

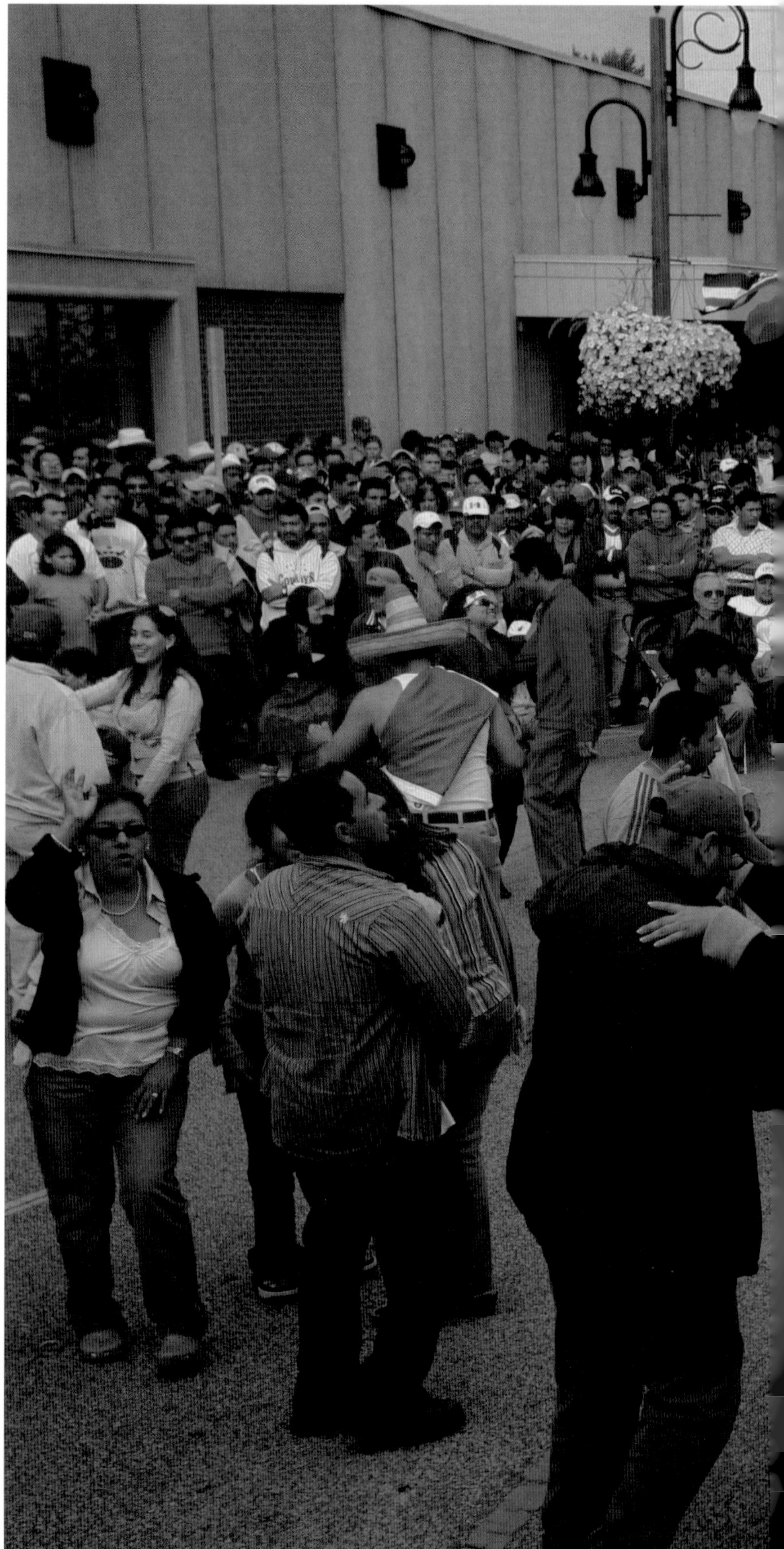

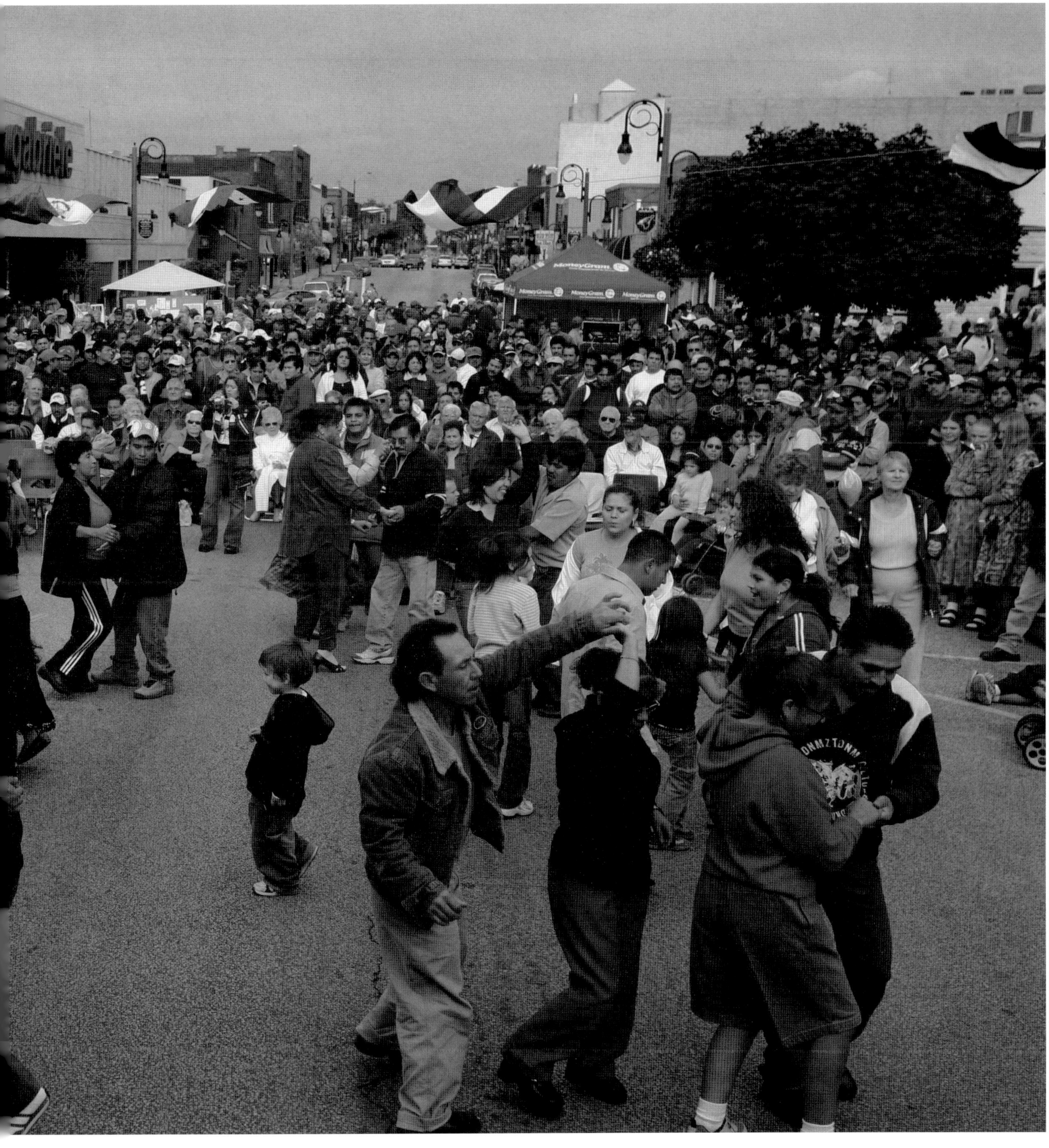
MoneyGram

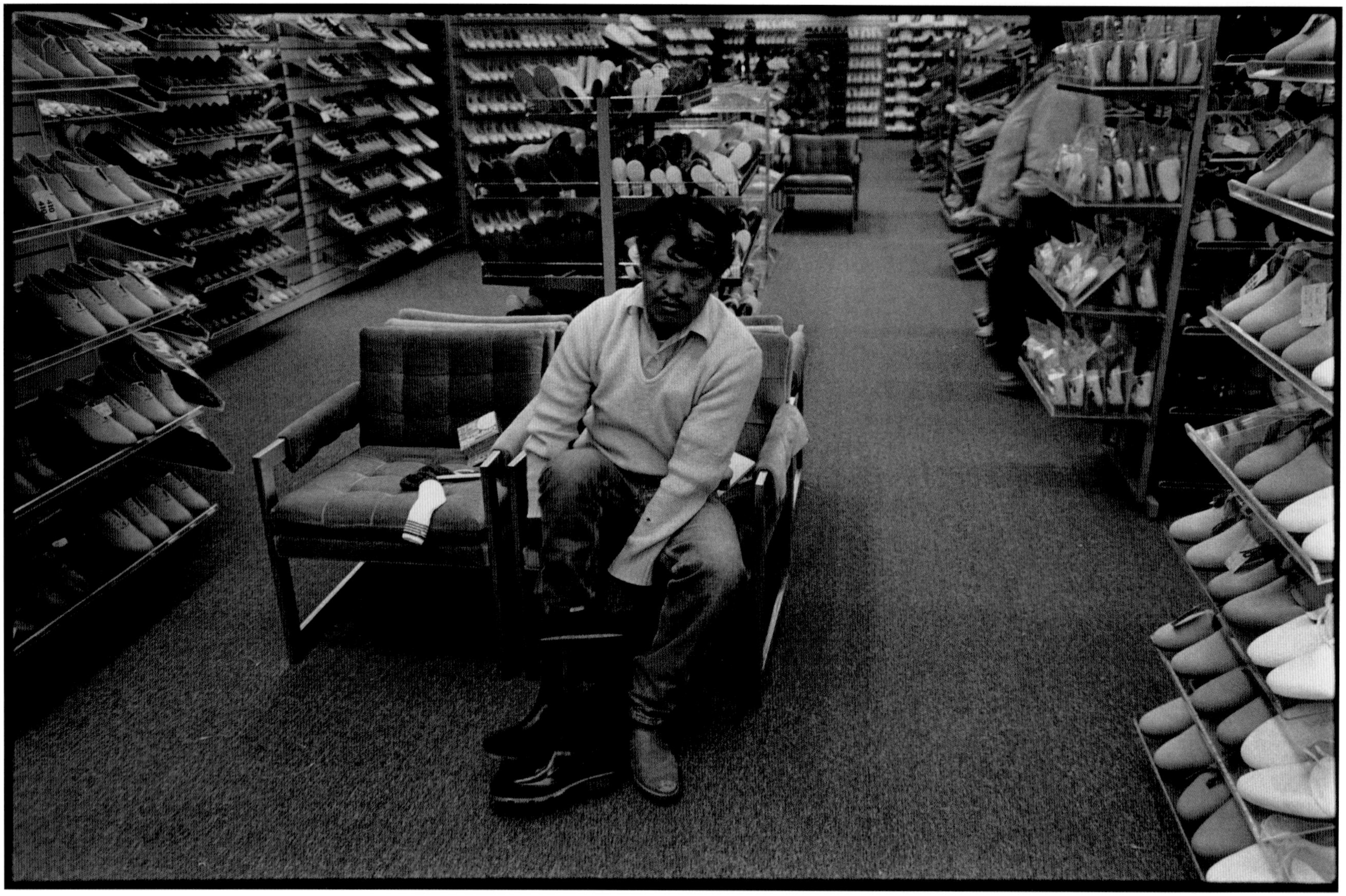

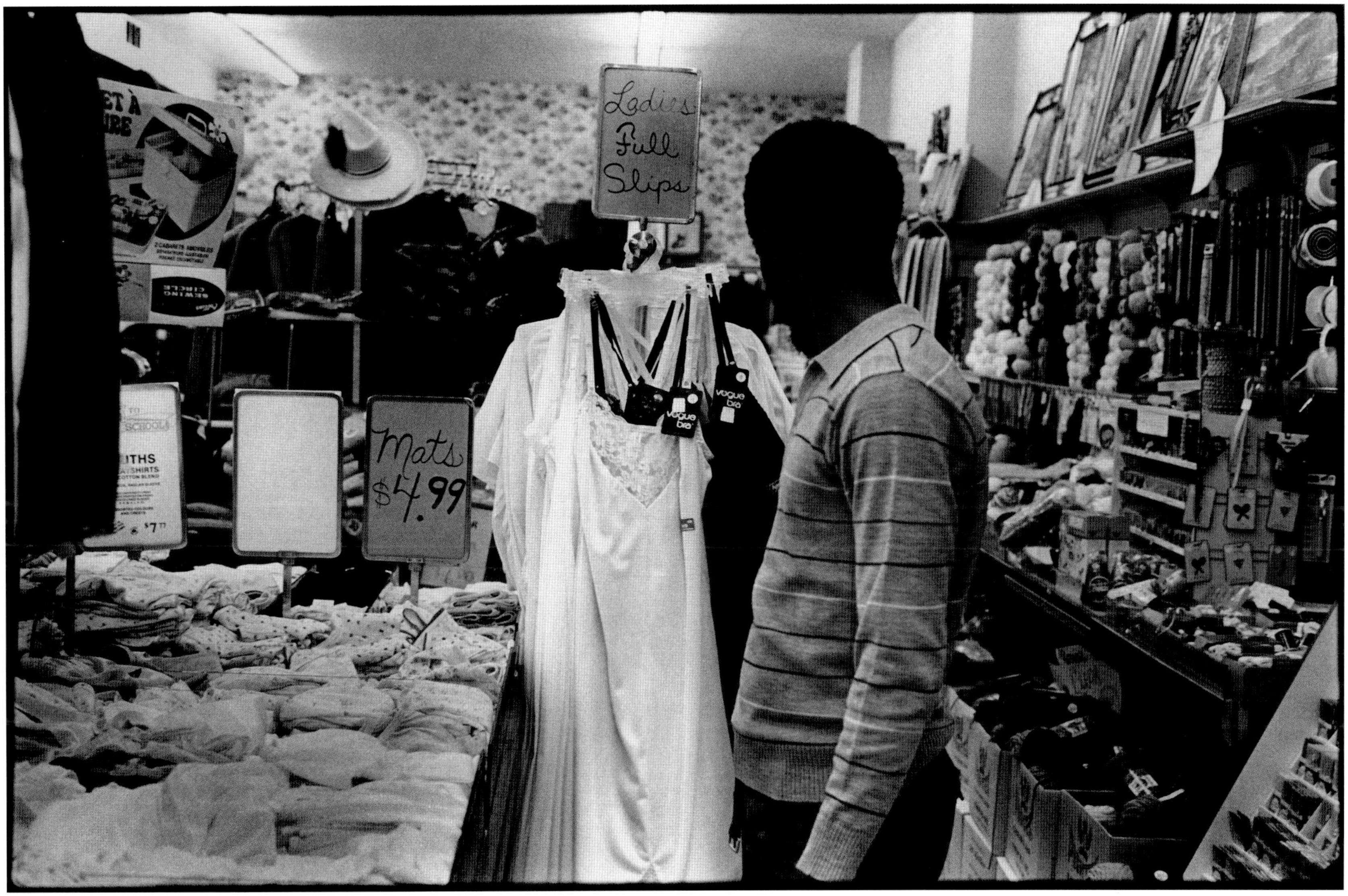

I'd like to stay. You just have to find a woman up here to get married to. Well, I guess there are not very many women. Yeah, but some [men], like where I was working, they got married and stayed. About four of them.

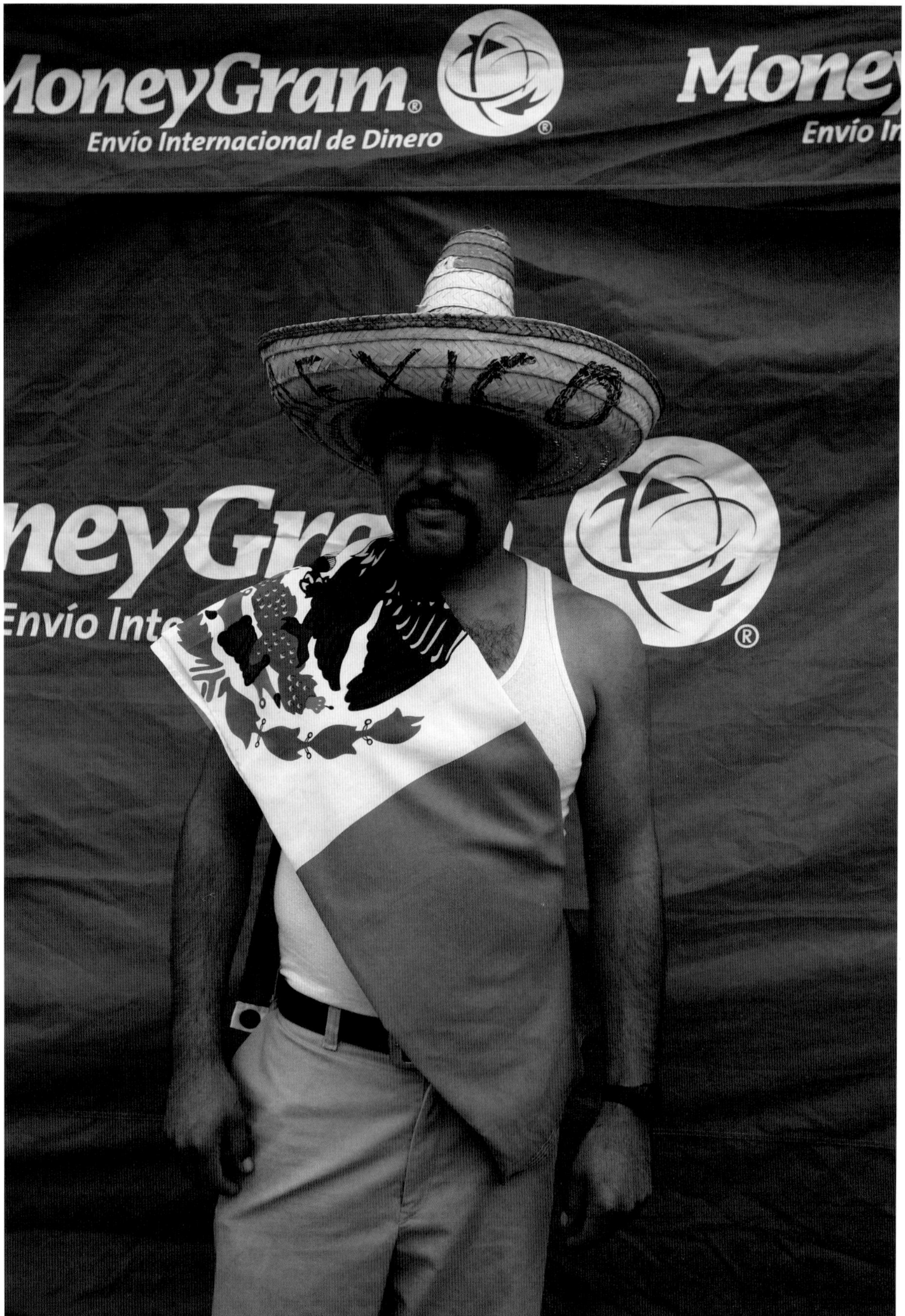
MoneyGram.
Envío Internacional de Dinero
neyGr
Envío Inte

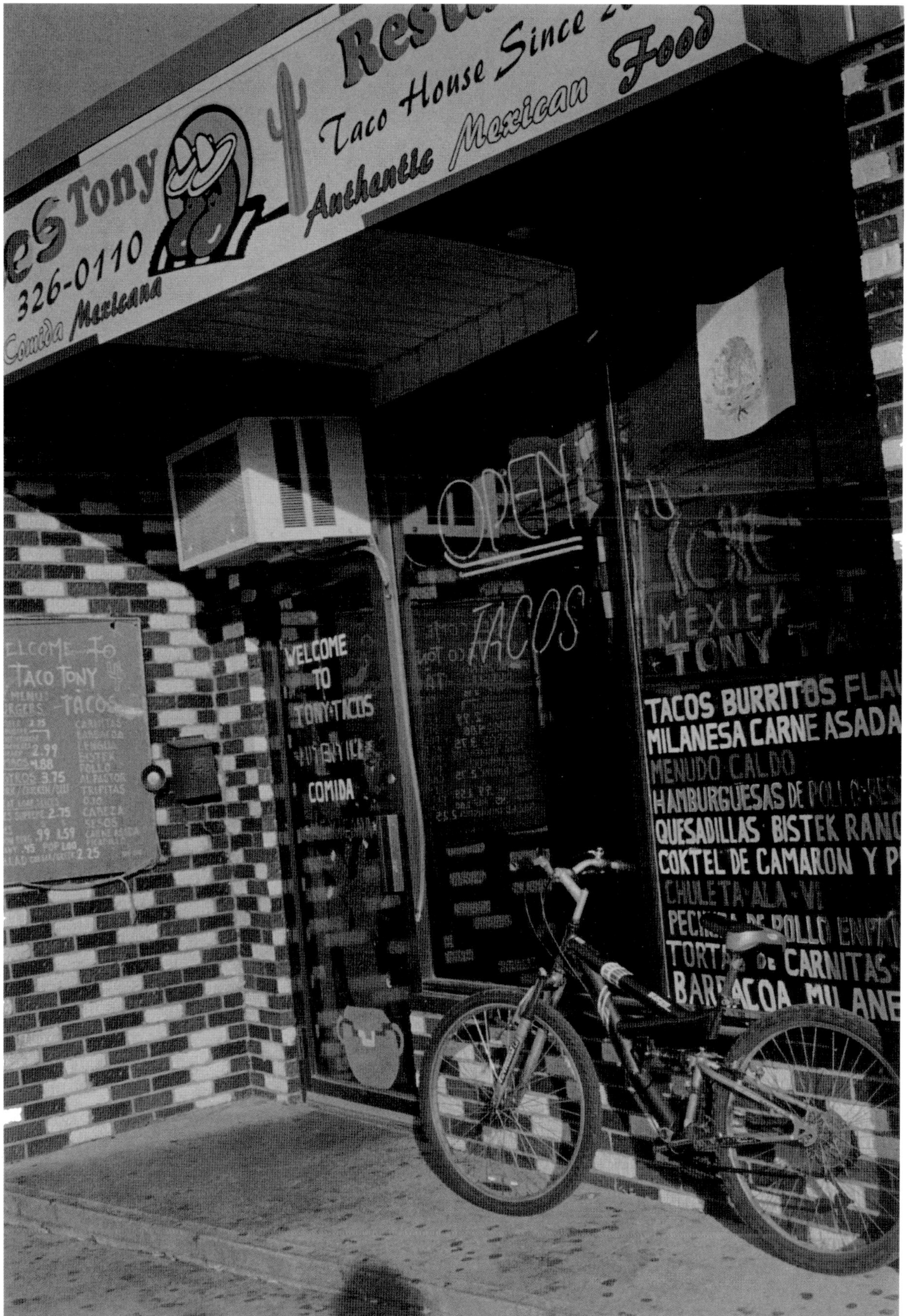
Tony
326-0110
Comida Mexicana
Taco House Since
Authentic Mexican Food
OPEN
TACOS
WELCOME TO TONY TACOS
COMIDA
MEXICA
TONY
TACOS BURRITOS
MILANESA CARNE ASADA
MENUDO CALDO
QUESADILLAS BISTEK
COKTEL DE CAMARON Y
CARNITAS

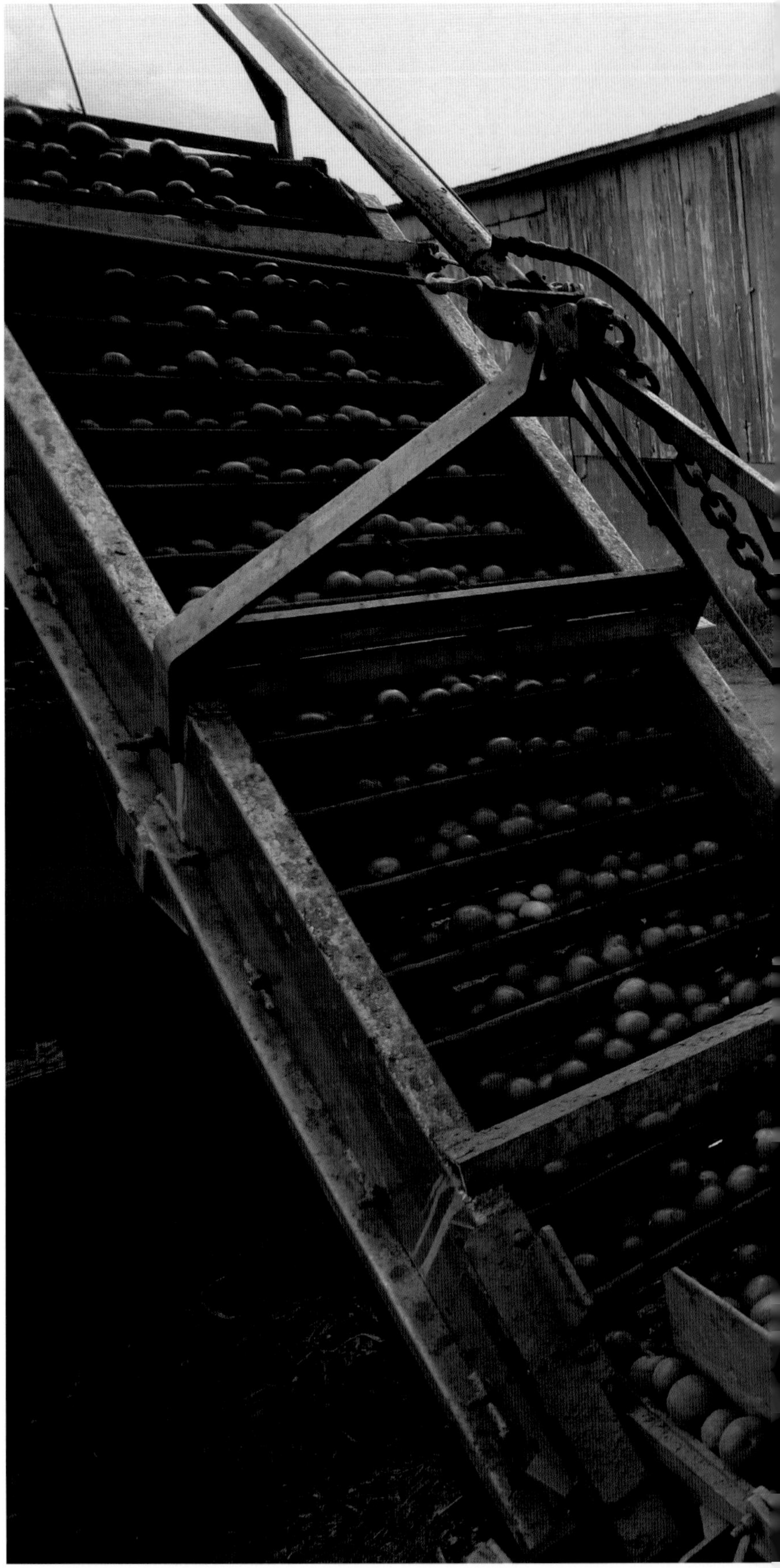

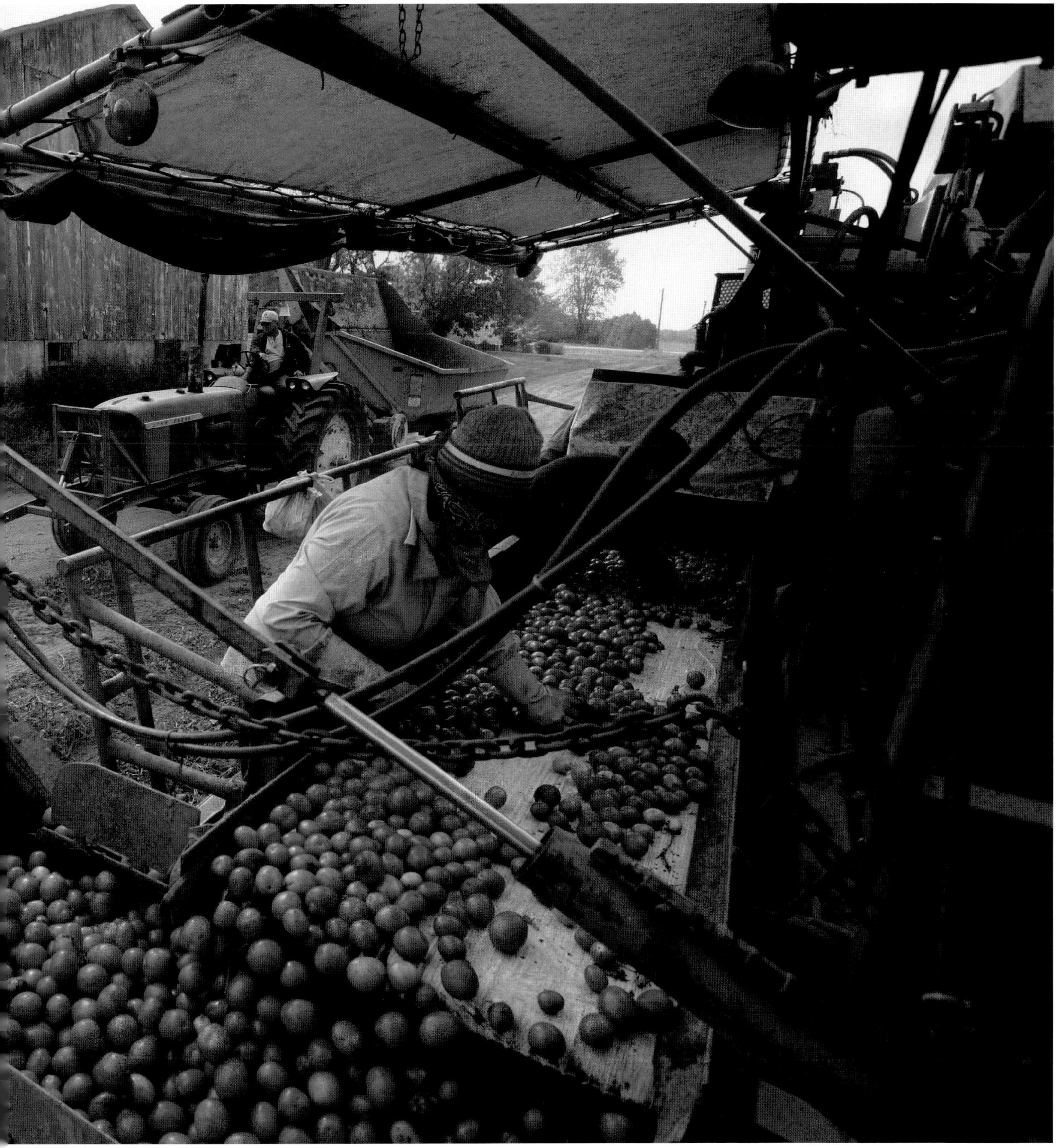

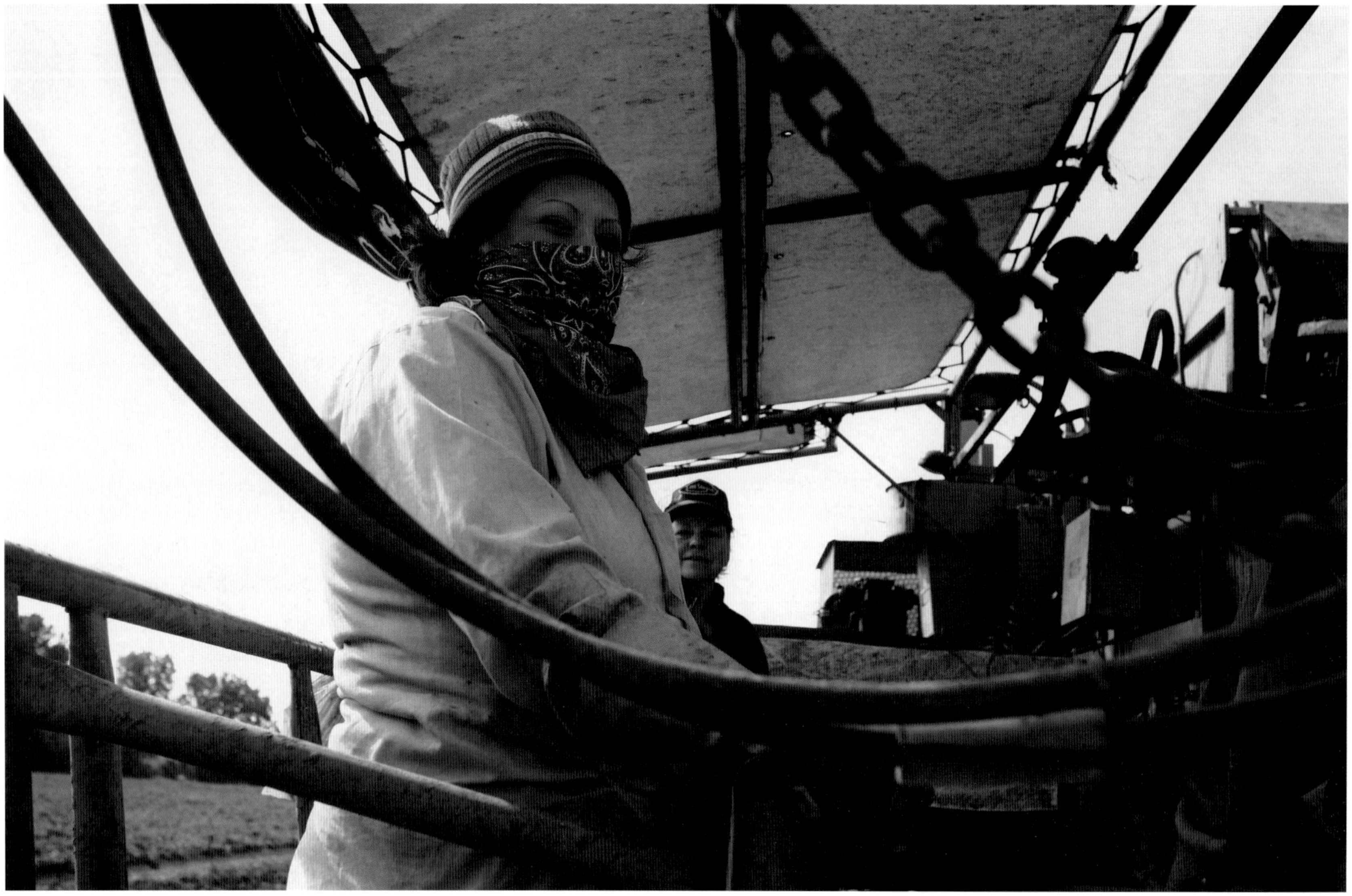

Well, emotionally it affects me a lot, because eight months seem a short time but being far from your family, well, it isn't that short. I'm used to working hard, I'm a hard worker, the only thing that bothers me, frankly, is that I'm separated from my family … yes, the work tires me out, I'm only human, after all. But no matter how tired, it's never enough to make me forget about my family.

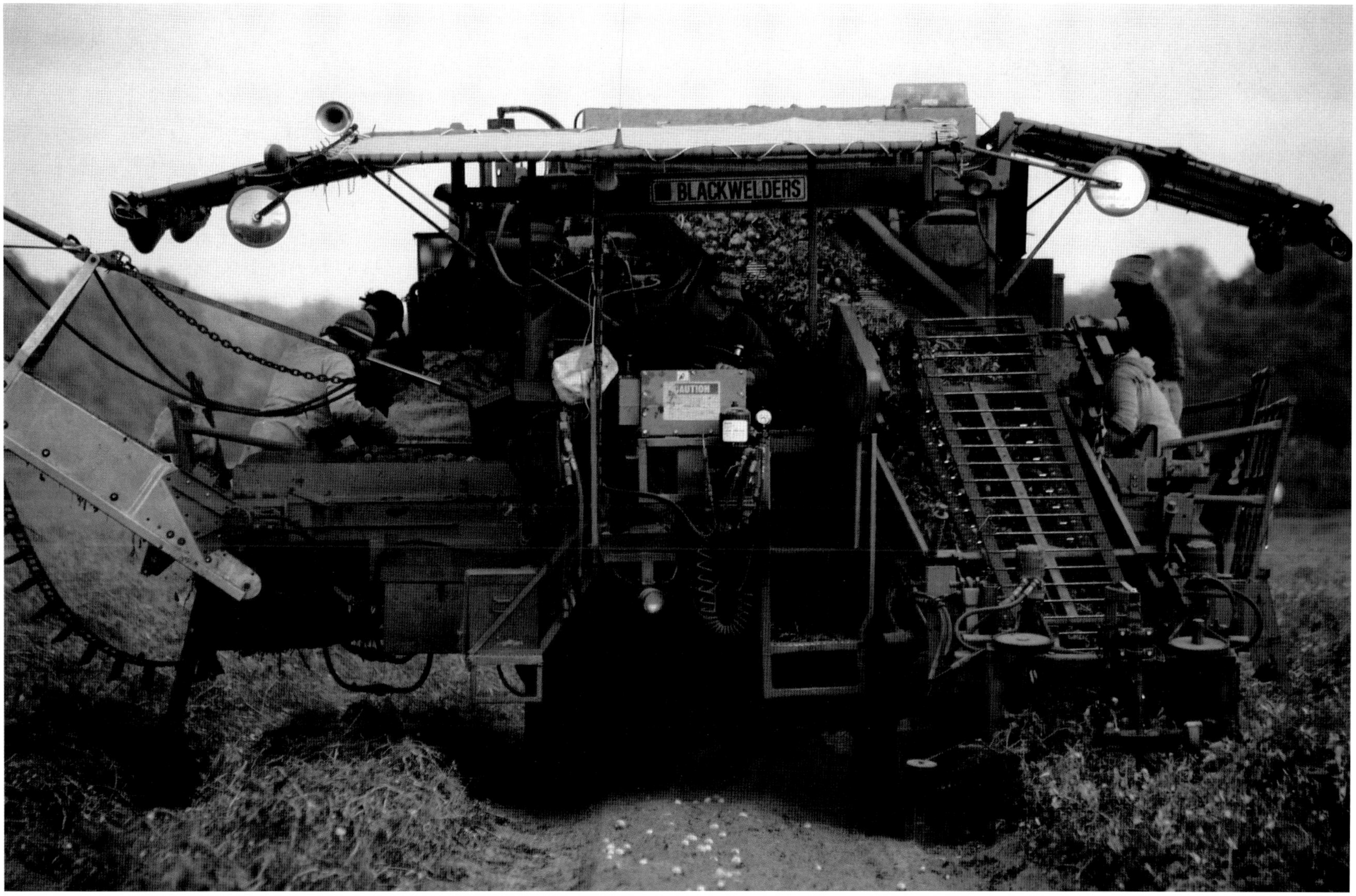
BLACKWELDERS
CAUTION

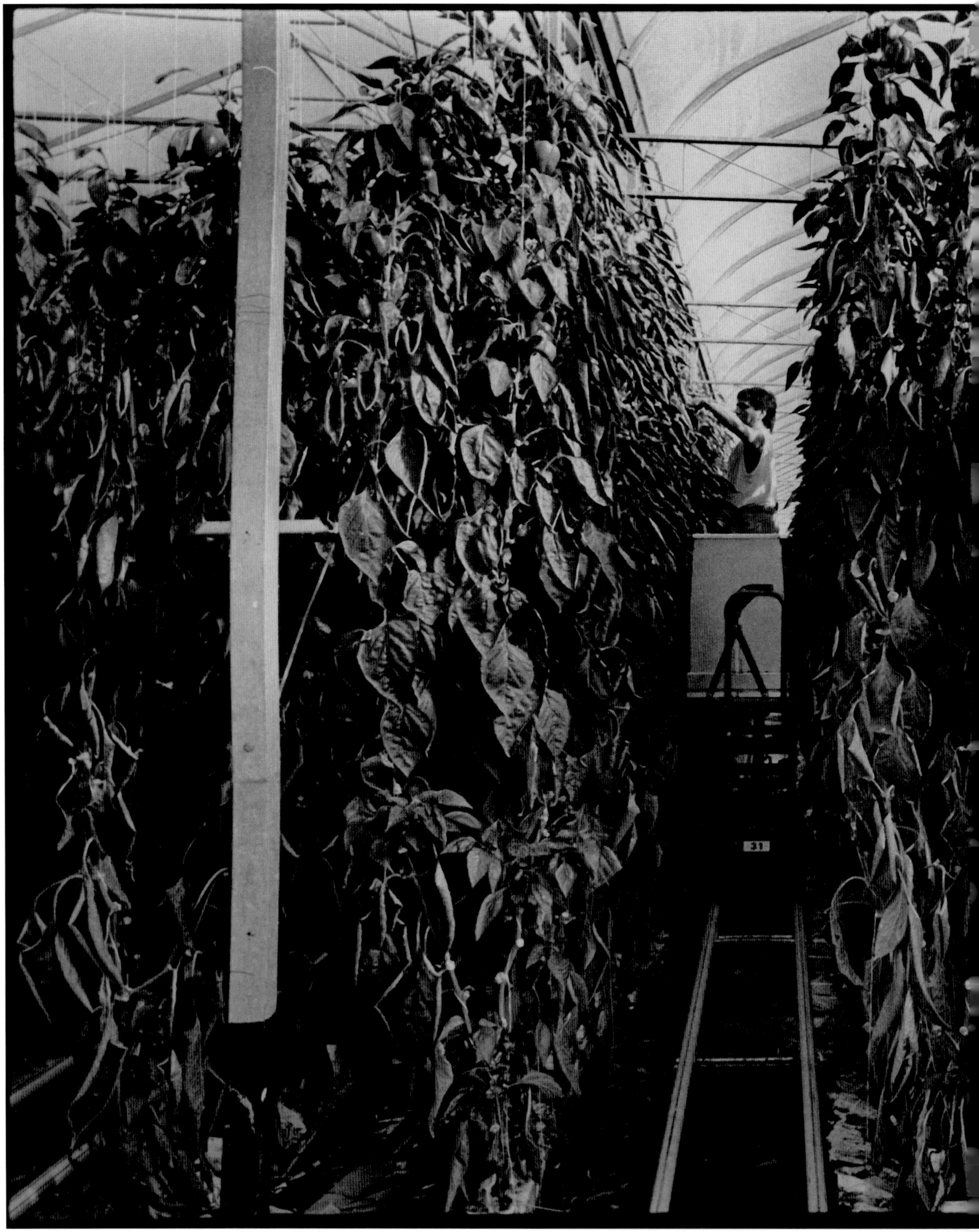

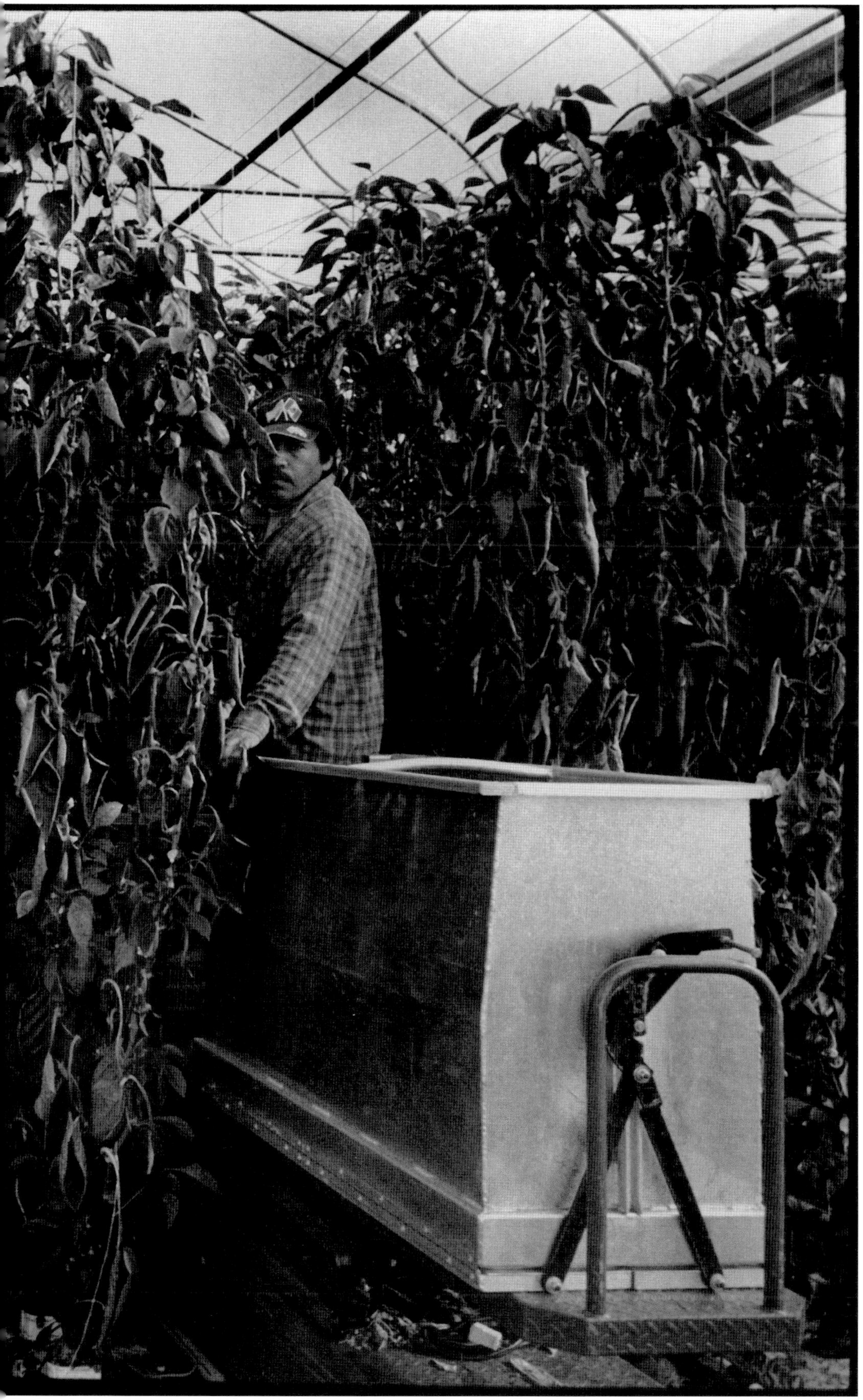

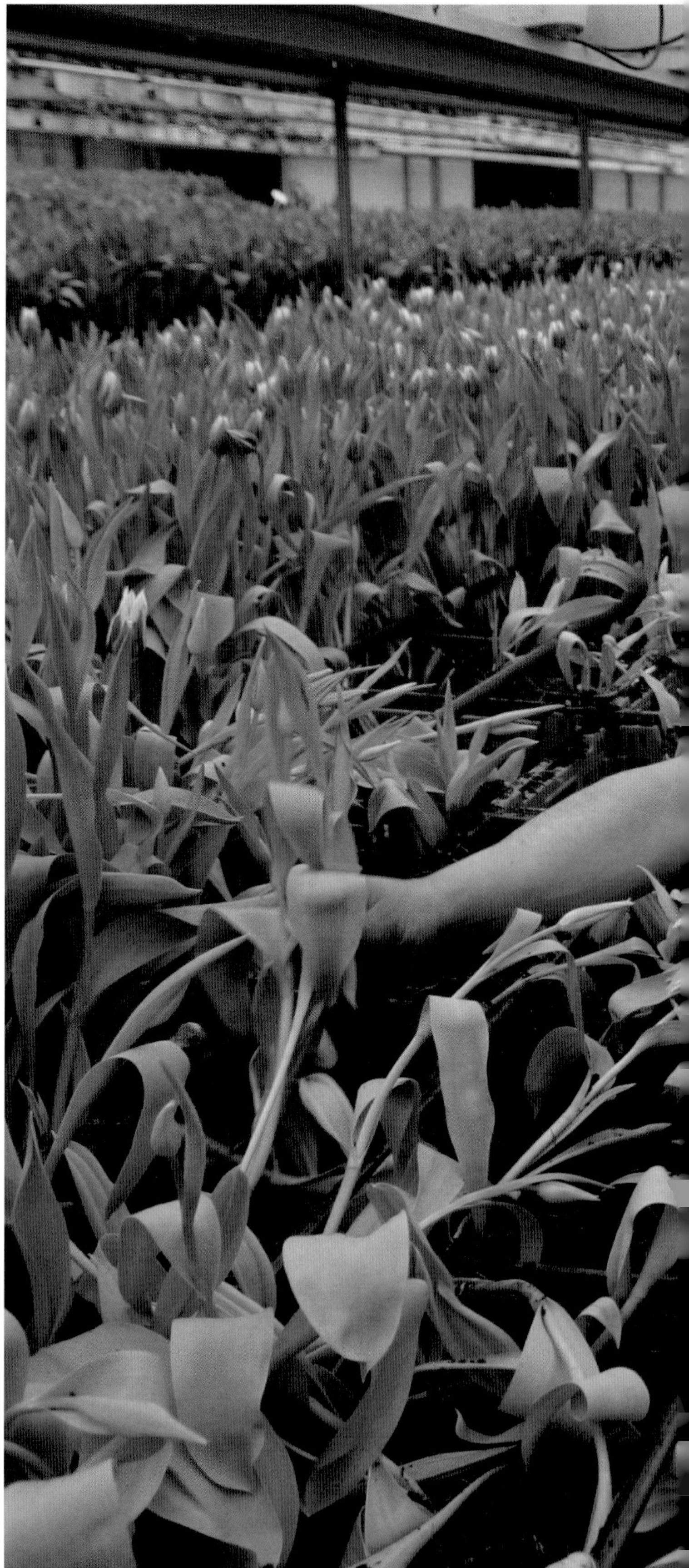

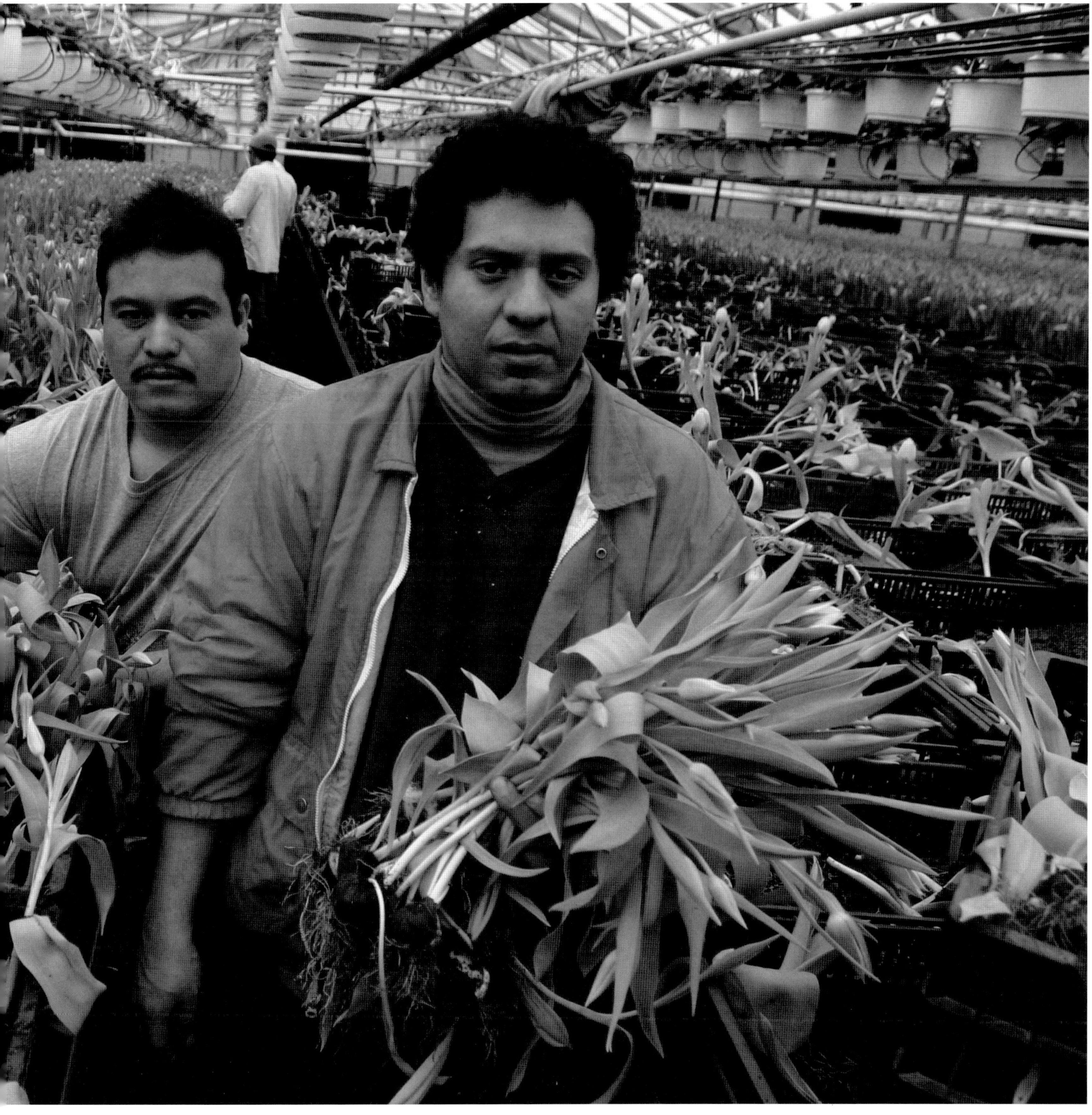

FURTHER RESOURCES

Books

Bacon, David, and Carlos Munoz Jr. and Douglas Harper (Foreword). *Communities without Borders: Images and Voices from the World of Migration*. Ithaca, N.Y.: ILR Press, 2006.

Barndt, Deborah. *Tangled Roots: Women, Work, and Globalization on the Tomato Trail*. Lanham, Md.: Roman and Littlefield, Publishers, 2007.

Berger, John and Jean Mohr. *A Seventh Man: A Book of Images and Words about the Experience of Migrant Workers in Europe*. Harmondsworth, Eng.: Penguin Books, 1975.

Castles, Stephen. *Here for Good: Western Europe's New Ethnic Minorities*. London: Pluto Press, 1984.

Coles, Robert. *Fields without Borders: An Anthology of Documentary Writing and Photography*. Durham, N.C.: Student Action with Farmworkers, 1998.

Cruz, Marco Antonio. *Cafetaleros*. Mexico City: Imagenlatina, 1996.

Emmet, Herman Leroy. *Fruit Tramps: A Family of Migrant Farmworkers*. Albuquerque: University of New Mexico Press, 1989.

Foster, Cecil. *Slammin' Tar* (a novel). Toronto: Random House Canada, 1998.

Hall, Douglas Kent. *The Border: Life on the Line*. New York: Abbeville Press, 1988.

Light, Ken, *To the Promised Land*. New York: Aperture Foundation, 1988.

Margaret, Poynter. *The Uncertain Journey*. New York: Atheneum, 1992.

Sassen, Saskia. *Guests and Aliens*. New York: New Press, 1999.

Shaw, Colin, and Phil Drabble (Foreword). *Farmwork: Men and Women on the Land*. London: Chatto & Windus, 1990.

Street, Richard Steven. *Everyone Had Cameras: Photography and Farmworkers in California, 1850–2000*. Minneapolis: University of Minnesota Press, 2008.

Weisman, Alan and Jay Dusard (Photographs). *La frontera: The United States Border with Mexico*. San Diego: Harcourt Brace Jovanovich, 1986.

Magazine and Newspaper Articles

"The Agriculture Issue." *Daylight Magazine*, Spring 2008: 1–55.

Amuchastegui, Maria. "Farming It Out." *This Magazine*, May-June 2006: 19–23.

Bain, Jennifer. "The Hands of Harvest." *The Toronto Star*, Sept. 24, 2003.

Bourrie, Mark. "Apple Growers Fear Losses Because of Picker Shortage." *The Globe and Mail*, Sept. 24, 1986.

Cohen, Nicole. "The Fruits of Their Labour." *Eye*, Oct. 28, 2004.

Dandurand, Andrée. "Migrant Workers in Québec and Canada." *Ovo*, 27/28 (1970).

Ferguson, Sue. "Hard Time in Canadian Fields." *Maclean's*, Oct 11, 2004.

Fitzgerald, Tony. "Fruits of Foreign Labour." *The Hamilton Spectator*, Oct. 6, 2001.

Grady, Wayne. "Tobacco Road." *Saturday Night*, July 1982.

Grez, Evelyn Encalada. "Migrant Workers Reap Bitter Harvest in Ontario." *The Toronto Star*, Oct. 28, 2008.

Johnson, Bryan. "Caribbean Commuters." *The Globe and Mail*, July 13, 1985.

Knox, Paul. "Migrant Laborers Reshape Two Lands." *The Globe and Mail*, May 12, 1987.

Lakey, Jack. "Caribbean Hands Vital to Fruit Harvest." *The Toronto Star*, Aug. 20, 1986.

Lazar, Barry. "The People behind Melons and Cabbages." *The Gazette* (Montreal), May 28, 1996.

Marr, Lisa. "Offshore Worker Bonanza." *The London Free Press*, Oct. 10, 1995.

__________. "Labourers of Our Fruits." *The Hamilton Spectator*, Aug. 10, 2002.

Milne, Mike. "The Migrant's Lot: Harvesting Our Feast." *The Observer*, August 1989.

Pietropaolo, Vincenzo. "Harvest Pilgrims." *This Country Canada*, 6 (Summer 1994).

__________. "Harvest Pilgrims." *The Globe and Mail*, Aug. 1, 1992.

__________. "Migrer au Rythme des Saisons." *Cérès: Revue de la FAO*. September–October 1995: 22–25.

__________. "Tobacco Road: Working the Fields of Southern Ontario." *Our Times*, September 1987: 26–33.

__________. "The Migrants." *This Magazine*, May 1988: 38–40.

Tatroff, David. "Fields of Fear." *Our Times*, December 1994.

Tracey, Lindalee. "The Dirt Workers." *Toronto Life*, May 1989.

Ward, Olivia. "Ontario Farmworkers: Hard Work, Few Rights." *The Toronto Star*, Oct 2, 1983.

Reports

Fairey, David et al. "Cultivating Farmworker Rights: Ending the Exploitation of Immigrant and Migrant Farmworkers in BC." Canadian Centre for Policy Alternatives, Justicia for Migrant Workers, Progressive Intercultural Community Services, and B.C. Federation of Labour, Vancouver and Ottawa, 2008.

Gibb, Heather. "Farmworkers from Afar." North-South Institute, Ottawa, 2006.

Films and Exhibitions

El Contrato. Directed by Min Sook Lee. Ottawa, NFB: 2005.

Migrants: Those Who Come from Within. Directed by Aaraon Diaz Mendiburo. Cuijingo, Mexico, 2007.

Salt of the Earth. Photographic exhibition by Carole Condé and Karl Beveridge. Toronto, 2008.

Music

Valles, Antonio et al. *Yo ya me voy amigos míos*. Mexico City: Dirección General de Culturas Populares e Indígenas/Instituto Coahuilense de Cultura/Ediciones Pentagrama, 2004.

Velázquez, Guillermo y Los Leones de la Sierra de Xichul. *Me Voy P'al Norte*. Mexico City: Discos Pentagrama.

Organizations

El Sembrador:
    www.stjohnchrysostom.on.ca.
Enlace:
    www.enlace.ca.
FERME:
    www.fermequebec.com/programmes_travailleurs_agricoles.html.
FARMS:
    www.farmsontario.ca.
Frontier College:
    www.frontiercollege.ca.
HRDC, Canada:
    Caribbean & Mexican Seasonal Agricultural Workers Program: http://www.on.hrdc-drhc.gc.ca/english/ps/agri/overview_e.shtml.
Justicia for Farm Workers:
    www.justicia4migrantworkers.org.
Leamington Arts Centre:
    www.leamingtonartscentre.com.
North-South Institute:
    www.nsi-ins.ca.
Ontario Fruit and Vegetable Growers' Association:
    www.ofvga.org/.
Ontario Greenhouse Vegetable Growers' Association:
    www.ontariogreenhouse.com/
United Food and Commercial Workers Canada union:
    www.ufcw.ca

INDEX TO THE PHOTOGRAPHS

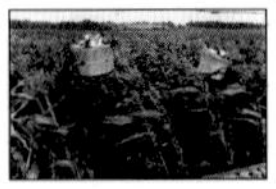

p.48–49. Jamaican workers with corn they have picked for market. Waterford, Ont., 1986.

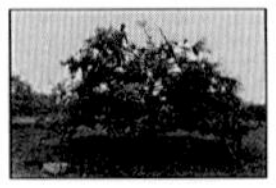

pp.50–51. Jamaican workers picking apples, Thornbury, Ont., 1986.

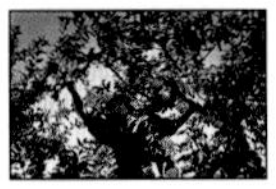

p.52. Delfina Valle Gutiérrez thinning the apple crop—removing imperfect or excessive bunching of fruit. Whitby, Ont., 1995.

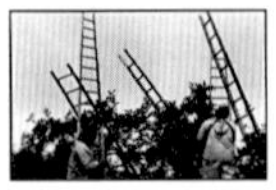

p.53. Jamaicans setting up ladders to pick apples. Thornbury, Ont., 1987.

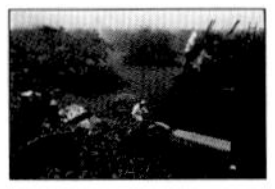

pp.54–55. Jamaican workers picking apples during an early morning rain. Thornbury, Ont., 1986.

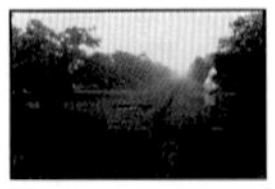

p.56. Early morning in the apple orchard. Clarksburg, Ont., 1986.

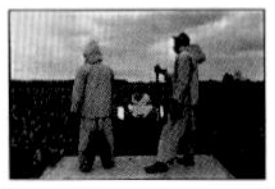

p.57. Workers from Montserrat setting off to work in a cauliflower field. Waterford, Ont., 1986.

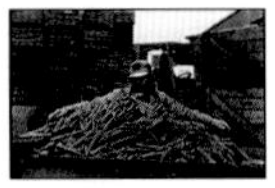

p.58. A Mexican worker crating carrots ready for shipping. Holland Marsh, Ont., 1987.

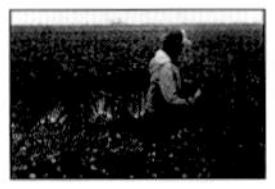

p.59. Mhado Mungal, a Trinidadian worker, harvesting celery. Holland Marsh, Ont., 1986.

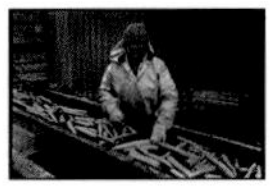

p.60. A Mexican worker inspects carrots passing along a conveyor belt. Holland Marsh, Ont., 1987.

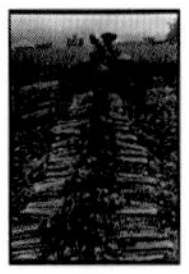

p.61. Trinidadian workers crating celery. Holland Marsh, Ont., 1986.

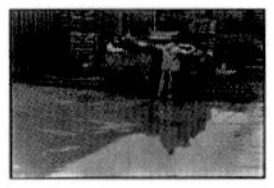

pp.62–63. Carrot-crating operation. Holland Marsh, Ont., 1987.

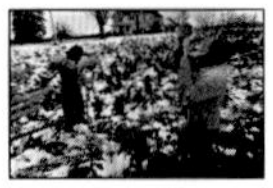

p.64. Two workers dig holes for staking apple saplings. Whitby, Ont., 1995.

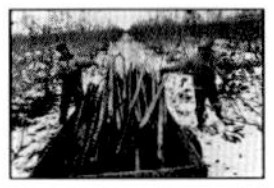

p.65. Trinidadian and Mexican migrant workers collecting stakes removed from mature trees. Whitby, Ont., 1995.

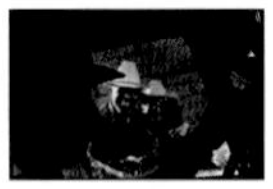

p.66. Manuel González is greeted by friends as he arrives home from Canada. Monte Prieto, Guanajuato, Mexico, 1993.

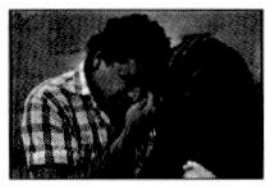

p.67. Manuel González greeting his sister Beda on his return home. Monte Prieto, Guanajuato, Mexico, 1993.

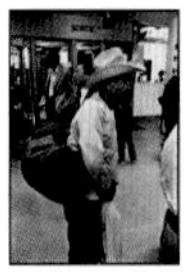

p.68. A Mexican worker arrives in Canada at the beginning of the work season. Pearson International Airport, Toronto, 1987.

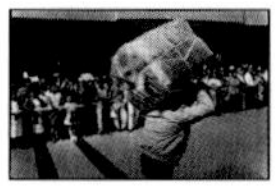

p.69. A Mexican worker returns home through Benito Juárez International Airport, Mexico City, 1993.

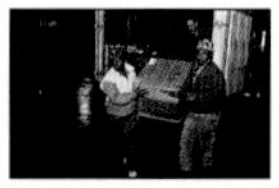

p.70. Two workers from Dominica prepare to return home. Pearson International Airport, Toronto, 1993.

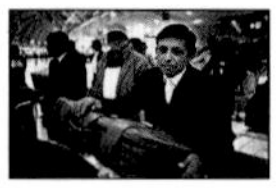

p.71. A man is accompanied to the airport by his employer for his return home. Pearson International Airport, Toronto, 1993.

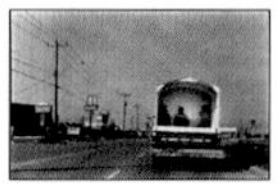

pp.72–73. On their first morning in Canada, Mexican workers are taken shopping for food and supplies. St. Catharines, Ont., 1987.

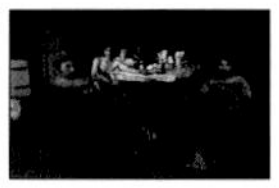

p.74. Mexican tobacco workers in their temporary home, a converted storage warehouse on the farm at which they are employed. The beer was supplied by the owner to welcome the photographer. From left to right: Fernando Martínez, Fermín Perez, Rosario [no last name given], Alfonso Antonio Hernandez, and Javier García Recendiz. Otterville, Ont., 1984.

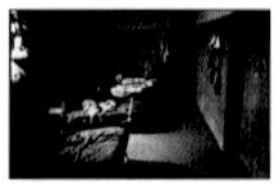

p.75. Bedroom facilities shared by four Mexican tobacco workers. Otterville, Ont., 1984.

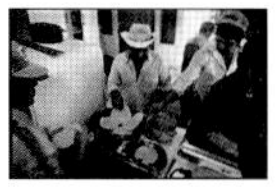
pp.76–77. A tortilla lunch. Beamsville, Ont., 1986.

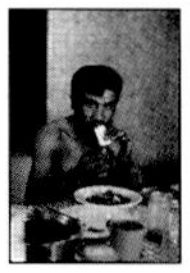
p.78. Fermín Perez, a Mexican tobacco worker. La Salette, Ont., 1984.

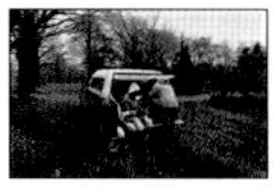
p.79. Jamaican workers at lunch in an apple orchard. Clarksburg, Ont., 1987.

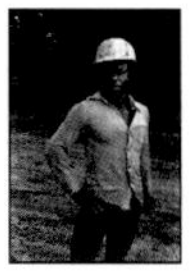
p.80. Errol Cain pauses before setting out on a new row of tobacco. Otterville, Ont., 1984.

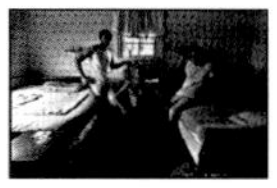
p.81. Caesar Uries, Errol Cain, and George Barber, tobacco workers from St. Vincent and the Grenadines, in their bedroom. La Salette, Ont., 1984.

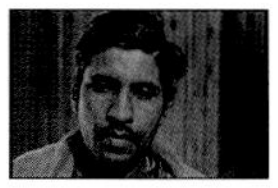
p.82. Samraj Sonny, a Trinidadian worker. Holland Marsh, Ont., 1986.

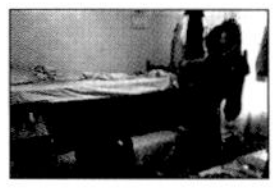
p.83. Das Raguba, a Trinidadian worker, Holland Marsh, Ont., 1986.

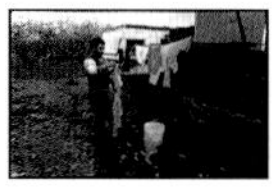
p.84. A Mexican worker doing his laundry. Beamsville, Ont., 1994.

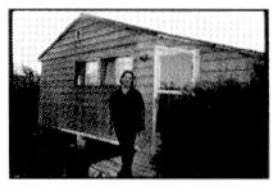
p.85. Maria Isabel Alejandra Hernández Cervantes in front of the house she lives in during her stay in Canada. Whitby, Ont., 1995.

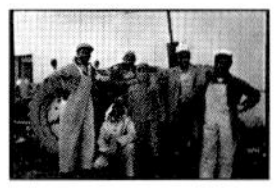
p.86. Tony Smyrecinsky, a vegetable-farm owner, with his Jamaican migrant workers. Waterford, Ont., 1987.

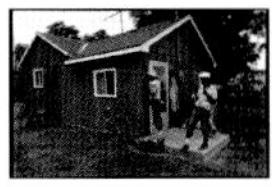
p.87. John Wekes and James Buffong, from Montserrat, in front of the house where they live while in Canada. Waterford, Ont., 1987.

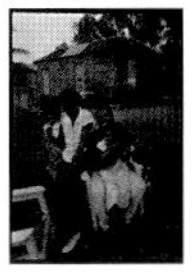
p.88. Stanley Rollston, who works as an apple picker in Thornbury, Ont., with his family at home in Jamaica. Clonmell, St. Mary's Parish, Jamaica, 1988.

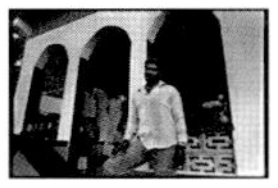
p.89. A migrant worker who works annually in Ontario, in front of a house that he is building at home. Aboukir, Jamaica, 1988.

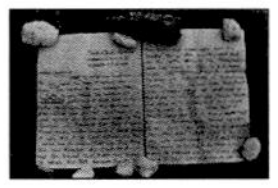
p.90. Part of a letter from Tony Peart to his wife, Maxine. Aboukir, Jamaica, 1988.

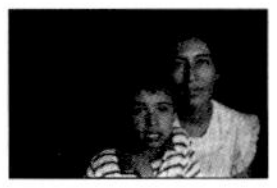
p.91. María Luisa González Frías with one of her children. Monte Prieto, Guanajuato, Mexico, 1994.

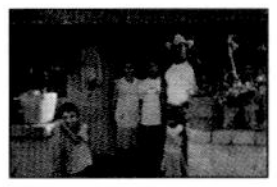
p.92. Rogelio González Martínez, who regularly works near London, Ont., at home with his family. Monte Prieto, Guanajuato, Mexico, 1994.

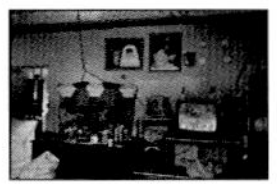
p.93. The home of Virginia and Manuel González, Monte Prieto, Guanajuato, Mexico, 1944.

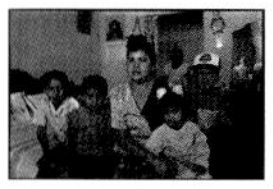
pp.94–95. Blanca Anaya Castillo and family. Monte Prieto, Guanajuato, Mexico, 1994.

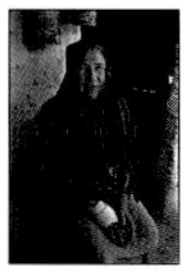
p.96. Beda González Gómez, the sister of a migrant worker. Monte Prieto, Guanajuato, Mexico, 1994.

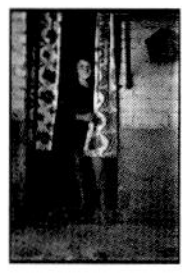
p.97. Rosaura González, the daughter of a migrant worker. Monte Prieto, Guanajuato, Mexico, 1994.

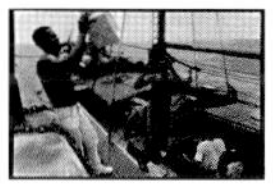
p.98. Reginald Cabey and an unidentified worker unloading a shipment of beer, a rare opportunity for local employment. Plymouth, Montserrat, 1986.

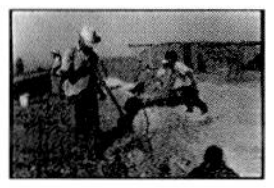
p.99. A small adobe brick operation, the only local industry in a village of migrant workers. Monte Prieto, Guanajuato, Mexico, 1994.

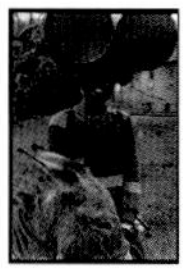
p.100. Tony Peart, a subsistence farmer in Jamaica and migrant worker in Canada. Akoubir, Jamaica, 1988.

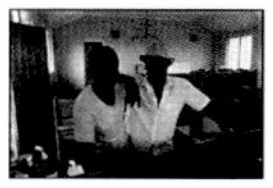
p.101. Two Jamaican workers just before the spring migration to Canada. Nine Miles, Spaldings, Jamaica, 1988.

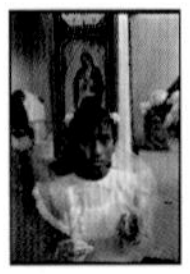

p. 102. A girl in her First Communion dress, on the day of the Feast of La Santa Patrona de la Concepción. Monte Prieto, Guanajuato, Mexico, 1993.

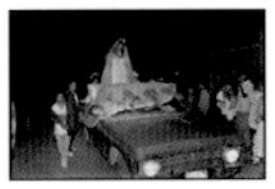

p. 103. During a procession a young girl portrays La Virgen de la Concepción, the local patron saint. Monte Prieto, Guanajuato, Mexico, 1993.

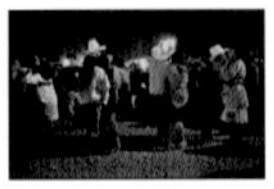

p. 104. A large celebration is held in the town square during the Feast of La Santa Patrona de la Concepción, December 8, by which time all the migrant farm workers have returned home. Monte Prieto, Guanajuato, Mexico, 1993.

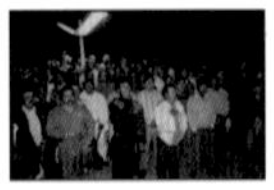

p. 105. Mexican workers singing their country's national anthem during Fiestas Patrias, Mexico's most important day of celebration. La Salette, Ont., 1996.

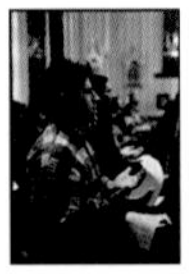

p. 106. A solemn moment during a mass celebrated for migrant workers in Spanish at Our Lady of La Salette Roman Catholic Church. La Salette, Ont., 1996.

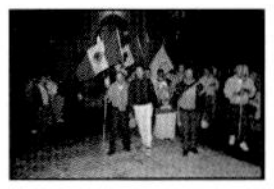

p. 107. Workers carry a statue of the Virgin of Guadalupe, Mexico's patron saint, in a short procession combined with the Fiestas Patrias celebrations. La Salette, Ont., 1996.

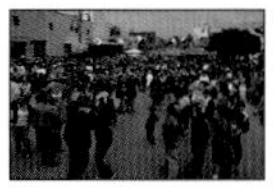

pp. 108–9. The Dos Culturas/Two Cultures street festival, held annually in recognition of the large migrant farm worker population in southwestern Ontario. Leamington, Ont., 2006 (digital photograph).

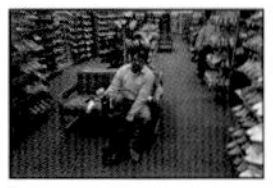

p. 110. On his first full day in Canada, a worker from Mexico shops for boots to begin his summer of work. St. Catharines, Ont., 1987.

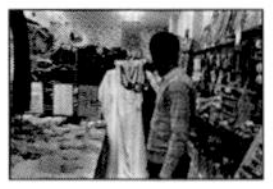

p. 111. A worker from St. Lucia browses for gifts to take home. Simcoe, Ont., 1984.

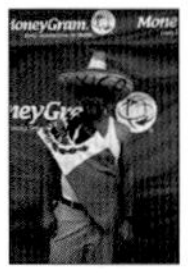

p. 112. A Mexican worker during the Dos Culturas/Two Cultures festival. Leamington, Ont., 2006 (digital photograph).

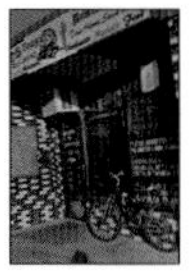

p. 113. Tacos Tony, a Mexican restaurant, a favourite gathering spot for migrant farm workers. Leamington, Ont., 2006.

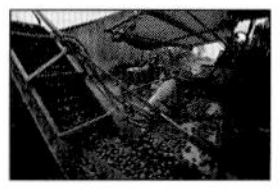

pp. 114–15. Erica Carreon-Acosta works on a field-tomato harvester, removing stones, clumps of soil, and other debris. The tomatoes travel on a conveyor belt to a bin towed alongside. Wheatly, Ont., 2006 (digital photograph).

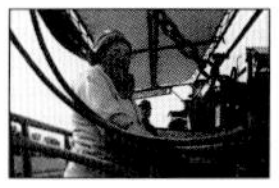

p. 116. Migrant and local farm workers on a field-tomato harvester. The dusty conditions force some of them to wear breathing protection. Wheatly, Ont., 2006 (digital photograph).

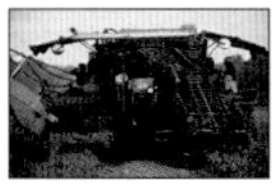

p. 117. A gigantic tomato-field harvester, operated by Frank Lehn, slices through the soil and scoops up the tomato vines, including the roots and fruit, which are then separated and sorted by mostly migrant workers who stand all day long on top of the moving machine. Wheatly, Ont., 2006 (digital photograph).

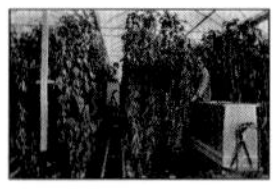

pp. 118–19. Mexican workers use cherry pickers to harvest greenhouse peppers in a completely mechanized operation. Leamington, Ont., 2005.

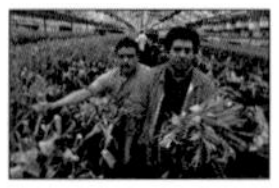

pp. 120–21. Ismael María López and Ulises Ramos work in a tulip greenhouse. St. Catharines, Ont., 2006.

Photographs from the Harvest Pilgrims series have appeared in these publications: *BorderCrossings*, *Bout de papier*, *Canadian Geographic*, *Ceres*, *Double Exposure*, *Eye Magazine*, *5 Photographers* exhibition catalogue, *Fotoseptiembre Latino Americano 96*, *Fotoseptiembre Latino Americano 94*, *Fronteras*, *Italian-Canadiana*, *Labour Times*, *New Internationalist*, *Now*, *Our Times*, *Photo Ed*, *Photo Life*, *The Globe and Mail*, *The Sunday Herald-Halifax*, *This Country Canada*, *This Magazine*, and the *Wall Calendar of the Workers Health and Safety Centre*; and in these books: *Harmony/Harmonie*, *Faces of Canada/Visage du Canada*, *Tortillas and Tomatoes*, and *Growing Strong: Women in Agriculture*.

Solo or group exhibitions have taken place at: Art Cite Gallery (Windsor), Art Gallery of Ontario, Art Gallery of Windsor, Camera Lucida (Montreal), Canadian Museum of Contemporary Photography (travelling show), Centro Hispano-Americano de Cultura (Havana), El Atrio (Embassy of Canada, Mexico City), El Mes de la Fotografía (Mérida, Mexico), (Galerie Montcalm (Gatineau), Leamington Arts Centre (Leamington, Ont.), Mayworks Festival (Toronto), Photo Union Gallery (Hamilton, Ont.), Pier 21 (Halifax), Pinacoteca José Antonio de las Cuevas (Puebla, Mexico), Stephen Bulger Gallery (Toronto), Universidad Michoacana de San Nicolás de Hidalgo (Morelia, Mexico), Harbourfront Centre (Toronto), Scotia Centre (Port-of-Spain, Trinidad and Tobago), National Gallery of Jamaica (Kingston, Jamaica), Universidad Nacional Autónoma de México (San Antonio, Texas), Universidad Autónoma Metropolitana (Xochimilco, Mexico), and Workers Art and Heritage Centre (Hamilton, Ont.).

Photographs are also in the collections of: the Art Gallery of Ontario, Canadian Museum of Contemporary Photography, and Library and Archives of Canada.

Harvest Pilgrims: Mexican and Caribbean
Migrant Farm Workers in Canada

First published in Canada in 2009 by
Between the Lines
720 Bathurst Street, Suite #404
Toronto, Ontario M5S 2R4
Canada
1-800-718-7201
www.btlbooks.com

Library and Archives Canada Cataloguing in Publication

Pietropaolo, Vincenzo
Harvest pilgrims : Mexican and Caribbean migrant farm workers in Canada / Vincenzo Pietropaolo.

ISBN 978-1-897071-54-0

1. Migrant agricultural laborers—Ontario—Pictorial works. 2. Documentary photography—Canada. I. Title.

HD1529.P54 2009 779'.9305563 C2009-902911-1

Cover and text design by David Vereschagin, Quadrat Communications
Printed in Canada by Thistle Printing Limited

Between the Lines gratefully acknowledges assistance for its publishing activities from the Canada Council for the Arts, the Ontario Arts Council, the Government of Ontario through the Ontario Book Publishers Tax Credit program and through the Ontario Book Initiative, and the Government of Canada through the Book Publishing Industry Development Program.

The Canada Council for the Arts since 1957 | Le Conseil des Arts du Canada depuis 1957

Canada

Ontario Arts Council
Conseil des Arts de l'Ontario